Imagining Armenia

Manchester University Press

Cultural History of Modern War

Series editors   Peter Gatrell, Max Jones, Penny Summerfield and
   Bertrand Taithe

Already published

Juliette Pattinson   *Behind enemy lines: gender, passing and the
   Special Operations Executive in the Second World War*

Jeffrey S. Reznick   *Healing the nation: soldiers and the culture of
   caregiving in Britain during the Great War*

Michael Roper   *The secret battle: emotional survival in the Great War*

Penny Summerfield and Corinna Peniston-Bird   *Contesting home
   defence: men, women and the Home Guard in the Second World War*

Colette Wilson   *Paris and the Commune, 1871–78: the politics of
   forgetting*

Imagining Armenia

Orientalism, ambiguity and intervention

JO LAYCOCK

Manchester
University Press

Manchester and New York

distributed in the United States exclusively by Palgrave Macmillan

Published by Manchester University Press
Oxford Road, Manchester M13 9NR, UK
and Room 400, 175 Fifth Avenue, New York, NY 10010, USA
www.manchesteruniversitypress.co.uk

Distributed in the United States exclusively by
Palgrave Macmillan, 175 Fifth Avenue, New York,
NY 10010, USA

Distributed in Canada exclusively by
UBC Press, University of British Columbia, 2029 West Mall,
Vancouver, BC, Canada V6T 1Z2

British Library Cataloguing-in-Publication Data
A catalogue record for this book is available from the British Library

Library of Congress Cataloging-in-Publication Data applied for

ISBN   978 0 7190 7817 0   hardback

First published 2009

18 17 16 15 14 13 12 11 10 09   10 9 8 7 6 5 4 3 2 1

Typeset in Minion
by Servis Filmsetting Ltd, Stockport, Cheshire
Printed in Great Britain
by CPI Antony Rowe, Chippenham, Wiltshire

In memory of Kathleen Laycock and Pat Greenwood

Contents

List of figures   viii

Acknowledgements   ix

List of abbreviations   x

Map 1: The Armenian Republic   xi

Map 2: Historical boundaries of Armenia   xii

Map 3: Armenia and the Near East   xiii

Introduction: From cradle of civilisation to victim nation:
Britain and Armenia 1875–1925   1

1   Imagining Armenia: otherness, orientalism and ambiguity   18

2   The boundary of the civilised world? Images of Armenia
    during the late nineteenth century   43

3   'The murder of a nation': representing the Armenian
    genocide of 1915   99

4   Armenian refugees: representation, relief and repatriation   144

5   Post-war Armenia: visions, realities and responses   182

Conclusions: The Armenian past, present and future in the
British imagination   218

Bibliography   231
Index   253

Figures

1 Armenia - The Lord Mayor of London Appeals for Help, Louis
   Raemaekers, 1917 (Source: IWM Collection)   127
2 *The Friend of Armenia*, cover illustration, April 1918   128

Acknowledgements

The writing of this book would not have been possible without the support and patience of my PhD supervisors at Manchester University, Dr Sian Jones and Prof. Peter Gatrell, who have provided invaluable guidance and encouragement at every stage. Other members of staff and postgraduates at Manchester University have also offered helpful feedback and opportunities for discussion during the process of research and writing for which I am very grateful. In particular thanks to Dr Rebecca Gill, Dr Sarah Croucher and Prof. Bertrand Taithe for their time and their insights.

Thanks also to all those involved with the University of Michigan Summer Armenian Programme 2003 not only for helping me learn Armenian but for broadening my knowledge of Armenian history, society and culture and opening up new opportunities for research.

Staff at the John Rylands University Library and the Portico Library, Manchester, the British Library, the Modern Papers Reading Room at the Bodleian Library and Rhodes House Library, Oxford provided me with assistance throughout this project. Thanks especially to Vahe Tachejian at the Bibliotheque Nubar for help in locating sources and for sharing ideas with me. The staff of the Armenian National Archives also provided important assistance with the later stages of my research.

I am grateful to all of my friends and family for providing both support and timely distractions from my research. In particular I would like to thank my parents Stella and Bill, my sister Emma and my grandfathers, Thomas Laycock and Fred Greenwood, for support of every kind during the ups and downs of writing my PhD thesis and this book. Thanks also to Kathleen Cunningham for putting up with me and providing me with many cups of tea. Finally special thanks to Ben Hill for sharing my enthusiasm for this project and providing the support and encouragement that I needed to persevere and complete this book.

Abbreviations

BAC	British Armenia Committee
ANDP	Armenian National Delegation Paris
LMF	Lord Mayor's Fund
NER	Near East Relief
AAA	Anglo-Armenian Association

Map 1   The Armenian Republic

Map 2   Historical boundaries of Armenia

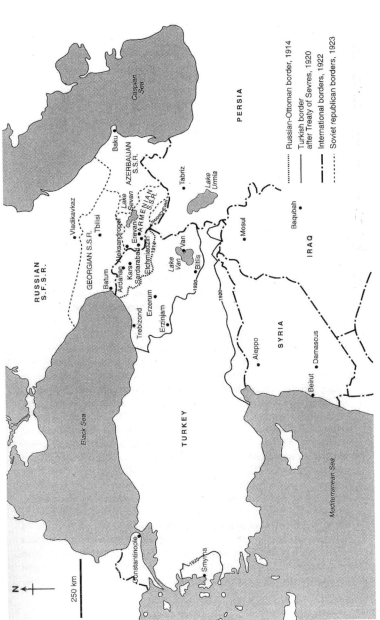

Map 3   Armenia and the Near East

RUSSIAN
S.F.S.R.

GEORGIAN S.S.R.

AZERBAIJAN
S.S.R.

ARMENIAN
S.S.R.

PERSIA

TURKEY

SYRIA

IRAQ

Black Sea

Caspian Sea

Mediterranean Sea

Lake Sevan

Lake Van

Lake Urmia

Baku
Vladikavkaz
Tbilisi
Batum
Aleksandropol
Ardahan
Kars
Erevan
Sardarabad
Etchmiadzin
Trebizond
Erzerum
Erzinjam
Van
Bitlis
Tabriz
Mosul
Baqubah
Aleppo
Damascus
Beirut
Smyrna
Constantinople

250 km

N

.... Russian-Ottoman border, 1914
———— Turkish border
       after Treaty of Sevres, 1920
—·—·— International borders, 1922
- - - - - Soviet republican borders, 1923

Introduction

From cradle of civilisation to victim nation: Britain and Armenia 1875–1925

At the beginning of the nineteenth century Armenia and the Armenians were unfamiliar to the majority of the British public, and were of little account so far as the British government was concerned. Encounters with the Armenians were occasionally described in travel narratives, whilst a few scholars demonstrated a familiarity with the medieval history of the Armenian Church and Armenian involvement in the Crusades. To that extent Armenia had already been 'discovered'.[1] To the vast majority of the British population however, Armenians remained obscure and largely irrelevant.

By the end of the century, however, this had changed: developments in international politics and imperialism had familiarised the British public with the Armenians. Their fate became an important international geopolitical question for the British government and a humanitarian cause occupying both prominent political, academic and religious figures and the general public. The Armenians thus became well known both as objects of romantic and scholarly interest and as victims of atrocity and massacre. Their fate became a 'cause' which occupied the British public until the aftermath of the First World War.

The 'Armenian question' and the representation of the other

The 'rediscovery' of Armenia and the Armenians in the second half of the nineteenth century was part of a broader encounter with new peoples and places as British and European imperial interests rapidly expanded across the globe. This period of imperial development was marked not only by the acquisition of colonies but also by increasing international trade, and improvements in transport and communications. These developments increased the possibility of travel to more remote regions not only for commercial and diplomatic reasons but also for pleasure or scholarly purposes.[2]

As a result of the expanded opportunities for travel during the nineteenth century increasing numbers of British individuals encountered the Armenians.[3] At the same time missionaries, principally from the USA, established a permanent presence in the Armenian homeland and focused their attention on the education and spiritual development of the Armenians.[4] A different type of encounter occurred closer to home, when merchants from the Ottoman Empire arrived in Britain and Armenian communities developed in London and Manchester.[5]

The travellers, merchants, scholars and diplomats of this period encountered a very different Armenia to that which exists in the early twenty-first century. During the latter part of the nineteenth century the Armenians were scattered across the Russian, Ottoman and Persian Empires. 'Armenia' had no definite borders, no concrete geographical existence and the 'Armenian nation' was a nebulous concept. The Armenians were yet another minority in regions inhabited by a mixture of Turks, Kurds, Greeks, Russians and other ethnic and religious groups. The situation remained this way until the establishment of a Soviet Armenian Republic after the First World War.

Armenians living in the Ottoman Empire captured British imaginations during the second half of the nineteenth century. Against a background of imperialist expansion, exploration and contact, the Ottoman Empire, and particularly its minority Christian populations, came to be the focus of a particular kind of British attention. This attention derived from concerns to preserve and protect the integrity of the strategically important Ottoman Empire. The attempt by Britain and the other European powers to halt the decline of the Ottoman Empire and manage the emergence of national movements within its territories, particularly the Balkans, became known as the 'eastern question'.[6]

In the latter part of the century this seemingly intractable 'question' became a focus of international politics and diplomacy. In Britain it impinged upon domestic party politics, generating unprecedented amounts of public interest in foreign policy. The 'eastern question' also provided an early forum for the extension of philanthropic ventures 'at home' in Britain to the so-called 'minorities' living beyond British borders. It was thus a forum for the development of discourses of humanitarianism which became more fully articulated over the next half a century.

The politics and diplomacy of the 'eastern question' have generated enormous scholarly interest. However, much of this scholarship has focused on the arenas of 'high' politics and European diplomacy. In the British case it has often focused upon the roles of leading politicians: Gladstone, Disraeli and Salisbury. The relationship between the 'eastern question', mass politics and the development of national and imperial identities is an issue which has also received significant attention. The examination of the 'Bulgarian horrors' agitation in terms of both the roles of Gladstone and Disraeli and its significance in the development of popular politics provides a good example of this scholarship.[7]

Bulgaria and the Balkans have been the geographical focus for most work on the 'eastern question'. Whilst images of the 'Bulgarian horrors' and the complex patterns of war and conflict in the Balkans are familiar elements of the historiography, the Armenian dimension is undoubtedly less well known. On the occasions when Armenia is addressed within the framework of the 'eastern question' it is often as an aside, a minor element of the broader issues at stake. When the Armenian dimension, the 'Armenian question' has attracted the attention of historians it has tended to have been once again in terms of 'high' politics and the workings – or in this case failings – of international diplomacy which culminated in the genocide of the Armenians during the First World War.[8]

More recently, scholarship on the 'eastern question' has developed in new directions. For example, Maria Todorova's work examines the representations of the Balkans that have been integral to the 'eastern question', questioning longstanding images of the Balkans as a fractured, violent region of endemic conflict or 'ethnic hatreds'. Other work, influenced by Edward Said's study of orientalism, has examined how and why these representations emerged and remained a powerful part of European imaginations.[9]

These developments were driven at least in part by the emergence of the conflicts in the former Yugoslavia in the 1990s or, more accurately, by the way in which Western Europe and the United States have perceived and represented these conflicts.[10] Representations of Armenia meanwhile have been neglected. Although they derived from a similar background and have some striking similarities to the representations of the Balkans, this kind of critical analysis of these representations is still lacking.

British representations of Armenia have been subject to little in-depth attention. British writings often refer to the role of Armenia as a 'cradle of civilisation', but this characterisation of the region is rarely subject to critical analysis. Christopher Walker's recent collection of British writing on

Armenia is a notable exception and hints at the complexities of British constructions of Armenia. Walker suggests that 'Making national general-izations is a way of approaching the shell of truths about oneself, not describing a people.' Yet the wider implications of the way that British observers imagined Armenia, in terms of both material relations with the region and the construction of British and Armenian identities, have not been fully examined.[11]

Just as recent scholarship on the Balkans draws attention to the effects which longstanding perceptions still have on shaping politics, conflict and international intervention, the current situation in Armenia highlights the need for investigation of perceptions of the region. Since the break-down of the Soviet Union and the creation of an independent Armenian nation in 1991, Armenian national identity has been intensely contested and reconstructed. Some of the visions of national identity which have emerged from this process are based on timeless, essentialist and exclusive constructions of the nation.[12] The conflict between Armenia and Azerbaijan over Nagorno-Karabagh has for example often been depicted in terms of longstanding 'ethnic hatreds'.[13] These trends draw attention to the need to investigate more thoroughly constructions of Armenian iden-tity, and particularly the uses of the Armenian past in the construction of national identity. The unresolved conflict with Turkey over the recogni-tion of the genocide and current debates about Armenia's place in the post-Soviet world also suggest there is a pressing need to address the way that Armenia has been, and continues to be, 'imagined' and represented by the rest of the world. These representations play a vital role in power, politics and the construction of identities.[14]

Armenian history and historiography in the twentieth century

The reasons for the failure to engage with these issues are embedded in broader patterns in the writing of Armenian history. During the twentieth century the history of Armenia has not been regarded as integral to the history of Europe or the history of imperialism. Armenian history has impinged on European history only at certain key flashpoints, for example, the genocide of 1915 or the breakdown of the Soviet Union. In itself this is a product of the ambiguity which has characterised British perceptions of and relations with Armenia since the late nineteenth century.

In the absence of such a broad perspective, the writing of Armenian history in the twentieth century has frequently been undertaken as a nar-rowly 'national' project, tracing the development of the people from the emergence of Armenian civilisation during 'ancient times' until the present day, focusing upon the 'golden ages' of the Armenian nation. The production of such a national narrative has been conditioned by the nature of twentieth-century Armenian history and particularly the genocide.

The genocide and mass displacement of the Armenian population of the Ottoman Empire which took place during the First World War unsurprisingly impacted deeply upon constructions of Armenian identity and particularly upon portrayals of the national past. Razmik Panossian has explained that the genocide has acted as a kind of 'prism, through which national identity is seen, politics interpreted and culture redefined'.[15] In the aftermath of genocide national history has played an important role in national reconstruction and the maintenance of identity and tradition. However these circumstances have tended to lead to a narrow focus on the writing of history as a work of national preservation. As R. G. Suny has pointed out:

> Often directed toward an 'ethnic' rather than a broader international or scholarly audience, Armenian historical writing has been narrowly concerned with fostering a positive view of an endangered nationality . . . Criticism has been avoided as if it might aid present enemies and certain kinds of inquiry have been shunned as potential betrayals of the national cause.[16]

The emphasis on writing history as 'national preservation' has been compounded by the post-war history of the Armenians. After the First World War the Armenians were dispersed not only across the Middle East and Transcaucasia, but also across Europe and the USA. As Richard Hovannisian explains, 'The genocide of 1915 dealt such a forceful blow that this time it thrust most survivors beyond their native lands into a diasporan existence.'[17] The experience of living as a diaspora has had a deep impact upon the writing of history and the importance attached to the past more generally, reinforcing the sense that the past must be protected and preserved.[18] On the other hand the writing of history in the Soviet Republic of Armenia has been shaped by the very different conditions of Soviet rule. In this context the nature and content of Armenian national histories has, to a large extent, been determined by the evolution of Soviet perspectives on the nature of nations and national identity and the limits and restrictions imposed under Soviet rule.[19]

Given these circumstances, the critical analysis of Armenian national history has not always been possible, nor has it been welcomed by sections of the Armenian community in the Armenian Republic and the diaspora.[20] There is nonetheless a need for more critical perspectives on the

Armenian past and its role in the construction of Armenian identities past and present. Such perspectives are necessary in order to move on from the treatment of the Armenian past as a heroic national epic.

Whilst genocide and dispersal has led to a defensive Armenian writing of history which focuses on national survival, it is a history which has attracted very little attention beyond diaspora communities in Britain and Western Europe. This is linked to politics of remembrance and denial of the fate of the Armenians at the hands of the Ottoman Empire during the First World War. In 2008, the Turkish government do not acknowledge that a genocide took place, whilst large sections of the international community have also failed to recognise the massacre and deportation of the Armenians as genocide. The impact of such denial upon the Armenians has been described by Richard Hovannisian:

> Armenians feel deeply that they cannot fully overcome that blow until it is acknowledged through acts of contrition and redemption. Hence in some ways they are imprisoned by their past and their liberation is dependent on actions of the perpetrator side.[21]

Turkish denial 'backed by the full force of a Turkish state machinery' has been difficult to counter. It has taken numerous forms, from outright denial to the 'provocation thesis', that the actions of the Armenians in the years before and in the early stages of war posed a threat to the Ottoman Empire and they were thus responsible for their own fate.[22]

International failure to recognise the Armenian genocide has a complex history.[23] As the following chapters demonstrate, during the First World War, the Allies were quick to condemn the actions of the Ottoman government. Though they failed to prevent the massacres and deportations, they expressed their outrage at these events, promising that Turkey would never again rule the Armenian population and raising hopes for the establishment of an independent Armenian nation state. At the same time American and British humanitarian agencies conducted a large-scale operation of relief and reconstruction amongst the displaced survivors of the genocide. In the post-war years, as the new Turkish Republic was established, a veil was drawn over the subject of the Armenian massacres.

Since the fiftieth anniversary of the genocide in 1965, which was marked by demonstrations in the Soviet Republic and the construction of the genocide memorial at Tsitsernakaberd, Yerevan in 1967, the campaign for recognition has gained momentum amongst the Armenian diaspora. Nonetheless, powerful countries such as the USA and Britain (motivated by their geopolitical interests and the desire not to antagonise

Turkey) still fail to recognise the massacre and deportations of the Armenians as a genocide.[24] From an Armenian perspective, the narrative is one of 'abandonment', of British failure to protect or fulfil promises to the Armenians.[25]

Despite the lack of international recognition it is clear that since Armenian independence, interest in the Armenians and their fate from outside the Armenian community and the field of 'Armenian studies' has increased. Additional public interest has been aroused by the international response to the murder of the outspoken journalist Hrant Dink by a Turkish nationalist in January 2007 and the attempts to prosecute leading Turkish authors, notably the Nobel Prize winner Orhan Pamuk in 2005, due to references made to the fate of the Armenians.[26]

In the academic world this interest in Armenia has taken the form of the consideration of the Armenian case in comparative works on genocide, ethnic cleansing or state violence. The Armenian genocide is frequently characterised as the first modern genocide and as a case study in the inadequacies of international responses to this type of crime. Patterns of denial and their implications for responding to genocide in the future have also occupied a prominent place in recent studies.[27]

Yet although recent events have drawn attention to the plight of the Armenians and the issue of denial, these issues are often addressed in isolation. There is still a need, as Suny suggests, to continue to 'promote an integration of the somewhat isolated historiography of Armenia into more general theoretical and historical concerns'.[28] My intention is to address this issue through examining the history of British relations with Armenia, focusing particularly on the ways in which Armenia was imagined and represented in Britain during the late nineteenth and early twentieth centuries. This approach illuminates a number of theoretical and historical concerns. It draws the case of Armenia into broader questions of representing the 'other' and the relationship of such representations to power. Such questions have been at the centre of recent historical scholarship.

Historical context

The British response to the 'Armenian question' was conditioned by the complex history of the 'eastern question' and previous experiences of the Christian minorities of the Ottoman Empire. Involvement in the 'eastern question' had its origins early in the century, during the Greek campaign for independence. During the 1820s a wave of philhellenism swept Europe as the Greeks fought for their independence. The war was marked by atrocities on both sides but the massacre of thousands of Greeks on the island of Chios by the Turks in 1822 in particular captured the public imagination. The Greeks were idealised as the originators of 'western civilisation' whilst popular beliefs regarding Turkish brutality and barbarism became more firmly entrenched.[29]

In the decades following the Greek revolution the ill treatment of Christian minorities in the Ottoman Empire and the growth of nationalism within its territories led to clashes between the Ottoman authorities and their subject populations. The situation was particularly bad in the Balkans, where the Ottoman Empire lost a great deal of territory.[30] For the most part the desire to 'prop up' the Ottoman government rather than the needs or aspirations of minorities shaped British responses. A central tenet of British foreign policy was that the integrity of the Ottoman Empire must be upheld at all cost. Fears that the weakening of the Ottoman Empire would allow Russian expansion, posing a threat to Constantinople, the Straits and ultimately to India, Britain's most prized imperial possession, motivated this policy.

On the other hand there was an increasing acceptance amongst the European powers that in order to survive, the Ottoman Empire would have to reform. The preferred approach was to encourage reform from within rather than to initiate international intervention which might destabilise the empire. This ushered in the period of Tanzimat reforms in the Ottoman Empire; the 1839 *Hatt-i-Gulhane* and the *Hatt-i-Humyan* Reform Act of 1856 which followed the Crimean War. On paper these reforms appeared to grant Christian subjects the same rights as their Muslim neighbours, bringing an end to religious discrimination and oppression.[31] In reality they made little difference.

In 1876 the exposure of the 'Bulgarian horrors' prompted widespread criticisms of British support for the Ottoman Empire.[32] The atrocities in Bulgaria were a product of clashes between Balkan nationalists and the Ottoman government. News of their occurrence led to an anti-Turkish campaign by the British press and leading public figures constituting a 'moral crusade on a vast scale'.[33] Gladstone's fiery condemnations of the Ottomans and his demand that they be removed from Europe 'bag and baggage' were echoed in a multitude of other publications.[34] Gladstone's rage was not restricted to the Ottoman Empire but also directed at those responsible for British policy, the Tory government and particularly Disraeli. From then onwards, the idea of responsibility for oppressed Christian minorities became entangled with the critique of Tory foreign policy and very much a part of Liberal imperial ideologies.

In the aftermath of the 'Bulgarian horrors' the Armenian cause began to gain ground in Britain. Not only had the Bulgarian campaign created public interest in 'minorities', it had also had international political consequences which made the fate of the Armenians a British concern. The peace treaties of San Stefano and Berlin demanded that the Ottoman government, the Sublime Porte, carry out reforms in the Armenian provinces of the empire and end the oppression of the Armenian population. Britain became involved in attempting to enforce these reforms. Despite these measures, the situation in the Armenian provinces deteriorated. In 1894 oppression and violence developed into widespread massacres which recurred over the next two years. The massacres prompted another outcry in Britain. A number of Liberal MPs, journalists, academics and churchmen expressed their support for the Armenians and condemned the government for failing to protect them. Meanwhile the government unsuccessfully searched for diplomatic solutions.

After the massacres the British government lost interest in the Armenian question, and so did the public. Nonetheless, an Armenophile movement had begun to emerge which continued to work on behalf of the Armenians. Organisations such as the *Friends of Armenia* and the *Anglo-Armenian Association* (AAA) provided humanitarian relief and pressed the government to intervene. As new conflicts emerged and attention shifted somewhat to the Balkan crises, Armenia moved to the background. The Young Turk revolution at first offered hopes that the situation in Armenia would be resolved but these were dashed by massacres which occurred at Adana, in Cilicia in South Eastern Anatolia in 1909. In the years before 1914 a new reform scheme was proposed by the European powers in order to improve the Armenian situation, but the progress of this scheme was halted by the outbreak of the Great War.

The war marked a disastrous new departure in the 'Armenian question'. The Ottoman Empire entered the war against the Allies in October 1914. In the months that followed, the authorities began to disarm the Armenian population, form Armenian units into 'labour battalions' and imprison Armenian men. In April 1915 the campaign against the Armenians intensified. On 24 April the Armenian leaders in Constantinople were imprisoned and executed and the deportation of the Armenian population began. The pattern of deportations was consistent: the men were rounded up, imprisoned and executed; women, children and the elderly were forced to leave their homes and join deportation marches into the Syrian Desert and Mesopotamian Valley. The pretext for the deportations was that the Armenians posed a threat to security as it was feared they would side with their fellow Armenians in Russia against the Ottoman Empire. Thus it was claimed that the Armenians had to be removed from vulnerable border regions.[35] In the process the Armenian population of Anatolia was practically destroyed.[36]

Around one million Armenians died as a result of the massacres and deportations. Those who were deported often suffered from sickness, starvation and exposure and were subject to ill treatment at the hands of their guards. Women faced added dangers of sexual violence. For those who survived the marches the situation was little better, as they were taken to camps without food, water, shelter or sanitation. The massacres not only resulted in the deaths of close to a million Armenians, they also created a refugee crisis in Transcaucasia and the Middle East, where thousands of Armenians were left destitute.

When they realised what was occurring, the Allies condemned the massacres and began the difficult attempt to bring humanitarian aid to the Armenians. As a result of the massacres and deportations, the Armenian population was scattered over Transcaucasia and the Middle East, and a fragile Armenian Republic temporarily emerged in Transcaucasia. The Armenian refugees were almost entirely dependent upon international aid, and organisations such as the British Lord Mayor's Fund (LMF) and American Near East Relief (NER) ran campaigns to raise funds.

The Allies made loud proclamations that the Turks should never again rule over the Armenians, and the Armenian diaspora in Europe attempted to convince the international community of the need for the creation of an independent state. Britain and the other powers initially appeared supportive of their claim. The form such a state should take, however, was a matter for some debate. By the end of the war, however, this support for the Armenians had evaporated and an independent Armenia failed to emerge. Instead the 'Armenian question' was brought to a close in a manner which no-one had envisaged, namely by the creation of a new Turkish nation which absorbed Western Armenian territories and by the establishment of Soviet power in Transcaucasian Armenia.

Imagining Armenia: ambiguity and intervention

The narrative of Armenian and British relations described above seems to conform to the idea of a British abandonment of Armenia after the First World War. This does not mean, however, that the precise nature of the British relationship with Armenia warrants no further attention. British relations with Armenia were bound up with the emergence of a particular set of representations of Armenia and the Armenians. My contention is that Said's account of orientalism offers a valuable starting point for gaining insight into the relationships between these representations and power. Considering British representations of Armenia from this perspective illuminates the way that they have shaped political and historical developments (and vice versa) and the construction of Armenian and British identities alike.

Such an approach also provides the possibility to build upon the theorising of orientalism and develop a more nuanced understanding of British constructions of 'the other'. Armenia does not fit easily into the dichotomous categories of 'East' and 'West' emphasised by Said. Instead images of Armenia have been characterised by ambiguity and fluidity. The ways in which ambiguity was bound up with power relations is a theme running through this book. This theoretical framework, which responds to Suny's call to integrate Armenian history with 'general theoretical and historical concerns', is addressed in depth in chapter 1.

Examining the ways in which the Armenians were imagined or represented in Britain during this period also offers insights beyond the focus on 'high politics' and diplomacy which have so far dominated the historical study of this period. In chapter 2 therefore, which concerns the 'rediscovery' of Armenia in the latter part of the nineteenth century, I draw upon representations of Armenia from a number of different fields, including travelogues, political pamphlets and the press. The chapter considers the frameworks and tools which were employed in conceptualising and categorising the world beyond Britain. It examines the discourses of orientalism, race, nation and gender which intersected to shape images of Armenia, drawing particular attention to the importance of the ideas of 'civilisation', 'degeneration' and 'progress' in conceptualising the Armenians and their relationship to Britain. This chapter also highlights the relationships of these concepts to paternalist ideologies, humanitarian interventions and power. Finally, it considers the ways in which images of Armenia help to shape, but were also shaped by, responses to the crisis constituted by the massacres of the Armenians 1894–96.

The issue of responding to crisis is followed through in chapters 3 and 4, which consider the representation of and responses to the Armenian genocide of 1915 and demonstrate the extent to which the fate of the Armenians impinged on wartime culture and politics. These chapters concern aspects of the war First World War which are not part of familiar British narratives of this period, which tend to focus on the Western Front. They draw upon a range of sources, from official government publications on the Armenians to less well-known Armenian nationalist propaganda and the reports of relief workers and officials.

These chapters examine the ways in which the image of the Armenians helped to determine the response to these events and also the way that ambiguous images of the Armenians were recast and manipulated according to particular historical circumstances. During the war, I suggest a new emphasis came to be placed upon the idea of Armenia as a 'nation', a change which related to specific wartime geopolitical agendas, but which also had important implications for the way in which the Armenian future was imagined. Chapter 3 also pays particular attention to how the genocide in Armenia was explained and categorised by contemporary observers. Whilst these explanations drew upon longstanding stereotypes, many British observers were insistent that they had witnessed an unprecedented kind of violence.

Chapter 4 addresses the fate of the Armenian refugees who survived the genocide. It focuses particularly upon British involvement in programmes of relief and repatriation. This offers important insights into the way Britain responded to population displacement on a massive scale, highlighting the motivations, practices and ethos that shaped the relief efforts. It also considers the particular ways that the Armenian refugee was represented and the relation of this to pre-existing images of Armenia and conceptions of Armenian identity. These images helped to determine the nature of British intervention in the region.

The final chapter examines British engagement with the question of the 'national' future of Armenia, tracing the shift from government support for the creation of an independent nation state to the abandonment of this project due to changing international aims and priorities. British attempts to gather information in order to determine the correct path for Armenian development are addressed, along with the various schemes which were proposed in order to bring peace and stability to the former Ottoman Empire. The British image of Armenia during the post-war period and the evolving responses to the idea of Armenian national independence and to the Sovietisation of the country are discussed in the final part of the chapter.

In conclusion I return to Armenia's position in relation to discourses of orientalism, examining the different factors which shaped images of British representations of Armenia and the changes that they underwent in the face of extreme violence and upheaval. I draw together the ways that shifting and ambivalent images of Armenia related to the realities of international politics. Finally I briefly examine hopes for the future of the

Introduction

Armenians, highlighting the way in which longstanding images of
Armenia as caught between East and West continued to shape visions of
the development of Soviet Armenia.

Notes

1 Some accounts are included in the collection edited by C. J. Walker, *Visions of
  Ararat: Writings on Armenia* (London: I. B. Tauris, 1997).
2 Felix Driver highlights the importance of empire for the development of
  exploration. 'The infrastructure of the British Empire was certainly significant
  for scientific exploration in the field; the imperial state's material resources and
  geographical reach provided unrivalled opportunities for scientific explorers
  to pursue their interests on a genuinely global scale.' F. Driver, *Geography
  Militant, Cultures of Exploration and Empire* (Oxford: Blackwell, 2001), p. 38.
  The development of empire was equally important for a general increase in
  possibilities for overseas travel.
3 After the 1820s the Armenian population were divided between these three
  empires. An explanation is provided in the introduction to M. Somakian,
  Empires in Conflict: Armenia and the Great Powers, 1895–1920 (London: I. B.
  Tauris, 1995). For population distributions of Armenians see R. Hewsen,
  Armenia: A Historical Atlas (Chicago and London: University of Chicago Press,
  2001).
4 American Protestant missionaries were present in the Ottoman Empire from
  the early nineteenth century. They were not allowed to carry out missionary
  work amongst the Muslim population so they turned their attention to the
  'improvement' of the Armenian Christians. S. E. Moranian, 'The Armenian
  Genocide and American Missionary Relief Efforts', in J. Winter, ed., *America
  and the Armenian Genocide of 1915* (Cambridge: Cambridge University Press,
  2003). In general see J. Grabill, *Protestant Diplomacy in the Near East*
  (Minneapolis: University of Minnesota Press, 1971).
5 J. George, *Merchants in Exile: The Armenians in Manchester, England, 1835–
  1935* (London: Gomidas Institute, 2002).
6 Hupchick explains that the term 'eastern question' 'lends general meaning to a
  complex web of nineteenth-century European Great Power relationships that
  dealt with the balance of power established at the congress of Vienna among
  Britain, France, Russia and the Hapsburg Empire . . . Ottoman destabilization,
  the rise of Romantic nationalism among the Empire's non Muslim subjects
  and the possible spectre of total Ottoman demise focused the issue of Great
  Power balance on the eastern Mediterranean and the strategically important
  Dardanelles and Bosporus straits.' P. Hupchick, *The Balkans, From
  Constantinople to Communism* (London: Palgrave, 2002), p. 245. In 1863 Sir A.
  H. Layard observed that 'This so called eastern question is undoubtedly one of
  the greatest problems that has ever been submitted to any generation of men.'

A. H. Layard, *The Condition of Turkey and Her Dependencies: A Speech Delivered in the House of Commons, Friday 29 May, 1863* (London: John Murray, 1863), p. 3.

7 See R. Shannon, *Gladstone and the Bulgarian Agitation, 1876* (London: Thomas Nelson, 1963) and A. Pottinger Saab, *Reluctant Icon: Gladstone, Bulgaria and the Working Classes 1856–1878* (Cambridge, MA: Harvard University Press, 1991).

8 Somakian, *Empires in Conflict*, A. J. Kirakosian, *Velikobritania i Armenianski Vopros: 90–e Gody XIX Veka* [Great Britain and the Armenian Question: 1890s] (Erevan: Aiastan, 1990). A more recent account is provided by D. Bloxham, *The Great Game of Genocide: Imperialism Nationalism and the Destruction of the Ottoman Armenians* (Oxford: Oxford University Press, 2005). On the 'Armenian question' and British party politics, R. Douglas, 'Britain and the Armenian Question 1894–97', *Historical Journal*, Vol. 19, No. 1 (March 1976), p. 117 and P. Marsh, 'Lord Salisbury and the Ottoman Massacres', *Journal of British Studies*, Vol. 11, No. 2 (May 1972).

9 See K. E. Fleming 'Orientalism, the Balkans and Balkan Historiography', *American Historical Review*, Vol. 105, No. 4 (October 2000). Fleming charts the use of Saidian approaches in the study of the Balkans.

10 M. Todorova, *Imagining the Balkans* (Oxford: Oxford University Press, 1997).

11 Walker, *Visions of Ararat*, Preface, p. xiii.

12 See R. G. Suny, 'Constructing Primordialism: Old Histories for New Nations', *Journal of Modern History*, Vol. 73, No. 4 (December 2001).

13 Conflict between Armenia and Azerbaijan over Karabagh, an autonomous region in Azerbaijan with a majority Armenian population, mounted during the 1980s and tensions escalated during the breakdown of the Soviet Union and independence. Armed conflict broke out during the 1990s. A ceasefire was declared in 1994 but the conflict remains unresolved. See M. Kurkchiyan, 'The Karabagh Conflict: From Soviet Past to Post-Soviet Uncertainty', in E. Herzig and M. Kurkchiyan, eds, *The Armenians: Past and Present in the Making of National Identity* (London: RoutledgeCurzon, 2005). On the Armenian Republic and the post-Soviet Caucasus see, E. Herzig, *The New Caucasus: Armenia, Azerbaijan and Georgia* (London: Royal Institute of International Affairs, 1999) and S. Cornell, *Small Nations and Great Powers. A Study of Ethnopolitical Conflict in the Caucasus* (Richmond: Curzon, 2000).

14 On Armenian identities see, Herzig and Kurkchiyan, *The Armenians*. They point out the complex ways in which Armenian identity is created and maintained by, 'as in all national communities the collective memory. Memory is not in itself history; it is a "socially constructed" selection from history that provides a shared account of where Armenians came from, the things that they did themselves and the things done to them by others, and how and why they came to be so widely dispersed today' (p. 2). Another recent contribution to scholarship on Armenian identity is L. Abrahamian, *Armenian Identity in a*

Changing World (Costa Mesa, CA: Mazda, 2006).

15 R. Panossian, *The Armenians: From Kings and Priests to Merchants and Commissars* (London: Hurst, 2006) p. 228.

16 Suny, 'Constructing Primordialism', p. 2. There are notable exceptions including Suny's *Looking Toward Ararat: Armenia in Modern History* (Bloomington and Indianapolis: Indiana University Press, 1993) and Hovannisian's many contributions.

17 Richard Hovannisian, 'Confronting the Armenian Genocide', in R. Hovannisian, ed., *Looking Backward, Moving Forward: Confronting the Armenian Genocide* (New Brunswick, NJ: Transaction, 2003), p. 2.

18 Susan Pattie points out that Armenian Studies courses in American universities respond in part to 'the anxiety that new generations may grow up knowing nothing about their past, and also to the fear that Armenians are being forgotten by a world where "no one knows about us". S. Pattie, 'Armenians in Diaspora' in Herzig and Kurkchiyan, *The Armenians*.

19 On the role of the past in Armenian national identity in the homeland and the diaspora see Panossian, *The Armenians*.

20 Suny documents the hostility that non-essentialist treatments of the Armenian nation can provoke in 'Constructing Primordialism'.

21 Hovannisian, 'Confronting the Armenian Genocide' pp. 2–3. Issues and implications of recognition and denial are also considered in R. W. Smith, 'The Armenian Genocide: Memory, Politics and The Future', in R. Hovannisian, ed., *The Armenian Genocide: History, Politics, Ethics* (London: Macmillan, 1992).

22 Provocation theses advocated, for example, by Stanford Shaw and Ezel Kural Shaw, are considered – and discredited – in R. Melson, *Revolution and Genocide: On the Origins of the Armenian Genocide and the Holocaust* (London and Chicago: University of Chicago Press, 1992), pp. 152–159 and Bloxham, *Great Game of Genocide*, pp. 209–211. Some scholars continue to deny that genocide occurred; others debate the causes and extent of the genocide. See also Gwynne Dyer, 'Turkish Falsifiers and Armenian deceivers. Historiography and the Armenian Massacres', *Middle Eastern Studies*, Vol. 12, No. 1 (1976) and Gerard Libaridian, 'Objectivity and the History of the Armenian Genocide', *Armenian Review*, 31 (Spring 1978).

23 Helen Fein outlines the issues at stake in denial of genocide in the twentieth century in Fein, *Denying Genocide: From Armenia to Bosnia* (London: LSE, Occasional Papers in Comparative and International Politics, 2001).

24 In America in October 2000, a recognition bill was removed at the last minute after Turkish protests. France recognised the genocide officially in 2001 and the European Parliament has also done so. The matter has become more pressing because of the issue of Turkish membership of the European Union.

25 Artin H. Arslanian, 'Britain and the Transcaucasian Nationalities during the Russian Civil War', in R. Suny, ed., *Transcaucasia: Nationalism and Social Change* (Ann Arbor: University of Michigan, 1983).

26 The charges against Pamuk were later dropped.

27 Comparative works include Melson, *Revolution and Genocide*, L. Kuper, *Genocide: Its Political Use in the Twentieth Century* (London: Penguin, 1982) and N. Naimark, *Fires of Hatred: Ethnic Cleansing in Twentieth Century Europe* (London: Harvard University Press, 2001). On responses see Samantha Power, *A Problem from Hell: America and the Age of Genocide* (New York: Basic Books, 2002).

28 Suny, 'Constructing Primordialism', p. 3.

29 See A. Wheatcroft, *Infidels: A History of the Conflict between Christendom and Islam* (London: Penguin, 2003), pp. 247–256.

30 M. Mazower, *The Balkans* (London: Phoenix, 2000), pp. 98–110, also Hupchick, *Constantinople to Communism*, Part 3.

31 Bloxham explains that 'The later *hat* (decree) was a restatement of the former, yet it went considerably further in its rhetoric of inter-religious equality and secularization and its view of a new form of inclusive common identity – patriotic Ottomanism – to replace the traditional theocratic order among the Sultan's subjects.' Bloxham, *Great Game of Genocide*, pp. 31–34.

32 In 1875 nationalist uprisings had occurred in Bosnia and Herzegovina, although these revolts were unsuccessful; by 1876 the unrest spread to neighbouring Bulgaria. The Bulgarian insurrection of May 1876 was violently suppressed by the Ottoman irregular troops, the *bashibasouks*, resulting in the death of 12–15,000 Christians and reports of widespread atrocities committed by the Turkish troops. Figures from Mazower, *The Balkans*, p. 100. See also R. Seton-Watson, *Disraeli, Gladstone and the Eastern Question* (London: Macmillan & Co., 1935) and R. Shannon, *Gladstone and the Bulgarian Agitation* (London: Nelson, 1963).

33 Wheatcroft, *Infidels*, p. 259.

34 W. E. Gladstone, *Bulgarian Horrors and the Question of the East* (London: John Murray, 1896), reprint of 1876 edition. This pamphlet sold 24,000 copies on the day it was published and 100,000 in the longer term. 'The appearance of Gladstone's great diatribe against the Turk in September 1876 was the point at which the anti-Ottoman cause became a juggernaut': Wheatcroft, *Infidels*, p. 262.

35 The most comprehensive cotemporary collection of accounts of the deportations and massacres is J. Bryce and A. Toynbee's *The Treatment of the Armenians in the Ottoman Empire* (London: Hodder and Stoughton, 1916). For an overview see 'Introduction' in Bloxham, *Great Game of Genocide*, pp. 1–5. Bloxham provides a longer term account of the process of the genocide in 'The Armenian Genocide of 1915–1916: Cumulative Radicalization and the Development of a Destruction Policy', *Past and Present*, No. 181 (November 2003), pp. 141–192. See also Hovannisian, 'The Historical Dimension of the Armenian Question', in R. Hovannisian, ed., *The Armenian Genocide in Perspective* (New Brunswick, NJ: Transaction, 1986) and Hewsen's maps of the

deportation routes and massacres (Map 224, The Armenian Genocide) in
Hewsen, *Armenia.*

36 Melson points out the difficulties at arriving at a precise figure due to a lack of
accurate pre-war statistics and subsequent attempts to minimise the killings.
He estimates that before the conclusion of the war around one million
Armenians, half the pre-war population, had been killed. Melson, *Revolution
and Genocide,* pp. 145–147.

1

Imagining Armenia:
otherness, orientalism and ambiguity

Introduction

> The Armenians have been a very typical element in that group of
> humanity which Europeans call the 'Near East' ... There has been
> something pathological about the history of this Near Eastern world. It has
> had an undue share of political misfortunes and has lain for centuries in a
> kind of spiritual paralysis between East and West, partaking, paradoxically
> of both.

The above quotation is taken from Arnold Toynbee's history of Armenia,
which he included as an appendix in his collection of documents on the
Armenian genocide, entitled *The Treatment of the Armenians in the
Ottoman Empire*.[1] Toynbee's characterisation of Armenia as a place
'between East and West' was by no means unusual; it drew upon a familiar theme in representations of Armenia since at least the late nineteenth
century, when British scholars, travellers and missionaries highlighted the
ambiguous position of Armenians.

For Toynbee, Armenia's borderland position was unnatural, dangerous, even pathological, because Armenia did not fit the ideal pattern of
a world divided into East and West, Orient and Occident. These geographical categories were also imbued with cultural significance, a
means of defining one's own identity and that of others, and were implicated in power relations and the maintenance of European imperial
domination.[2] Toynbee's anxieties over the paradoxical position of
Armenia in relation to these categories represented only one dimension
of a complex array of British perceptions of this region. Not all observers

viewed this paradoxical position as a matter for anxiety. Others believed that it offered potential for cultural exchange and development rather than 'spiritual paralysis'.

Toynbee's approach to Armenia reflected the circumstances in which he wrote. He produced *The Treatment of the Armenians* during the First World War, under the auspices of the Ministry of Information, the propaganda department of the British government.[3] Toynbee's agenda was to demonstrate that the Ottoman Empire constituted despotic government, unfit to rule over Christian minorities. That Toynbee sought to interpret the situation of the Armenians in accordance with prevailing political agendas was not unique. British images of the Armenians were never produced in a vacuum; popular images of Armenia which appeared during the late nineteenth century had been conditioned specifically by the 'eastern question' and more generally by imperial considerations. Following the genocide, Britain's international interests governed its stance towards Armenian independence and indirectly affected representations of Armenia. Toynbee's interpretation is significant because of the way in which he utilised the image of the Armenians as 'in-between' to suit his own purpose, namely to 'claim' the Armenians unambiguously for the West.

This chapter addresses the 'in-between' status of Armenia in order to provide a framework for understanding how Armenia and the Armenians were imagined, represented and responded to in Britain. It examines the relationship of representations to the growth of political and humanitarian interest and intervention in the region. Edward Said's account of orientalism as a 'Western style for dominating, restructuring and having authority over the Orient' is taken as a starting point.[4] This approach has had a powerful impact upon the ways in which the relationship between European representations of the 'other' and the maintenance of imperial power are understood.[5]

The interrelatedness of representations and imperial dominance is significant for understanding how Armenia was imagined in Britain but Said's influential ideas, which centre upon the western construction of the East as opposite and inferior, cannot be applied straightforwardly to images of Armenia. Examining British representations of Armenia poses a challenge to the idea of orientalism, highlighting the need for an examination of the complexities of these categories, especially in the case of regions considered to be borderlands or in-between spaces. In this chapter I begin by examining Said's account of orientalism and the critiques that it has provoked before going on to consider how and why his approach can nonetheless be productive in analysing British representations of Armenia.

Orientalism at the crossroads: imagining Armenia

Edward Said draws upon Foucault's conceptions of discourse and power in order to examine the ways in which knowledge and representations of the Orient were implicated in European imperial dominance or 'the degree to which the West's systems of scholarship, and its canons of aesthetic representation, have been implicated in the long history of the West's material and political domination of the non-western world'.[6] Imperial power, according to Said, was not simply exercised at a state level, but rather permeated through society. As Said explained:

> Because of Orientalism the Orient was not (and is not) a free subject of thought or action. This is not to say that Orientalism unilaterally determines what can be said about the Orient but that it is the whole network of interests inevitably brought to bear on (and therefore always involved in) any occasion when that peculiar entity is in question.[7]

Orientalist discourse produced a particular set of images of the East for the West which allowed a distant place to be 'known', that is understood, managed and ruled. This process was not simply the work of the academic study of the Orient but of cultural production in a much broader sense. As Catherine Hall points out, 'Said's contribution was to link culture inexorably with colonialism – a link which has been taken up in different ways by many scholars.'[8] Numerous different forms of knowledge were involved in reproducing and elaborating upon the Orient. Literary texts (upon which Said focuses), art, history, travel writing, anthropology, linguistics and geography were all bound up with orientalist discourse:

> There emerged a complex Orient suitable for study in the academy, for display in the museum, for reconstruction in the colonial office, for theoretical illustration in anthropological, biological, linguistic, racial and historical theses about mankind and the universe, for instances of economic and sociological theories of development, revolution, cultural personality, national or religious character.[9]

As Said points out, it was the consistency and cohesion of images of the Orient produced across different forms of knowledge which made orientalism powerful. Orientalist discourse was therefore wide ranging yet highly systematic. This is what secured western hegemony over the East.[10]

Power over the East stemmed not only from the fact that the West could produce knowledge about it, but also from the particular ways in which the Orient was represented. According to Said, this related more to the needs of imperial power than it reflected any 'real' Orient. Orientalist discourses first and foremost created a binary distinction between the East and the West. In Said's interpretation, the Orient figured in the western imagination as its opposite or 'other', as exotic, feminine, barbaric, lustful, unchanging and irrational. This vision of the East always implied inferiority to the West, and as such helped to re-affirm and legitimise the superiority of the European world and therefore European imperial power. In Said's words, 'European culture gained in strength and identity by setting itself off against the Orient as a sort of surrogate and even underground self.'[11]

Notwithstanding the criticism that it has generated, Said's approach in *Orientalism* has generated fresh understanding of imperialism and representations of the 'other'. As Patrick Williams and Laura Chrisman indicate:

> It is perhaps no exaggeration to say that Edward Said's *Orientalism*, published in 1978, single handedly inaugurates a new area of academic inquiry, colonial discourse . . . Michael Foucault has said that discursive constraints – the rules governing what can and cannot be said within the boundaries of a particular discourse – should be understood as productive as well as limiting; and certainly if we see Orientalism as setting out various discursive boundaries for colonial discourse analysis, then, judging from the work that has followed, they appear to have functioned much more as an incitement than as an impediment.[12]

If Orientalism is regarded as an 'incitement', its relevance to representations of Armenia becomes clearer. Looking at representations of Armenia through the lens of orientalism not only enhances understandings of the representation of this particular 'other', it also contributes to the process of critiquing and developing the idea of orientalist discourse. The case of Armenia, a place which was accepted as neither 'eastern' or 'western', offers an opportunity to examine the complexities and ambiguities of constructions of the 'other', complexities which may be glossed over by overarching theories of orientalism.

Orientalism: critiques and developments

Critiques of *Orientalism* have arisen from a variety of perspectives and have addressed a number of problematic elements within Said's approach. One of the most significant has been the charge that Said fails to acknowledge the capacity of the colonised to resist or 'answer back' to orientalist discourse. In effect, this renders them powerless and reinforces the power relations created by the orientalist discourses he sets out to challenge. This has proved to be a productive area of study, particularly in postcolonial theory.[13] Most pertinent to the question of the British encounter with Armenia are critiques of Said's emphasis on the 'systematic and invariant nature of the orientalist discourse'.[14]

In *Orientalism*, Said tried to demonstrate that European representations of the East were not objective reflections of the realities of the region or simply the expressions of those who produced the representations. Instead, Said argued that European representations of the Orient were a product of orientalist discourse which shaped and constrained what could and what could not be said about the region. This resulted in a highly coherent and regularised understanding of the Orient.[15]

However, Said's employment of Foucault's concept of discourse has been subject to numerous critiques. One of the principal issues at stake is whether orientalist discourse should be understood as monolithic, consistent and unchanging, or as dynamic and heterogeneous. In the words of Dennis Porter, 'because he overlooks the potential contradiction between discourse theory and Gramscian hegemony, he fails to historicize adequately the texts he cites and summarises, finding always the same triumphant discourse, where several are frequently in conflict'. This suggestion that Said has failed to acknowledge the heterogeneity and historical and geographical specificities of orientalist discourse has been made from a variety of disciplinary perspectives.[16]

Although he focuses on the period of 'high' imperialism during the nineteenth century, Said traces a lineage of 'orientalism' from the ancient world. In doing so he is in danger of presenting orientalism as a 'natural' way of perceiving the world and confusing his argument that orientalist discourse is specifically linked to the age of imperialism.[17] Other critics have pointed out that discourses of orientalism are geographically as well as historically specific. As Sarah Mills suggests, 'each colonial relation develops narrative and descriptive techniques particular to its setting and history, which draw on a range of discursive practices'.[18]

Critiques from a feminist perspective have tended to suggest that it may be inadequate to assume that only one orientalist point of view will emerge even in relation to one particular setting.[19] In *Gendering Orientalism*, Reina Lewis points out that, for Said, orientalism 'is a homogenous discourse enunciated by a colonial subject that is unified, intentional and irredeemably male'.[20] Rejecting this viewpoint, she and other scholars have stressed the range of voices and perspectives that are involved in the production of orientalist discourse.[21] Lisa Loew has suggested that orientalism is more helpfully understood as an 'apparatus through which a variety of concerns with difference is figured'.[22] This work draws attention to the generation of orientalist discourse from multiple sites, and its intersection with discourses of class, gender or race. As a result of these approaches the dichotomy drawn by Said between 'self' and 'other' is disrupted. What constitutes the 'self' appears less unified and instead as a number of fragmented, sometimes conflicting or competing voices.

Orientalism, imperialism and the question of minorities

Even though Armenia was never a British imperial possession, imperialism provided the context for British encounters with Armenia. The regions inhabited by Armenians had a strategic, geopolitical relevance for the British imperial project. Armenia lay on the edge of the Russian and Ottoman Empires, in a region vital for the defence of India.[23] The British government feared Russian advances in this region and as a result was keen to prevent instability which would provide a pretext for Russian intervention. Britain therefore became involved in the development of reforms in the Armenian provinces of the Ottoman Empire. Involvement in reform schemes for Armenia gave British power in the region a material form. Administrative reforms such as the appointment of European military consuls represented an attempt to control the development of the region.

Imperialism also conditioned British relations with Armenia in a more general sense, having a cultural, social and political influence beyond the regions under colonial rule. Discourses of imperialism impinged upon understandings of domestic life and culture, playing a role in the shaping of identities at home as well as abroad. In the words of Reina Lewis, 'As a pervasive economic, social, political and cultural formation, the imperial project could not but influence how people thought, behaved and created.'[24] It follows therefore that imperialist discourse (which encompassed not only orientalism, but also, for example, discourses of race and religion, civilisation and progress) affected the construction of British images of Armenia and the Armenians. It also had an equally powerful effect upon political and humanitarian intervention undertaken in the region.

From the late 1870s onwards, Armenia became entangled in discourses of imperialism in a very specific way. As the 'eastern question' developed, the Armenians came to be portrayed as a Christian minority, suffering under Ottoman rule. The fate of the Armenians rapidly progressed from the status of a relatively minor political problem or 'question' to that of a passionate cause. The emergence of a network of dedicated British

Armenophiles was central to the transformation of the status of the 'Armenian question'.

This pro-Armenian cause or Armenophile movement did not develop in isolation. Maria Todorova has highlighted an emerging preoccupation with the condition of 'minorities', national or religious groups thought to be subject to oppressive rule at the hands of the Ottoman Empire and deemed deserving of British support: 'there was always a plurality of British sympathies in the East and there is hardly a single group or nation that had not attracted the support of some group in English society at some time'.[25] The start of this prolonged incursion of the Christian minorities of the Ottoman Empire into British political and cultural life was marked by the popular agitation over the 'Bulgarian horrors' in 1876.

The fates of the Armenians, the Bulgarians and later the Macedonians all became the subject of popular interest in Britain during the late nineteenth and early twentieth centuries. Although these 'causes' shared similar features and were all shaped by discourses of Ottoman barbarism, Christian suffering and European (specifically British) civilisation, the Armenian cause was distinct in a number of ways. Firstly the Armenian diaspora were particularly engaged in promoting the Armenian cause and in many cases worked closely with their British supporters. Secondly the Armenians, in the eyes of the Armenophiles at least, had a particular association with the origins of civilisation (Mount Ararat, the Armenian national symbol, was thought to be the final resting place of Noah's Ark) and a special capacity for progress, which were thought to make them worthy of British attention. Lastly the cataclysmic events of the First World War ensured that the Armenian cause remained the object of political and humanitarian intervention until at least the mid-1920s.

During the last three decades of the nineteenth century espousing these minority causes became a key dimension of Liberal critiques of British imperialism, a way of critiquing Disraeli's supposedly aggressive foreign policy. For Liberal public figures it provided a way to demonstrate moral and political convictions and credentials. In expressions of their concern for a minority such as the Armenians they demonstrated their commitment to a progressive approach to empire, their humanitarian ethos and also their Christian beliefs.[26]

The need to demonstrate a particular vision of imperialism through taking up the cause of a minority was directly linked to the development of mass politics and the increasing significance of public opinion in matters of imperial and foreign policy. In the latter decades of the nineteenth century imperialism had been increasingly a matter of public interest and debate.[27] Attempts to popularise the idea of empire and utilise imperialism as a source of patriotism and a force for social cohesion have been closely associated with Disraeli. His approach helped ensure that empire became an increasingly important aspect of British identity and a source of pride and prestige. Colin Matthew explains that 'Recognising the power of symbol, Disraeli created for the new electorate the myth of the imperial party with the patriotic underpinnings of Queen, Church and Empire.'[28]

Minority 'causes' were one way in which the public could be drawn into foreign and imperial matters. Graphic depictions of the suffering of Christians under Ottoman rule brought Britain's imperial role home to the public in a highly emotive manner. However, the relationship of this concern for minorities to British politics was complex and shifting. In the late nineteenth century, 'minority' causes were an arena for protest and could be utilised in order to motivate public opinion; not against imperialism as such, but against the particular form of imperialism associated with the Tories and personified by Disraeli.

This is not to say that the espousal of minority causes was a straightforward matter of party allegiances and politics. Many Armenophiles were keen to stress the 'non-party' nature of their interest in the cause. Concerns for minorities were connected to other developments beyond the sphere of high politics and imperialism. Most importantly, concern for minorities abroad must be examined in the context of discourses of philanthropy and humanitarianism circulating in Britain in the late nineteenth century. Concerns for minorities such as the Armenians were framed in strikingly similar ways to the increasing concerns for the British poor. As Todorova points out, 'the coincidence between the discovery of the oppressed Christian nationalities and the discovery of the Victorian poor with their respective discourses after the middle of the century was especially remarkable'.[29] During the late nineteenth century both of these groups found themselves the object of scrutiny as well as sympathy. Thus the Armenians not only became the subjects of intense political debate, but also the objects of concern in terms of health, welfare and education and consequently the recipients of charity.

The leading lights of minority campaigns were frequently Liberal academics and politicians, along with religious leaders from the Nonconformist and Anglican churches. Their support for minorities usually went hand in hand with a number of other 'moral', progressive or humanitarian causes, for example the anti-slavery movement, the peace movement, the pro-Boers and the campaign to reform the Belgian

Congo.[30] These humanitarian ventures were framed as a common cause.[31] During the First World War interest in the welfare of minorities reached new heights as campaigns were mounted on behalf of various nationalities and minorities said to be suffering under German, Ottoman or Habsburg rule.

The centrality of 'minority campaigns' to imperialism is highlighted by Said in *Orientalism*:

> Near the centre of all European politics in the East was the question of minorities, whose 'interests' the powers, each in its own way, claimed to protect and represent. Jews, Greek and Russian Orthodox, Druses, Circassians, Armenians, Kurds, the various small Christian sects: all these were studied, planned for, designed upon by European powers improvising as well as constructing their Oriental policies.[32]

However, the case of 'minorities' raises important questions regarding the dichotomy between East and West which underpins Said's argument. None of the Christian minorities which attracted the support of the European nations (Armenians, Bulgarians and for example, Maronite Christians in Lebanon) fitted neatly into the opposing categories of East or West. Nor did they completely fulfil all of the criteria of civilisation and barbarism that they entailed. On the one hand, they were portrayed as having close historical and cultural bonds with their European supporters – in particular through their Christian faith. In the eyes of their supporters this bestowed on them the potential to be 'civilised' and rendered them deserving of British support. Nevertheless, these minorities were not treated as 'the same'; they were inhabitants of distant and exotic lands, with 'eastern' characteristics, unfamiliar customs and ways of life, incapable of improving their situation without British intervention.

As the fate of the Armenians began to impinge upon the British political world, an increasing amount of time and energy was spent trying to untangle such complexities through observing, studying and classifying the Armenians. Although interest in Armenia was driven by contemporary politics it was not just the current situation of the Armenian people that was considered to be of importance, but also their history, society and culture. Thus British interests in Armenia were wide ranging, spanning from ancient history to contemporary religious practice. In their efforts to 'understand' the nature of the Armenians, British scholars, travellers, officials and missionaries employed the practices, categories and theories associated with orientalism. Theories of race, of progress and degeneration and concepts of civilisation and barbarism which had been elaborated in order to deal with the diversity encountered through imperialist expansion, were all utilised in order to fit the Armenians into the hierarchical worldviews of the nineteenth century.[33]

This effort to become 'experts' on Armenia should be viewed in the light of James Clifford's observation that one of the most significant contributions of *Orientalism* is to highlight, 'The paternalist privileges unhesitatingly assumed by Western writers who "speak for" a mute Orient or reconstitute its delayed or dismembered truth, who lament the passing of its authenticity and know more than its mere native ever can.'[34] British scholars, politicians and Armenophiles made the paternalist assumption that with access to 'authentic' information about the Armenian past and present, they could ascertain what was in their 'best interests' for the future.

Both officials and interested members of the public contributed to this process. Consular and diplomatic staff in the Ottoman Empire provided the British government with first-hand information about the Armenians in order to help determine policies of reform and intervention.[35] The information they gathered was augmented by that of individuals, including politicians, scholars and the clergy, who travelled in the region in the hope of gaining an 'authentic' insight into the life of the Armenian population; in fact travelogues soon became the most important source of information about Armenia.[36] As public interest in the 'Armenian question' grew, journalists such as E. J. Dillon supplemented travel accounts by providing 'up to date' reports on the situation in Armenia. These were frequently sensationalist reports which graphically depicted violence and suffering.[37]

Since the Bulgarian atrocities British observers had attempted to understand the 'problem' of the nineteenth-century Ottoman Empire. Journalists, politicians and academics all sought to explain why, in their eyes, atrocity and massacre were inescapable features of Ottoman rule.[38] Race, religion, culture and history were incorporated into these arguments but their overarching theme was that Ottoman rule represented barbarism and had no place in the modern world.

Those interested in the Armenian cause sought more specific and indepth information. Their interest was not restricted to the present condition of the Armenians. On the contrary, an understanding of the present was thought to depend upon on a thorough knowledge of Armenian society, culture, politics and particularly the Armenian past. Armenophiles such as James Bryce and later Noel and Harold Buxton did not draw the line at political criticism and activism; they positioned themselves as 'experts' on all things Armenian.[39]

Attempts to 'find out' about and define the Armenians were not a one-way process. Armenian scholars and social, political and religious leaders had already begun to undertake this project. The Armenian cultural 'renaissance' spearheaded by the work of the Armenian Mekhitarist monks in Vienna and Venice preceded the work of the British Armenophiles in bringing the Armenians to the attention of Europe. From the end of the eighteenth century these monastic communities res-urrected and reprinted important works of Armenian literature and medieval histories, and promoted Armenian education.[40]

This 'renaissance' continued amongst the Armenian communities in the Ottoman and Russian Empires as scholarly and commercial contacts abroad developed, educational opportunities increased and a national press emerged.[41] As a result of this process, 'Armenian intellectuals began to articulate a new idea of what it meant to be Armenian, a secular myth appropriate for the modern world.'[42] Cultural renaissance preceded the development of political forms of nationalism and Armenian nationalist parties were established during the 1890s.

Although the Armenian nationalist movement was by no means united, a common theme running through pro-Armenian propaganda was the appeal to Western Europe, and particularly Britain, to come to the aid of the Armenians. The appeal to Britain had its roots in the great power diplomacy of the 'eastern question' and as the 'Armenian question' pro-gressed diasporan Armenians, in Britain at least, showed a willingness to work with the Armenophile movements, providing them with informa-tion and in some cases working in close association with them.

Between East and West: the ambivalent image of Armenia

Though the Armenian cause was associated with the critique of a partic-ular type of imperialism, it was not necessarily 'anti-imperialist'. Rather, it implicitly sanctioned British imperial dominance, reaffirming imperialis-tic worldviews. Minority causes were enmeshed in the formation of British imperial identities and the delineating of the boundaries of the 'self' or the civilised European world. Yet the image of minorities did not conform to the orientalist East/West division of the world which has come to be associated with imperialism. Rather than 'eastern' or 'western', Armenia was imagined as a borderland, 'in-between' East and West. The image of the Armenians, therefore, was characterised by ambiguity.

The Armenian population was dispersed across the borders of the Russian, Persian and Ottoman Empires, a region frequently portrayed as the boundary between civilisation and barbarism or Europe and Asia. It was also perceived as a religious borderland, the meeting place of Christianity and Islam. Armenia was problematic as it seemed to straddle these borders. The Armenians were considered an 'ancient nation' with a long history of 'civilisation' and Christianity and the potential to be 'resurrected'. These features distanced them from stereotypical images of the East as unchristian, uncultured and barbaric. In these respects Armenia belonged to the West.

The violence and upheaval which the Armenians was subjected to during the nineteenth and early twentieth centuries also confirmed their status as part of the West, for acts of 'barbarism' played an important part in defining the East. This would become particularly evident after the Armenian massacres of the 1890s and again following the genocide of 1915. Committing 'atrocities' came to be seen as characteristic behaviour of 'orientals'. Their victims became part of the West by default, by virtue of the nature of their enemies rather than their own characteristics.

The oppression of minorities was regarded as representative of an ongoing clash between East and West or barbarism and civilisation. The Quaker relief workers Rendel and Helen Harris, on a journey through Armenia in the wake of the massacres of 1894 exemplify this point of view. They felt they were experiencing this clash at first hand, reporting that they were very 'impressed' by what they saw 'as regards the conflict between civilisation and barbarism'.[43]

Yet even the writings of the most ardent British Armenophiles expressed the belief that the Armenians were 'different' to the British population. This difference was articulated in a number of ways. For example, those who encountered the Armenians in the Ottoman or Russian Empires were disillusioned by what they witnessed of day-to-day life. The 'otherness' of the Armenians was expressed through mundane details of food, clothes, manners and dress, none of which matched the standards of the British observers. Secondly, differences between the Armenians and the British were theorised in terms of national development and the argument that the Armenians had not yet reached the same levels of civilisation and progress as western European nations.[44] Armenia therefore occupied an ambiguous border space in the British imagination, part eastern, part western; not fully civilised yet not totally alien, worthy of British support and protection, yet subordinate and inferior.

To an extent the Armenians occupied a similar place in the turn of the century British imagination to that of the Jews. The work of scholars such as Bryan Cheyette demonstrates that the Jews, like the Armenians, did not fit neatly into existing categories or worldviews but also occupied an ambiguous place on the margins.[45] British perceptions and representations of the Jews, Cheyette suggests, cannot be easily divided into 'antisemitic' and 'philosemitic'. Rather the image of the Jew was flexible and shifting, and 'the Jew' could represent a multitude of different characteristics. British perceptions of the Armenians were equally ambiguous.

Scholars of Jewish history and culture have also argued that such ambiguity was not 'neutral', but rather could provoke anxiety or hostility. In particular, Zygmunt Bauman has suggested that it is precisely because the Jews do not fit the categories and divisions that characterise modernity, that they have been a source of anxiety and fear and have therefore been targeted. 'Doing something about the Jews was not just an effort to make the world pleasingly uniform again but an effort to fight the world's contingency, opacity, uncontrollability. In other words to fight ambivalence.'[46]

Bauman's arguments regarding ambivalence and the fate of the Jews in twentieth-century Europe are very specific and cannot of course be applied in full to case of the Armenians.[47] However his perspectives regarding ambivalence and the desire to intervene that it may provoke offers insights for the Armenian case. Like the Jews, the Armenians were dispersed rather than a homogenous nation state. They were thought to have origins and history in common with Europe but a present which had diverged. They were a Christian people but they lived on the fringes of the Christian world, surrounded by Islam. In summary they were regarded as 'special' and worthy of British attention, but also as 'different' or a 'problem'. Often these two perspectives overlapped in producing a desire to intervene on their behalf and 'resolve' their troublesome position.

As Bryan Cheyette has pointed out, in the British Liberal framework Jews were only tolerated under the assumption that they would ideally overcome and transcend what made them 'different'. That is, they were regarded as close enough to the British ideal of the good citizen that there was potential for them to overcome their distance from this and become the ideal.[48] The same was true of Liberal approaches to the Armenians which centred upon encouraging the development of Armenian 'civilisation' towards British standards. Although the 'otherness' of the Armenians was obvious to the British scholars, travellers and diplomats who encountered them, it was firmly believed that with British intervention and assistance this 'otherness' could be tamed and a model Armenian nation created.

Defining the boundaries of Europe

The Jewish case is not the only one to offer important insights into British understandings of the Armenians. In her work on European representation of the Balkans, Maria Todorova refers to discourses concerning the region as 'Balkanism'. This term is used in direct reference to Said's account of 'orientalism'. Todorova's purpose however is to draw attention to the fact that 'Balkanism' is something different to 'orientalism', not merely a variety or 'subspecies' of the same phenomenon.[49] K. E. Fleming reinforces Todorova's point, warning against making generalisations about orientalism: 'Orientalism cannot simply be a catchall category that denotes something along the lines of making gross and vaguely depreciating generalizations about other (especially non-western) peoples and cultures.'[50] Nevertheless, the idea of orientalist discourse provides a frame of reference for both of their arguments.

As Fleming points out, there is a two-way exchange; just as the concept of Orientalism illuminates the study of the Balkans, so examining the representation of the Balkans challenges and develops the theorising of orientalism:

> The Balkans once again eludes Said's criteria. Their liminality, their status as an 'inside other', their own claims to European primacy, their geographical location (on the borders of but nevertheless within Europe), Western Europe's uncertainty as to where to place them all make the Balkans ripe with theoretical possibility.[51]

Liminality and the notion of being 'borderlands' are characteristics frequently attributed to both the Balkans and Armenia. As the quotation from Toynbee at the start of this chapter illustrated, the Armenians were, like the Balkans, thought of as, 'between East and West', belonging fully to neither.[52] This perceived status was not exclusive to Armenia and the Balkans. Eastern Europe for example, has been, in the words of Larry Wolff, 'a paradox of simultaneous inclusion and exclusion, Europe but not Europe. Eastern Europe defined Western Europe by contrast, as the Orient defined the Occident, but was also made to mediate between Europe and the Orient.'[53]

In *Inventing Eastern Europe*, Wolff historicises the way that the margins of Europe have been imagined, demonstrating the contingency of the meaning of 'Europe' and undermining ideas regarding 'natural' divisions between the East and the West. He does not dispense with the orientalist idea of contrast between East and West altogether; the idea of Eastern Europe, he says, evolved alongside that of orientalism and is closely related to it. Like Orientalism, the invention of Eastern Europe was essential to the parallel process of inventing the West. It was a process by which Western Europe 'identified itself and affirmed its own precedence'.[54] What is most interesting for the Armenian case is his observation that the construction of Eastern Europe as an ambiguous, paradoxical or 'in-between' place is not merely accidental. It is not a matter of the region having 'slipped through the net' of dichotomous worldviews. Imagining Eastern Europe in this way could be deliberate and productive; it was a concept which 'flourished on its own instability'.[55]

Wolff also highlights the close relationship of the invention of Eastern Europe to the elaboration of concepts such as civilisation and backwardness, concepts which are frequent reference points in 'minorities' discourse. The region is imagined as both contrasting with European civilisation and providing a space that 'mediates' between the East and the West or civilisation and barbarism. This theme of mediation recurs in British images of Armenia. Armenia often represents a space through which civilisation was first passed from the East to the West and through which civilisation may once again be rekindled in the East. The idea of mediation also relates to power. As an intermediate region Armenia was thought to be open to change and progress, a site where the spread of British 'civilisation' could occur on a practical, material level.

Wolff's arguments raise important questions regarding the ways in which Western Europe has defined itself and its 'others'. However the Enlightenment encounter with Eastern Europe which is the focus of Wolff's work was somewhat different to the British encounter with the Armenians. Although Armenia, like Eastern Europe, has been viewed as a kind of 'internal other', there are particular aspects of the British image of Armenia which differentiated it from the image of Eastern European regions. Just as it is unhelpful to apply the concept of orientalism in a blanket manner, it is unhelpful to subsume British representations of Armenia into those of 'Eastern Europe'. For this reason it is necessary to focus more closely upon the context in which the Armenians were encountered.

Orientalism, Balkanism, ambiguity

In terms of historical context, British encounters with the Balkans had much in common with the encounter with the Armenians. Both Armenians and Balkan minorities (Bulgarians, Serbs and Macedonians) were Orthodox Christian peoples ruled over and thought to be oppressed and exploited by the Ottoman Empire. They were also commonly regarded as part of the same problem, the 'eastern question'. In both cases Britain had to grapple with the issues of Ottoman decline and emerging national movements. Both of these issues posed seemingly intractable problems.

Both regions were deemed worthy of special interest and attention by British observers. However, they were also perceived as 'problem' areas, prone to violence and unrest. They were a source of anxiety for two reasons: firstly because of the destabilising threat they posed to the international balance of power and secondly because they transgressed the conceptual boundaries that ordered the world. Their liminal position blurred the border between 'self' and 'other' and presented a confusing mix of characteristics and features. For this reason representations of Armenia and the Balkans alike sometimes encompassed a reassertion of a 'natural' order, addressing the question of how and why these regions deviated from the 'proper' path of development, and how this situation could be rectified through British intervention in the future. Of course this also presented an opportunity to shore up the boundaries of the European, 'civilised' self.

Todorova's claim that orientalism is a discourse about opposition, whereas 'Balkanism' is a discourse about 'imputed ambiguity', is suggestive for the case of Armenia.[56] This ambiguity is clearly demonstrated in the response to the Orthodox Churches of the Balkans and Armenia. In both cases the Eastern Church was regarded as an inferior form of faith, based on superstition and ignorance. Nevertheless Orthodoxy was not, like Islam, thought to be the 'enemy' or antithesis of European Christianity. Rather there were thought to be 'bonds' between the two faiths and many Western European observers believed that the Orthodox churches simply needed corrective reform. Racial difference was understood in a similar way. Although the Slavic peoples of the Balkans were thought to be different they were not as different as the inhabitants of Africa or Asia. In Todorova's formulation, difference is characterised as a variation 'within' rather than 'between' types.[57]

But although they shared the characteristic of ambiguity, British images of Armenia and the Balkans were not identical. Specific meanings were attached to Armenia, differentiating the region from the Balkans. These meanings were derived from the history and geography of Armenia and from the particularities of the encounter between Armenia and Britain. The geographic location of the Armenians also distanced them from Europe and the Balkans, allowing them to be more closely identified with the Near East. Thus Francis Seymour Stevenson of the AAA could confidently assert that in 1876 'the condition of the Christians in Asia Minor

. . . was not a subject which concerned European politics. Armenia was not in Europe.'[58]

Nor was Armenia fully part of the 'East'. As the 'Armenian question' developed there was an increasing tendency to view Armenia as a part of the civilised European world. Geographical distance or disunity was compensated for through the ideas of cultural proximity and shared origins. The idea of Armenia as a 'cradle of civilisation' became a recurrent theme in British images. This theme drew upon the idea of Armenia as the site of biblical origin myths, racial theories and the diffusionist belief that culture and civilisation had been passed from East to West. It was notably absent from representations of the Balkans. Although the Balkan nationalities were idealised for their endurance of sufferings, their contribution to European civilisation and culture was rarely remarked upon.[59]

Rather than being viewed as outsiders within Europe, the Armenians were sometimes portrayed as a kind of civilised outsider in the eastern world, a part of Europe which had been displaced. During the late nineteenth century the British Armenophiles adopted the idea of Armenia as the last outpost of Europe, the final defence of Christianity and civilisation against incursions from the East. In an 1877 pamphlet, J. W. Probyn described the convents, monasteries and churches of Armenia as 'a kind of advanced post of European civilisation'.[60] Around this notion was built the idea of a special bond between Europe and Asia, of British duty and responsibility to the Armenians.

The emphasis placed on Armenia as a 'cradle of civilisation' was not simply Armenophile rhetoric designed to evoke British sympathies. Characterising Armenia in this way was also conditioned by British discourses of identity. Through making links between the origins of ancient civilisation and Britain, the nation's role as a model of civilisation in the contemporary world could be reaffirmed. Through claiming shared origins and close kinship with Armenia, a 'cradle of civilisation', the ancient Armenian past was portrayed as integral to British development.

The past played a vital role in the construction of British national identities; a long and illustrious national past was used to legitimate the existence of the nation in the present.[61] Identifying with Armenia proved to be an ideal forum for extending the scope of the national past. It provided an opportunity to identify the British past with the broad history of 'civilisation', demonstrating its continuity from the ancient inhabitants of Armenia to contemporary Britain. By identifying themselves as the defenders of Armenia, the Armenophiles were also making a statement regarding the continued role of Britain in the defence and propagation of 'civilisation'.

This approach was not exclusive to the Armenophiles. In fact it was part of a much broader process of identifying with and 'reclaiming' sites considered part of the British heritage of civilisation and culture. The representation of Armenia was conditioned by the way in which classical Greece had been, and continued to be, adopted as part of British heritage. David Roessel explains that the Hellenist movement of the early nineteenth century had viewed the modern Greeks as the direct inheritors of classical civilisation. This had fed into support for the ending of Ottoman rule in the region:

> For if the modern Greeks were descended from the victors of Marathon, then they were Europeans and siblings of the West. And if they were Europeans, indeed the ancestors of the founders of European civilisation, then they should not be the subjects of Eastern barbarism.[62]

Idealised images of a civilised past also underpinned Armenophile visions of liberation and freedom from Ottoman rule. British Armenophiles were clearly working from the same framework of romantic attachment to the past as the Hellenists had before them, setting the origins of European civilisation against Ottoman barbarism.[63] Yet by the time the case of Armenia came to the attention of the British public, the consequences of Greek independence had already sounded warning signs for Western Europe, which had rapidly become disappointed with the realities of modern Greece.[64] This experience led to caution regarding capabilities of the modern Armenian population. Though British Armenophiles drew upon Armenian national narratives that identified Armenia as a key site for the evolution of civilisation, they doubted that the 'golden ages' of the Armenian nation could easily be recreated.

It was in this mismatch between the 'claiming' of the Armenian past and disillusionment with present (from the violence and massacres that were thought endemic in the region, to the perceived 'backwardness' of the rural Armenian people) that the ambiguity of Armenia was most clearly manifested. It was the same kind of ambiguity which, in the aftermath of independence, became characteristic of the image of Greece. As Michael Herzfeld explains, 'If this region is ancestral to "us", it is removed from us through mythic time; if merely exotic, then its distance is merely one of cultural space. In either case it is not us, though we claim it as "our own".'[65]

The complex methods of 'claiming' and distancing which shaped British representations of Armenia required a vocabulary which went beyond romantic attachment or orientalist 'othering'. To negotiate this ambiguity and ambivalence a number of overlapping concepts and categories were employed. They were all based around the notion of civilisation and how this might be acquired or lost. The Armenian past and present were fitted into a broader pattern of the growth of civilisation and its movements through space and time through processes of progress and degeneration. Needless to say, this approach served to reaffirm the British position at the 'top' of hierarchies of development. Meanwhile the ambiguity of Armenia meant that it could be manipulated according to prevailing political and cultural agendas.

This approach not only accounted for the position of Armenia, it also reinforced, through a vivid example, a critique of the Ottoman Empire. The in-between image of the Armenians came to be treated as negative 'evidence' of the effects of Ottoman rule. Like modern Greece, Armenia was thought to have been 'polluted by the Taint of Turkish culture – the taint that late medieval and renaissance Europe viewed as the embodiment of barbarism and evil'.[66] Implicit in this critique was the notion that the Western European way of life and mode of imperial government was 'right'. It suggested that Britain, with an empire based on progress and the spread of civilisation, should guide the region's development rather than the degenerate and despotic Ottoman Empire. This theme recurred from the initial stirrings of the 'Armenian question' during the 1870s through to the attempts to create an Armenian nation state at the end of the First World War.

Conclusions

The case of Armenia, like that of Greece and the Balkans, highlights the fact that during the nineteenth century an orientalist division of the world into two distinct spheres of East and West was not the only way of understanding the world beyond Britain. This is not to suggest that the concept of orientalism should be abandoned completely. The link between knowledge, power and representations described in *Orientalism* provides a fundamental starting point for understanding the ways in which the 'other' is represented. Even images of regions perceived as 'in-between' were shot through with orientalist concepts, categories and images.

Ambiguous images of borderland regions such as Armenia played an important role in the articulation of British worldviews. Conceiving of a place like Armenia as 'in-between' did not mean that it was exempted from imperial power relations; in fact ambiguity was deeply embedded in power relations. Precisely because of their ambiguity, images of borderlands were open to manipulation and reconstruction in the face of changing social or political circumstances. This would prove important for the maintenance of power, in the broadest sense of the word, through periods of international conflict and rapidly shifting geopolitical agendas.

Nor was 'in-betweenness' unique to Armenia. Representations of Eastern Europe and the Balkans were also characterised by ambiguities, albeit of a different nature. Images of Armenia and of these other regions provided a forum in which differences between 'self' and 'other', 'East' or 'West', 'civilisation' and 'barbarism' could be played out. In particular, British writings on Armenia demanded an exploration and an attempt at definition of what it meant to be 'civilised' and what it meant to be 'European'.

Between 1878 and 1925 the ambiguous, unstable meanings of Armenia were deployed and manipulated according to different sets of political circumstances and shifting power relations. The continuities and developments in representations of Armenia during this period were both shaped by, and helped to shape, interventions in the region, political and humanitarian, against a backdrop of war and violence. In the longer term these shifting representations helped shape visions of the Armenian future and impinged upon Armenian articulations of the Armenian nation and national identity.

Notes

1 Bryce and Toynbee, *The Treatment of the Armenians*, p. 595.
2 E. Said, *Orientalism* (London: Penguin, 1995). Originally published 1978.
3 See chapter 3.
4 Said, *Orientalism*, p. 3.
5 Said, *Orientalism*. See also his later work, *Culture and Imperialism* (London: Vintage, 1994).
6 Introduction to B. Moore-Gilbert, G. Stanton and W. Maley, eds, *Postcolonial Criticism* (London: Longman, 1997), p. 22.
7 Said, *Orientalism*, p. 3.
8 C. Hall, 'Thinking the Postcolonial, Thinking the Empire', in C. Hall, ed., *Cultures of Empire: A Reader* (Manchester: Manchester University Press, 2000), p. 15.
9 Said, *Orientalism*, pp. 7–8. Williams and Chrisman remind us that 'such is the power of orientalist or colonialist knowledge that even those discourses which are not formally or ideologically aligned with it may be pulled in an orientalist direction, or may simply be appropriated by Orientalism and utilised as if they were just another facet of its world view'. P. Williams and L. Chrisman, 'Colonial Discourse and Post-Colonial Theory: An Introduction', in P. Williams and L. Chrisman, eds, *Colonial Discourse and Post-Colonial Theory: A Reader* (London: Harvester Wheatsheaf, 1993), p. 8.

10 Said integrates Gramci's theory of hegemony with Foucault's concept of discourse. The theory of hegemony '. . . seeks to demonstrate the role that culture plays in soliciting the consent of the subordinate (or subaltern) social constituencies in the rule of the dominant order'. Moore-Gilbert et al., *Postcolonial Criticism*, p. 22.

11 Said, *Orientalism*, p. 3.

12 Williams and Chrisman, 'Colonial Discourse', p. 5.

13 On postcolonial studies, B. Moore-Gilbert, *Postcolonial Theory: Contexts, Practices, Politics* (London: Verso, 1997), chapters 3, 4 and 5 on the work of Homi Bhabha and Gayatri Spivak. One of the important aspects of postcolonial studies has been to turn attention to the colonised and the construction of their identities. See also Williams and Chrisman, *Colonial Discourse*, Part 1 and H. Schwarz and S. Ray, eds, *A Companion to Postcolonial Studies* (Oxford: Blackwell, 2000).

14 J. Clifford, 'On Orientalism', in J. Clifford, *The Predicament of Culture: Twentieth-Century Ethnography, Literature, and Art* (Cambridge, MA: Harvard University Press, 1988), p. 258.

15 Said, *Orientalism*, p. 20.

16 D. Porter, 'Orientalism and its Problems', in Williams and Chrisman, *Colonial Discourse*, p. 160. Clifford points out Said's contradictory approach to the reality of 'the Orient': 'frequently he suggests that a text or tradition distorts, dominates or ignores some real or authentic feature of the Orient. Elsewhere, however, he denies the existence of any "real Orient" and in this he is more faithful to Foucault.' Clifford, 'On Orientalism', pp. 255–276.

17 John Mackenzie is amongst the critics who have claimed that Said's approach to orientalism is as inadequate as it is ahistorical, although his claims have been subject to less forgiving criticism than those of Said. See Mackenzie, *Orientalism: History, Theory and the Arts* (Manchester: Manchester University Press, 1995). Mackenzie suggests that Said does not leave room for sympathetic representations of the Orient, however the possibility of representations of the Orient which are not implicated in imperial power relations has been doubted by many critics. 'For Said, what is at issue is not so much the question of whether identification with Eastern culture in such scholarship was sympathetic or not, but the fact that (as he sees it) all western discourse about the East is determined in the last instance by the will to domination over Oriental territories and peoples.' Moore-Gilbert et al., *Postcolonial Criticism*, p. 22.

18 S. Mills, *Discourses of Difference: An Analysis of Women's Travel Writing and Colonialism* (London: Routledge, 1991), p. 87.

19 R. Lewis, *Gendering Orientalism: Race, Femininity and Representation* (London: Routledge, 1996), Mills, *Discourses of Difference* and R. Lewis and S. Mills, eds, *Feminist Postcolonial Theory: A Reader* (Edinburgh: Edinburgh University Press, 2003).

20 Lewis, *Gendering Orientalism*, p. 17.

21 In 'Orientalism and its Problems' Porter also draws attention to the conflicting voices which exist within what are considered to be orientalist texts – in
this case T. E. Lawrence's *Seven Pillars Of Wisdom.*

22 L. Loew, *Critical Terrains: French and British Orientalisms* (Ithaca and London:
Cornell University Press, 1991), p. 8.

23 The journey of John MacDonald Kinneir in 1813 and 1814 is a reminder of the
strategic interest in Armenia. Kinneir, a captain working in the East India
Company, travelled through Armenia, collecting detailed geographical information, in an attempt to 'visit all the countries through which a European
army might attempt the invasion of India'. Sir John MacDonald Kinneir,
Journey through Asia Minor, Armenia and Koordistan in the years 1813 and
1814 (London: John Murray, 1818), p. vii.

24 Lewis, *Gendering Orientalism,* p. 13.

25 Todorova, *Imagining the Balkans,* p. 97.

26 For Gladstone's rhetoric on minorities see W. E. Gladstone, *Bulgarian Horrors*
and also the pamphlet, *Mr Gladstone on the Armenian Question* (reprint of his
speech at Chester Town Hall, 6 August, 1896).

27 For details see J. Mackenzie, ed., *Imperialism and Popular Culture* (Manchester:
Manchester University Press, 1986) p. 2, pp. 4–5. Mackenzie lists a series of
'imperial' events which capture the public imagination from the 1870s
onwards, from the death of Livingstone to the Boer War.

28 H. C. G. Matthew, ed., *The Gladstone Diaries,* Vol. IX, January 1875–December
1880 (Oxford: Clarendon Press, 1986), Introduction, p. xxxv. Eric Hobsbawm
describes the way that imperialism was utilised in order to try to gain popular
support for the government and the social order. 'More generally, imperialism
encouraged the masses, and especially the potentially discontented, to identify
themselves with the imperial state and nation, and thus unconsciously to
endow the social and political system represented by that state with justification and legitimacy. And in an era of mass politics even old systems required
new legitimacy': Hobsbawm, *The Age of Empire: 1875–1914* (London: Abacus,
1987), p. 70.

29 Todorova, *Imagining the Balkans,* p. 100.

30 James Bryce, C. P. Scott (editor of the Manchester Guardian which consistently
supported the Armenian cause), G. P. Gooch, Gilbert Murray and H. A. L. Fisher
were all involved in the pro-Boer movement, as well as the Armenian cause. See
Arthur Davey, *The British Pro-Boers 1877–1902* (Cape Town: Tafelberg, 1978).
On the Congo reform campaign, see K. Grant, *A Civilised Sauagery: Britain and
the New Slaveries in Africa 1884–1926* (London: Routhedge, 2005) and also M.
Ward, *European Atrocity, African Catastrophe: Leopold II, the Congo Free State
and its Aftermath* (London: RoutledgeCurzon, 2004). Bernard Porter highlights
the inconsistent and varied approach to empire amongst the Liberal party.
Porter, *Critics of Empire, British Radical Attitudes to Colonialism in Africa 1895–
1914* (London: Macmillan, 1968), pp. 5–18.

31 Grant, *A Civilised Savagery*; P. Laity, *The British Peace Movement 1870–1914* (Oxford: Clarendon Press, 1990). Noel Buxton provides a good example of the kind of cross section of interests of those involved in the Armenophile movement. Not only was he also a member of the Balkan Committee, which campaigned on behalf of the Macedonians, but he was also involved in the peace movement and a member of the parliamentary committee of the Anti-Slavery and Aborigines Protection Society. On Buxton see T. P. Conwell-Evans, *Foreign Policy from a Back Bench, 1904–1918. A Study Based on the Papers of Noel Buxton* (London: Oxford University Press, 1932) and M. Anderson, *Noel Buxton: A Life* (London: Allen and Unwin, 1952).

32 Said, *Orientalism*, p. 191.

33 On discourses of progress, degeneration and civilisation see chapter 2.

34 Clifford, 'On Orientalism', p. 258.

35 See information collected by consuls and the British Foreign Office on social conditions in Eastern Anatolia and the grievances of the Armenian population in National Archive (NA) FO 424/181 – FO 424/183, 1895 and NA FO 881/6621, Report on the populations of Asia Minor, Colonel W. Everett, 11 May 1895.

36 Travelogues are considered in chapter 3.

37 The reports of E. J. Dillon were typical. Dillon reported on the massacres of the 1890s for the pro-Armenian Journal, the *Contemporary Review* in 1895 and 1896.

38 The historian E. A. Freeman provided a powerful historical condemnation of the Ottoman Empire in his works *The Ottoman Power in Europe: Its Nature, its Growth and its Decline* (London: Macmillan, 1877) and *The Eastern Question in its Historical Bearings* (Manchester: National Reform Union, 1876). Freeman played an important role in the Bulgarian agitation: his scholarly background gave his analysis legitimacy but his work remained highly propagandist. For other 'scholarly' analyses of the 'eastern question', see J. Bryce, *Russia and Turkey* (London, 1876) and Frederic Harrison, *Cross and Crescent* (London, 1876). Liberal academics, particularly historians, played an important role in the Bulgarian and Armenian campaigns. Their analysis of the need for reform in Armenia was not only based on current suffering but also upon long-term historical factors.

39 J. Bryce, *Transcaucasia and Ararat* (London: Macmillan & Co., 1877), N. Buxton MP and Rev. H. Buxton, *Travels and Politics in Armenia* (London: Smith, Elder and Co., 1914).

40 Kevork Bardakjian, *The Mekhitarist Contributions to Armenian Culture and Scholarship* (Cambridge, MA: Harvard College Library, 1976) and Suny, *Looking Toward Ararat*, Introduction and chapter 1; J. Etmekjian, *The French Influence on the Western Armenian Renaissance* (New York: Twayne Publishers Inc., 1964) and H. J. Sarkiss, 'The Armenian Renaissance 1500–1863', *Armenian Review*, Vol. 23, Part 3, reprinted from the *Journal of Modern History*, December 1937.

41 Anahide Ter Minassian describes the impact of Armenian scholars educated at the University of Geneva on the development of Armenian nationalism. Ter Minassian, 'Elites Arméniennes en Suisse: Le Rôle de Genève dans la Formation des Elites Arméniennes au Début du XXieme Siècle', in Hans-Lukas Kieser, ed., *Die Armenische Frage und die Schweiz: 1896–1923* (Zurich: Chronos Verlag, 1999).

42 Suny, *Looking Toward Ararat*, p. 22.

43 J. Rendel Harris and H. B. Harris, *Letters from the Scenes of the Recent Massacres in Armenia* (London: James Nisbet and Co., 1897), p. 41.

44 See chapter 3.

45 B. Cheyette and N. Valman, eds, *The Image of the Jew in European Liberal Culture 1789–1914* (London: Vallentine Mitchell, 2004), B. Cheyette and L. Marcus, eds, *Modernity, Culture and the Jew* (Cambridge: Polity Press, 1998), B. Cheyette, *Constructions of the Jew in European Liberal Culture: Racial Representations 1875–1945* (Cambridge: Cambridge University Press, 1996).

46 Z. Bauman, 'Allosemitism: Premodern, Modern, Postmodern', in Cheyette and Marcus, *Modernity, Culture and the Jew*, p. 151.

47 For a discussion of Bauman's perspective see Bauman 'Allosemitism' and also B. Cheyette, 'Introduction', in Cheyette, ed., *Between 'Race' and Culture: Representations of 'the Jew' in English and American Literature* (Stanford: Stanford University Press, 1996).

48 B. Cheyette and N. Valman, 'Introduction', in *The Image of the Jew*, p. 5.

49 Todorova, *Imagining the Balkans*, p. 8.

50 Fleming, 'Orientalism', p. 1231.

51 Ibid.

52 Bryce and Toynbee, *The Treatment of the Armenians*, p. 595.

53 Larry Wolff, *Inventing Eastern Europe: The Map of Civilization on the Mind of the Enlightenment* (Stanford: Stanford University Press, 1994), p. 7.

54 Ibid., p. 360.

55 Ibid., p. 358.

56 Todorova, *Imagining the Balkans*, p. 17.

57 Ibid., p. 18.

58 F. S. Stevenson, MP *The Case for the Armenians* (London: Harrison and Sons, 1893), p. 36.

59 Fleming differentiates between orientalism and the study of the Balkans, claiming that the Balkans, unlike the East, were not thought worthy of scholarship. 'There is no history or tradition of western European academic interest in the Balkans that is remotely comparable to the history of western academic study of the colonized Orient': Fleming, '*Orientalism*', p. 6. This was different in the case of Armenia which was often considered to be part of the Near East, as studied by western academics.

60 J. W. Probyn, 'Armenia and the Lebanon', in Eastern Question Association, *Papers on the Eastern Question* (London: Cassell, Peter & Galphin, 1877), p. 12.

61 Amongst many, one influential articulation of this argument is Eric Hobsbawm, 'Mass Producing Traditions: Europe 1870–1914', in E. Hobsbawm and T. Ranger, eds, *The Invention of Tradition* (Cambridge: Cambridge University Press, 1983). On the use of the past in contemporary Armenian national identity see R. Panossian, 'The Past as Nation: Three Dimensions of Armenian Identity', *Geopolitics*, Vol. 7, No. 2 (2002).

62 David Roessel, *In Byron's Shadow: Modern Greece in the English and American Imagination* (Oxford: Oxford University Press, 2002), p. 17.

63 In the case of Armenia it was the ancient civilisations of the Near East, not the classical past, that was of interest.

64 'The new complaint was that the Greeks were incapable of governing themselves': Todorova, *Imagining the Balkans*, p. 95.

65 M. Herzfeld, *Anthropology through the Looking Glass: Critical Ethnography in the Margins of Europe* (Cambridge: Cambridge University Press, 1987), p. 7. See also p. 21 for a discussion of how the West 'claimed' Greece as its ancestor. He explains the differing interests of the Greeks and Western Europe: 'Unlike their European patrons the Greeks were not seeking a return to the classical past, they were instead seeking inclusion in the European present.' A similar conflict between Europeans who idealised Armenia yet decided it was 'unready' to become a nation state, and Armenian nationalists who wanted autonomy reached a peak in the failure to create a nation state following the First World War.

66 Herzfeld, *Anthropology through the Looking Glass*, p. 7.

2

The boundary of the civilised world? Images of Armenia during the late nineteenth century

Introduction

During the last two decades of the nineteenth century the British government and the British public became increasingly aware of the plight of the Ottoman Armenians. In response to reports of the Armenians' declining condition a British Armenophile movement emerged with the aim of protecting them and ensuring their future security and development, along with providing material aid to ease the current crisis.

The British representations of Armenia and the Armenians that developed in conjunction with the Armenophile movement were complex and multilayered; images of both people and place were characterised by ambiguity. In this chapter I examine the particular ways in which the British population characterised the Armenians and negotiated their position on the borders of East and West.

During the second half of the nineteenth century what may be termed a 'rediscovery' of Armenia occurred. I use the term 'rediscovery' to reflect not only renewed British interest in Armenia but also the attitude of those who now encountered Armenia, and regarded it very much as 'unchartered territory'. British observers treated people and place as passive and inert, waiting for British interest to bring them 'alive' for the rest of the world. Over the course of the century this interest in Armenia developed from occasional passing encounters to the more specific interest in the Armenian population which emerged alongside the 'Armenian question'.

In this chapter I focus upon British attempts to define and categorise the Armenians and examine how discourses of nationalism and imperialism shaped understandings of the Armenian past, present and future.

This leads on to a consideration of the ambivalences of images of Armenia and the means used by British writers to idealise both people and place, along with the simultaneous process of differentiating and creating distance between Britain and Armenia.

The final part of this chapter concerns the massacres of Armenians in the Ottoman Empire during the 1890s. These massacres were the first real crisis faced by the British Armenophile movement and they had a striking effect upon British responses to the Armenians. Representations of the massacres drew heavily upon an image of Armenia which had been constructed over the previous two decades. The image of Armenia as a cradle of civilisation, for example, was central to British portrayals of the massacres as a barbarian attack on civilisation. Examining the representation of the massacres therefore provides insight into the ways that representations of Armenia were subject to manipulation and change, according to specific sets of historical circumstances.

The development of an 'Armenian question'

The emergence of the 'Armenian question' was, as I have explained, part and parcel of the 'eastern question'. In particular, the peace settlements following the Russo-Turkish war (1877–78) entangled the British government in the fate of the Ottoman Armenians. During the war, the Russian army had occupied a large part of the eastern Vilayets, (provinces) of the Ottoman Empire: Kars, Ardahan, Bayazid and Alashkert. These regions were heavily populated by Armenians. The initial peace settlement, San Stefano, stipulated that Russian troops would not withdraw from these Vilayets unless reforms to ameliorate the situation of the Armenians were implemented.[1] However, these terms allowed Russia a level of influence in a strategically important region which was unacceptable to Britain. The British government therefore supported the Ottoman Empire and engineered a new peace settlement, the Treaty of Berlin, reducing Russia's gains.[2] In return for their support of the Ottoman Empire the British government gained control of Cyprus. Both the Cyprus Convention and the Treaty of Berlin committed the Ottoman government to reform. Article 61 of the Berlin Treaty stated that:

> The Sublime Porte undertakes to carry out, without further delay, the ameliorations and reforms demanded by local requirements in the regions inhabited by the Armenians, and to guarantee their security against the Circassians and the Kurds. It will periodically make known the steps taken to this effect to the powers, who will superintend their application.[3]

Article 61 had little practical effect. There was nothing to compel reforms and the European military consuls sent to the region could do little other than document the continued oppression of the Armenian population.[4] Nonetheless the Berlin Treaty had turned the 'Armenian question' into an issue of international significance.[5] Article 61 proved to be a constant reference point for Armenians active in the diaspora and the 'homeland' and for Armenophile organisations. Their core argument that Britain had a legal responsibility for the Armenians was based upon this clause.[6]

In the 1870s the British Armenophile movement had emerged from the Eastern Question Association (EQA), the political pressure group formed as a part of the Bulgarian agitation. Like the EQA, the Armenophiles counted numerous Liberal politicians, academics and churchmen amongst their ranks. James Bryce, the Liberal MP and scholar, after travelling through Armenia, directed the attention of the EQA to the Armenians.[7] From then onwards the fate of the Armenians became incorporated into their cause.

Bryce was in contact with prominent members of the Armenian diaspora in London, and in July 1878 held a meeting at Westminster Abbey for the Armenian community and British politicians in order to raise awareness of the Armenian situation.[8] After the disappointments of the Berlin Treaty this embryonic movement continued to grow, and a number of Armenophile organisations began to emerge, including the Grosvenor House Armenian Relief Committee and later the AAA.[9] At the same time the British Armenian diaspora became increasingly politically engaged and organisations such as the Armenian Patriotic Association and the Armenian United Association (in Manchester) emerged.

The internationalisation of the 'Armenian question' also affected the perspectives of Armenian nationalist organisations in the Ottoman and Russian Empires. Whilst some of these organisations looked to Russia for protection (conditions for the Armenians in the Russian Empire, whilst far from ideal, were far better than those in the Ottoman Empire), others pinned their hopes on British intervention.[10] This tendency to look to Britain was reflected in the visit of an Armenian delegation led by Patriarch Khrimian, leader of the Armenian church, to Britain and Europe in order to try and draw attention to the Armenian cause in the lead up to the Berlin Conference. This appeal to the European powers must be placed in the broader context of Armenian nationalism, an important dimension of which was the self-perception of Armenian nationalists as members of the European world.[11]

Armenian communities in Britain were based in the commercial centres of Manchester and London. A large proportion of these communities were involved in international trade and in frequent contact with Armenians in the Ottoman Empire via networks of family and friends.[12] These British Armenians worked hard to bring the plight of the Armenians to the attention of the British public, and to put pressure on the government to act on their behalf. They appealed to the idea of Britain as the protector of oppressed Christians. The 1888 pamphlet, *The Cry of Armenia*, typified this approach:

> The Armenian nation has the right of claiming great things from Great Britain, for it has seen that she has in many parts of the world stood forth as the powerful champion of the down-trodden Christians. Indeed great is our hope that this our cry will not remain without an echo in your hearts and that the humane government of England will not delay in extending her helping hand and saving the unhappy people of Armenia from this miserable and intolerable state.

In addition, diaspora contacts with Armenians in the Ottoman Empire provided a vital source of information for the British Armenophile movement.[13] Thus the idea of Armenia as an ancient civilised nation or the Armenians as a martyred people was promoted as much by the Armenians as by their British counterparts.

A cradle of civilisation?

By the end of the 1870s, the 'Armenian question' had emerged as an international political problem, the solution to which was thought to lie in diplomacy and reform. But despite the emphasis placed on diplomatic solutions, interest in Armenia and the Armenians extended beyond high politics. News of the suffering of the Armenians provoked wide curiosity about this obscure and distant people – who they were, where they came from and how they had fallen upon such difficult times: what may be broadly termed a 'cultural' or 'scholarly' interest in Armenia which blossomed alongside, and as a product of, the politics of the 'Armenian question'. A general interest in the geographical regions inhabited by the Armenians developed into a specific interest in the 'condition' of the population.[14]

Britain and Armenia: early encounters

British contacts with Armenia had a long history, stretching back at least as far as the Crusades.[15] Although nineteenth-century Armenophiles made frequent reference to these 'ancient bonds', contact with the Armenians in the intervening period was minimal.[16] John Cartwright provided the earliest known account of a visit to Armenia in 1593; he was followed by John Fryer, a doctor travelling on behalf of the East India Company in 1688.[17] The works of early travellers like these provided only fragmentary information. During the nineteenth century, the information that they had amassed was augmented by that of the travellers, scholars, missionaries and diplomats who visited or studied Armenia.

The Armenian renaissance and the development of an Armenian national history were also vital to the nineteenth-century resurgence of interest in Armenia. The literary and historical texts written or translated by Armenian scholars of this period, for example Chamichian's *History of Armenia*, were relied upon by European historians and archaeologists trying to piece together a narrative of the Armenian past.[18] In the early part of the nineteenth century it was French scholars who paid the most attention to Armenia. The orientalist Jean Antoine de Saint-Martin persuaded the French government and the Société Asiatique to fund an archaeological excavation at Van in 1827 and his *Mémoires Historiques et Géographiques sur L'Arménie* became a reference point for later European scholars and travellers.[19]

Whilst the Armenians were objects of study for a number of Armenian and European scholars, during the mid-nineteenth century they were more often encountered by the British in the context of travel and exploration. Accounts of these journeys featured regularly in the *Journal of the Royal Geographical Society* (*JRGS*).[20] They were enormously wide ranging, encompassing not only physical geography but also geology, climate, agriculture and trade, botany, population distribution, and ethnography. Barbara Korte's observations on Victorian travel writing demonstrate that this was by no means unusual: 'Victorian accounts of exploration tend to include increasingly lengthy descriptions of natural and anthropological phenomena, as well as extensive scientific appendices and precise illustrations.'[21]

These early travellers branched out into ancient history and archaeology, recording ancient monuments and sites and providing histories for the places that they encountered. K. E. Abbott, for example, described at length his visit to the ruined city of 'Anni, the capital of the Pakadian kings'. William Hamilton, a geologist who travelled through Armenia in 1835, besides providing detailed geographical information, also carefully recorded archaeological monuments.[22] Hamilton's aim was to locate classical sites in the landscape, an approach which incorporated Armenia into a history of 'civilisation' familiar to the educated British public, rendering the Armenian past relevant for a British audience and creating the sense of a shared past.[23]

These early reports of travel in Armenia are extremely detailed, recounting vast numbers of facts and measurements and describing scientific observations in great depth. Temperatures, times, heights, depths, pressures and distances are all meticulously measured, rock types, soil types and vegetation are noted and inscriptions are copied or observed. The emphasis is placed firmly on the empirical observation of the surrounding environment. When local populations figure in the text they become part of the landscape; their appearance, characteristics or way of life may be briefly described but people themselves play a passive role. They are rarely accorded a voice of their own, and the authors express little concern for the conditions in which they live.[24]

'Rediscovery' of Armenia

In 1876 James Bryce had travelled through Transcaucasia in order to climb Ararat, supposed resting place of Noah's Ark and potent spiritual and national symbol for the Armenian people. The publication of his travelogue *Transcaucasia and Ararat* coincided with the emergence of the Armenians in the realm of international politics.[25] In many ways Bryce's account was no different from others, providing 'scientific' information accompanied by elements of adventure and dramatic encounters with the dangerous, exotic and bizarre. However, Bryce's travel narrative differed in that it concluded with 'political reflections' on the future of the region, utilising the information he gained on his travels to evaluate the current condition of the region and its future prospects.[26]

Bryce's work spurred on public interest in the Armenians and marked the beginning of the publication of numerous works which, although not always overtly political, engaged with the 'Armenian question'.[27] The most popular format for such works was the travel narrative, already a well-established and popular genre. The fact that 'Armenia' could be the subject of a travel narrative, a genre which also addressed the 'savage' populations of the dark continent, in itself distanced the Armenians from their British audience. The journey through Armenia was presented as a quest for knowledge, truth and authenticity and the traveller as risking close encounters with dirt and danger in order to fulfil this quest.

Travellers were quick to profess their impartiality and authenticity. Seasoned traveller and author of *Journeys in Persia and Koordistan* Isabella

Bishop, for example, claimed to come to Turkey as a 'perfectly neutral and impartial observer'.[28] Bishop's gender possibly allowed her to position herself outside of the political conflicts over the regions, which were primarily the domain of male politicians, scholars and journalists. Even so, claims of impartiality were equally common from male authors who often prided themselves on objectivity and clear judgement. But despite these claims to provide a unique, objective viewpoint, travel writers engaged in a constant process of extracting information from and cross-referencing against existing texts. This process created consistency, so that although British writings on Armenia varied in subject and tone, texts employed the same concepts, categories and interpretive frameworks.

Categories and definitions: nation, religion, race

During the last decades of the nineteenth century Armenia was still regarded as unknown and mysterious. This increased its appeal for travellers seeking adventure or knowledge. In 1842, William Ainsworth observed that:

> The ancient state of this country is among the least known to the learned and curious of Europe, and it is one of the countries of the East that has hitherto attracted the least attention. There can be no doubt, that were the literature of this ancient people more studied, the comparative geography of the country drawn from its present obscurity, and a new light thus thrown upon its history, a feeling of real interest would be excited in the present fallen condition of its people.[29]

The sense that Armenia lay waiting to be 'discovered' by western observers persisted through the century. Bryce thought it was 'as if every nation that passed from North to South or East to West had left some specimens of its people here to found a kind of ethnological museum'.[30] Alexander MacDonald, journalist and author of *The Land of Ararat* made equally grand claims, suggesting that 'Armenia contains more mysteries awaiting the solution of naturalists, geographers, philologists, and historians than Africa, America and Hindoostan together.'[31]

Such statements ostensibly reinforced the idea of Armenia as a rewarding site for exploration and investigation, but in reality they had more complex effects. Firstly, they marginalised the contemporary population of the region, who appeared passive or absent. This 'emptying' of the contemporary population reinforced British authority over the landscape. In the case of Armenia this meant an appropriation of the region and particularly its past as part of the heritage of European civilisation.[32]

Secondly, they highlighted the perceived difference and distance, not only spatially but also in terms of status, between Armenia and its British observers. They suggested that Armenia could not be understood by the British on an equal footing, but had to be observed, classified and analysed from a perspective of superiority.

The process of 'making sense' was complex. In fact people and place defied contemporary classifications and categories. Even defining what Armenia 'meant' was not straightforward. It did not exist as a political or territorial entity; an autonomous Armenian state had not existed for centuries. Even so, there was a tendency to territorialise; 'Armenia' was used by travellers and scholars as a geographical term denoting a region stretching from Eastern Anatolia into Transcaucasia. However the boundaries of the 'Armenia' they referred to were fluid and ill-defined.[33]

Difficulties in defining 'Armenia' were compounded by the dispersion of the Armenian population, spread across the Ottoman, Persian and Russian Empires. By the nineteenth century, the diaspora reached as far as India and the Far East. In the Ottoman Empire the Armenians rarely formed a clear majority of the population; the regions they inhabited were characterised by a 'mixed' population of Armenians, Kurds, Turks and other groups. This population distribution was regarded as undesirable by the vast majority of British observers, as the source of potential racial or religious conflict.

Regions with such 'mixed' populations were also perceived as difficult to rule. A report into the populations of Asia Minor for the British Government, for example, reflected upon the problems a 'mixed population' posed for implementing reforms on the basis of nationalities: 'In the eastern districts the impossibility of finding any area of large dimensions inhabited only by one race or religion would have rendered the attempt abortive.'[34] Fifteen years later the issue was still problematic. H. F. B. Lynch, who travelled extensively in Armenia in the early 1890s, produced a memorandum for the British government in which he attempted to define 'Armenian' territory based on population distribution. As British involvement in the reform of the Ottoman Empire failed, his ideas were never implemented.[35] The idea of the 'mixed population' as a 'problem' was not only an 'administrative' issue but also a product of the nature of dominant late nineteenth-century discourses of nationalism, which held that the world was 'naturally' divided into discrete national units.[36] The dispersed Armenians clearly did not conform to this model.

The idea of the Armenians as a dispersed or dismembered nation became integral to British constructions of Armenia as a site of suffering and oppression. This was reliant upon a particular reading of the Armenian past which held that the Armenians were the remnants of an ancient nation which had survived through centuries of conquest and oppression. These understandings of the Armenian past drew upon the constructions of the national past which had been undertaken by Armenian scholars and nationalists.

The importance of 'national pasts' and origin myths in the construction of national identities is well documented. Hobsbawm suggests that the four decades before the First World War were a particularly intensive period of inventing traditions in Europe. This climate of emerging nation states and nationalism affected Armenian constructions of their own national past and also shaped British interpretations of the Armenian past.[37] For nationalists and Armenophiles alike, 'Armenia' came to mean the territories which (it was believed) the Armenians had inhabited for thousands of years before their conquest by invaders from 'the East'. Historical sites, notably the medieval cities of Ani and Van, as well as the hundreds of distinctive Armenian churches which dotted the landscape, provided tangible evidence of their 'great antiquity as a nation'.[38]

The relationship between these conceptions of 'historic Armenia' and the modern Armenian population were not straightforward. Some British observers viewed a long 'national' past as a sound basis for the development of Armenia. Others were keen to associate themselves with the achievements of Armenia in the past, but were less impressed with Armenia in the present. In any case, nineteenth-century nationalist discourses, which held that nations were timeless and rooted in ancient homelands, shaped the way that the British conceptualised people and place. In a climate of emerging nationalism, Ottoman decline and European reform, reconciling constructions of the historic Armenian homeland with nineteenth-century realities proved problematic.[39]

Discourses of nationalism played an important role in British attempts to define Armenian identity as well as territory. This was also a complex process, for whilst Armenian nationalists attempted to draw attention to Armenia's status as a 'nation', many British observers were sceptical about such claims.[40] During the last two decades of the nineteenth century, as international efforts to improve the situation of the Armenians failed to have any effect, Armenian nationalist sentiments had begun to be expressed in increasingly radical forms.[41] In 1887 the first of the two most significant Armenian nationalist parties, the *Hnchaks*, was established in Geneva. Three years later another group of socialist-leaning nationalists founded the *Dashnaksutiun* (Armenian Revolutionary Federation) in

Tbilisi. These Armenian revolutionaries aimed to 'liberate' fellow Armenians suffering under Ottoman rule, and were prepared to use violent methods to draw attention to their cause.[42]

Revolutionary nationalism aroused little sympathy amongst British Armenophiles. Numerous moderate Armenian activists were also keen to distance themselves from the revolutionary elements, and focused on the need for reform. In a speech to the AAA, Nubar Pasha (a well-respected diasporan Armenian working for the Egyptian government) emphasised Armenian conservatism, claiming that, 'The Armenians do not aim at independence, or at a distinct political existence. All they ask for is civil liberties and the establishment of institutions calculated to guarantee their personal safety . . .'[43] Even so, when addressing the 'Armenian question' the issue of nationality was difficult to avoid. Writings on Armenia therefore tend to be couched in terms of an evaluation of national potential, drawing upon essentialised national characteristics, weighing virtues against failings and measuring national 'sentiment' or unity. Bryce concluded that:

> They may in time recover as their awakened national feeling ripens and strengthens the courage and political self-confidence which would enable them to hold their own; as yet they have not given such evidences of these sterner qualities as the Greeks and Servians [Serbians] gave in winning their freedom.[44]

But whereas Bryce was hopeful about the national future of the Armenians, others were less positive. Fanny Blunt, resident of the empire and wife of a British Consul, for example, claimed to have witnessed little 'patriotism':

> When the first cravings of their hearts for peace and security had been satisfied, they settled down in communities, forgot their country and its past history, and assimilated their external forms and customs with those of the nations amongst whom they lived, with the philosophic non-chalance of the Asiatic.[45]

Another layer of confusion was added to the uncertainty about Armenian nationhood through the use of other categories in order to define or classify the Armenians. Primarily, the issue of whether the Armenians were a national or a religious community posed a troubling question. For it was clear that Armenian national and religious identities were closely entwined, but the precise relationship between the two was a matter of some debate. Some observers suggested that religion and nation could be reduced to the same thing or that religion was the only defining feature of the Armenian nation. Others suggested that the Armenians were simply a religious community and not a nation. An alternative viewpoint was that religion reinforced or preserved nationality. Isabella Bishop was amongst those who suggested that the Armenians clung to religion as a means to maintain 'national existence'.[46]

In reality the relationships between religion and the nation were complex. Although the Armenian Apostolic Church was commonly presented as a 'national' religion, the Armenians were in reality members of a number of different churches. Catholic missionaries had converted significant numbers of Armenians and under the influence of American missionaries the number of Armenian Protestants was increasing. Relationships between the churches were sometimes strained. This did not go unnoticed; Henry Barkley, who described his journey through Armenia in somewhat negative terms in his book, *A Ride through Asia Minor and Armenia*, rather dramatically observed that 'If the Turks were removed out of the way for a short time, the three denominations of Christians would cut each other's throats.'[47] However these divisions were glossed over by British Armenophiles who were keen to create an image of Christian solidarity between Britain and Armenia and referred to the Armenians simply as 'Christians'.

The category of race also played an important role in classifying the Armenians. Understandings of race were difficult to disentangle from those of nation, especially as some strands of popular nationalism held that ancient races corresponded with modern nations. However the use of 'race' had meaning beyond the definition of national boundaries. Armenian 'characteristics' and capabilities were racialised, and race became an important tool in explaining differences between Britain, the Armenians and the other peoples who inhabited Asia Minor.

By the late nineteenth century 'race' had become a primary method of classifying and comparing the human diversity encountered through imperialist expansion.[48] It also became a powerful explanatory tool, thought to determine physiognomy, mental capabilities and behavioural characteristics. The Armenians were recognised as a distinctive racial 'type' with a distinctive physical appearance. Alexander MacDonald gave his assessment of Armenian racial 'types' a scholarly tone claiming that, 'Ethnological opinion has led to the recognition of the Armenians as the oldest type of the species. As a race they have large eyes and mouths, long noses, and dark olive complexions, and, like the Jews have theirs, they have retained these distinctive facial peculiarities.'[49]

Others reflected further on the characteristics of the Armenians, most reaching a positive conclusion about their 'nature'. James Creagh suggested that they were 'a high bred race of the purest Caucasian type; and as blood always tells in men as well as in animals, they still survive, but display symptoms of a steadily-increasing vitality'.[50] Isabella Bishop, equally enthusiastic, highlighted the commonalities of the Armenians and the British:

> It is not possible to deny that they are the most capable, energetic enterprising and pushing race in Western Asia, physically superior, and intellectually acute and above all they are a race which can be raised in all respects to our own level, neither religion, colour, customs, nor inferiority in intellect or force constituting any barrier between us.[51]

The assignment of positive racial characteristics to the Armenians was counterbalanced by negative stereotypes which were often also racialised. They were perceived to be cunning and greedy, untrustworthy and quick to take advantage of the unsuspecting English traveller. William Ramsay refers to the common perception of the Armenians as 'rich and tyrannical, ignorant and grasping, tradesmen who have made money in narrow, sordid business in towns'.[52] As in the case of the Jews this image sprung from the Armenians' success in their roles as merchants and bankers but was generalised across all sectors of the population.

The idea of 'race' had its roots in an earlier period, but during the nineteenth century it became fully elaborated as an accepted 'scientific' concept.[53] By 1900 evolutionary theory had rendered polygenic understandings of race (the belief that human groups were descended from separate racial origins) defunct, but some of its essential premises, the separateness of races, racial hierarchies and undesirability of racial 'mixing', were retained in one form or another.[54] Discourses of race based on the premise that humanity was divided into distinct groups, with inherent mental and physical characteristics, remained powerful. In popular thought races were still imagined to be identifiable from physical attributes and characteristics while 'blood' and 'inheritance' remained important metaphors.[55]

Racial categories provided a framework for the conceptualisation of difference and 'otherness', but these categories were by no means fixed and were utilised in flexible and overlapping ways. Thus in the Armenian case, the concept of race played a key role in differentiating them from their Turkish and Kurdish neighbours. Racial categories were often interchangeable or overlapped with the categories of 'civilisation' and 'barbarism'. To add to the complexity, religious and racial identities were also frequently conflated or confused.

Understanding the nature of the various races living in the Ottoman Empire was thought key to resolving the 'eastern question'. In consequence,

British travellers elaborated at length upon the nature of racial difference in these regions. They suggested that the people who now inhabited the Ottoman Empire represented the descendents of 'races' that had invaded or migrated into the region over the past centuries. Describing the physical characteristics of these peoples, their 'condition' and 'character' was a standard feature of the travel writing genre. Fanny Blunt provided descriptions of each of the different 'races' of the Ottoman Empire, dedicating chapters to each of the races living under Ottoman rule and describing their current conditions and future prospects. She approached 'race' in a hierarchical manner, remarking upon the 'vast superiority' of the Greeks. Blunt assumed her readers recognised the stereotypical characteristics of different races, claiming that they were 'fairly enlightened as to the manners of the Turk'. This reflected the contemporary belief in a direct and static relationship between race and character.[56]

The overlapping categories of race, religion and nation provided the framework for British constructions of Armenia and the Armenians. But even though the use of these categories and concepts by writers was remarkably consistent, they drew varied conclusions. The process of studying and categorising the Armenians was in itself ambivalent. Whilst it demonstrated a keen interest in the Armenians, it placed them in a subordinate position, rendering them unable to 'speak' for themselves.

The racial, national and religious categories employed in the construction of British images of Armenia all related to the broader question of where the Armenians 'belonged' in the wider world. These questions were in turn related to defining the boundaries of civilisation and of Europe.

Armenia as a cradle of civilisation

> Below and around, included in this single view seemed to lie the whole cradle of the human race, from Mesopotamia in the south to the great wall of the Caucasus that covered the northern horizon, the boundary for so many ages of the civilized world . . . If it was indeed from here that man first set foot again on the unpeopled earth, one could imagine how the great dispersion went as the races spread themselves from these sacred heights along the courses of the great rivers down to the Black and the Caspian seas and over the Assyrian plain to the shores of the southern oceans, whence they were wafted away to other continents and isles, no more imposing centre of the world could be imagined.[57]

Thus did James Bryce respond to the panoramic view of the Transcaucasian landscape he encountered from the summit of Ararat.

His words evoked a sense of wonder and awe and appear spontaneous and emotional, but in reality his depiction of the region as a 'cradle of civilisation' drew upon an established repertoire of themes and images. His idealised construction of this landscape, with Ararat at its heart, epitomised the image of Armenia in late nineteenth-century Britain.

Bryce produced his account of his journey to Transcaucasia in the late 1870s just as the 'Armenian question' began to impinge upon British consciousness. The timing is highly significant. The transformation of the fate of the Armenians into an international 'question' led to the reworking of fragmentary images into a more coherent image of Armenia. The idea of Armenia as a 'cradle of civilisation' drew upon the development of Armenian nationalism and the creation of national narratives which traced the distant past and described the achievements of past national 'golden ages'.[58] It was also the product of the work of European scholars who had addressed the Armenian past in the context of the history of the 'great civilisations' and the search for the origins of European civilisation and Christianity.

Both aspects of the writing of Armenian history would be utilised when the politics of the 'Armenian question' created the imperative for the construction of an appealing image of Armenia for European audiences. The resulting image stressed Armenia's historical, cultural and spiritual bonds with Europe, emphasising the role it had played in the development of 'civilisation'. In a parallel process, the image of the contemporary Armenian population as a suffering nation fed into the development of heroic images of the Armenian past. In the last three decades of the nineteenth century such idealised readings of the Armenian past were not only present in 'histories', they also permeated travel writing and journalism and were the standard fare of pro-Armenian pamphlets.

The notion of Armenia as a 'cradle of civilisation' was complex and often vague. It drew upon both biblical imagery and theories of European racial origins. It also related to the belief that Armenia belonged to the world of the 'great civilisations' of the Near East. These themes were impossible to separate. At their centre was a romantic attachment to Mount Ararat, an imposing symbol of Christianity, civilisation and endurance.

That Ararat lay at the core of the myth of Armenia as the site of human origins was due to the association of Armenia with biblical origin myths. For example, Armenian traditions located the Garden of Eden within the Armenian homeland.[59] Better known to British audiences, however, was the claim that the Armenia was the site of biblical Ararat, the final resting place of Noah's Ark.[60] Doubts as to the veracity of these claims do not seem to have detracted from the fascination with Ararat. Many of those who came close to the mountain, such as Douglas Freshfield, a traveller in the Caucasus in the late 1860s, were so impressed by what they encountered that they were prepared to suspend their disbelief. 'We agreed that no single mountain we knew presented such a magnificent and impressive appearance as the Armenian giant . . . One is ready immediately to admit that the Ark must have grounded there, if it grounded anywhere in these parts.'[61]

The interest generated by Ararat must be understood in the context of wider interest in the biblical landscape and the attempt to ascertain the historical truth of the Bible through exploration and archaeology in the Holy Land. The Palestine Exploration Fund, for example, had been created in 1865 and had focused the attention of both scholars and the public upon the Near East.[62] Transcaucasia lay beyond the scope of these investigations, yet the Ararat myth created a similar kind of connection between Armenia and the biblical past. Like that of Palestine, the Transcaucasian landscape came to be regarded as having a sacred or spiritual dimension; claimed as a vital part of a British heritage of civilisation and Christianity. The Ararat legend created an island of Christianity, a symbol of the endurance of the faith in a predominantly Islamic region.

The adoption of Ararat as a symbol of Christian heritage related to the tendency of British travellers to 'empty' the Armenian landscape of its contemporary inhabitants in order to imbue it with meaning for British audiences. Similarly, Mark Mazower has remarked of travellers to Salonica that, 'it would not be too much to say that the educated European felt far closer in spirit to the ancient inhabitants of the lands through which he passed than he did to those he actually met'.[63] This tendency comes through particularly strongly in Bryce's narrative of his ascent of Ararat and his survey of the surrounding landscape. Bryce, an Englishman in a foreign land, surveyed the landscape from a vantage point which, as he repeatedly reminds his audience, was thought to be inaccessible by the local population.[64] Even the spatial arrangement of British observer on high and the Armenian landscape spread out below reinforces the inequality of Armenia and Britain.

This scene constitutes what Mary Louise Pratt has termed 'monarch of all I survey' scenes in Victorian travel writing, in which a European observer, 'discovers', 'describes' and 'masters' a landscape from a commanding viewpoint. This kind of narrative, she suggests, implies a 'power if not to possess, at least to evaluate this scene'.[65] Although Bryce does not claim to discover this view, he appears to have mastered its geography and history which he considers his own and in which the contemporary population have no part. He re-claims this landscape, makes a strange place meaningful by integrating it into familiar historical narratives.

The importance accorded to Ararat also drew upon theories of racial origins and archaeological investigations into the origins of 'civilisation'. In the case of the Armenians, racial origins were of particular interest as they, in common with the British, were identified as an 'Indo-European' race. The idea of an 'Indo-European' racial type was based upon a conflation of linguistic and biological categories. In the late nineteenth century it was commonly taken for granted that linguistic groups would correspond clearly to racial and cultural entities which had their origins in clearly defined territories. Linguistic and cultural change was thought to be the product of invasions or migrations (in other words a diffusionist approach) which scholars attempted to map through space and time.

This understanding of racial and linguistic identity was in part a product of essentialist discourses of nationalism which suggested that linear histories of bounded racial or national groups could be traced into the distant past.[66] The identification of the Armenians as Indo-Europeans gave credence to the belief that the Armenians were an ancient people and enmeshed them further in the quest for the origins of European civilisation, which the Indo-Europeans were believed to have played a vital role in bringing from the East.[67] For scholars and travellers such as Lynch, this provided an important framework for understanding the contributions of the Armenians to the modern world: 'The Asiatic, for all his debility, is not the African; he is our father, from whose lips we received our first lessons.'[68] The Indo-European connection thus strengthened the claim that Armenia was culturally, if not territorially, part of Europe, a claim fully exploited in Armenophile and diaspora propaganda.

In the popular imagination the status of the Armenians as Indo-Europeans created the impression of similarity between the British and the Armenians. It suggested the two regions had a common heritage and language, sharing characteristics and capabilities. By the late nineteenth century 'Indo-European' seems to have been a category with connotations for popular audiences. Frequent references to Armenians as Indo-Europeans implied much more than a linguistic category.[69] For those with a more scholarly interest in the Armenians, however, the question of origins proved trickier. The problem arose from investigations into the kingdom of Urartu, in the Armenian homeland.[70]

In 1850 A. H. Layard, famed for his discoveries in Mesopotamia, visited Van in order to study cuneiform inscriptions copied earlier in the century by the German scholar, Schulz.[71] Layard published the details of his visit to Van along with plans and sketches of the cliff apartments in *Discoveries in the Ruins of Nineveh and Babylon: With Travels in Armenia*, describing his travels and his time at Van, 'chiefly engaged in copying the cuneiform inscriptions, and in examining its numerous monuments of antiquity'.[72] Layard's work helped construct the image of Armenia as worthy of historical and archaeological investigation and the Kingdom of Urartu as the pinnacle of civilisation in the region. It also reconsidered the linguistic problems posed by the inscriptions for those interested in Armenian origins. Layard had some doubts about the language family to which the inscriptions belonged:

> It is yet doubtful to what family of languages the Wan [Van] inscriptions must be assigned. Some believe it to be a tartar dialect: or, at least to be largely intermixed with the Mongolian element. Dr. Hincks, on the contrary, is of the opinion that it is indo-Germanic, and adduces, in proof, various instances of case endings corresponding with the Sanskrit.[73]

It later became clear that the Van inscriptions were not Indo-European and therefore unlike the language spoken by the contemporary Armenian population. In a framework where language, race, culture and nation were thought to be congruent, the discovery that the language of Urartu was not the same as that of the Armenians had important implications. It disrupted the idea of an Armenian nation or race continuously occupying the same territory for 'time immemorial' and conflicted with the national histories provided by Armenian chroniclers such as Khorenatsi, who linked the Armenians with the remains of the Urartu.[74] The location of the Urartian archaeological remains in the territory of Armenia had played a role in attracting European attention to the region; it had also drawn the Armenians into the realm of the ancient Near Eastern civilisations. If the Armenians were not the direct descendents of the Urartians, then the issue of origins was once again a puzzle, and their place in the history of 'civilisation' was called into question.

The answers to these issues were also framed in terms of the migrations of racial and linguistic entities in the distant past. The Van cuneiforms were eventually translated and published in the *Journal of the Royal Asiatic Society*, 1882–1932. This firmly established that Urartian was not Indo-European. It was suggested that, in simple terms, the indigenous population who formed the Kingdom of Urartu were not Indo-European speakers, but that Indo-European speakers had later migrated into the region and their language had been adopted by the indigenous populations. The question of Armenian origins was however highly complex and subject to numerous competing explanations and interpretations.[75] In 1902 Lynch argued that the cuneiform script was neither Semitic nor Indo-European, and should be attributed to a new people in 'the museum of the Oriental world'; the Khaldians or Urartians.[76]

Although Lynch devoted much time to the question of origins, many of his contemporaries seemed unaware or uninterested in the nuances of academic debates about the inscriptions and archaeology of Van. However, evidence of the existence of the remains of an 'ancient civilisation' in a region now considered Armenian retained its symbolic power. Most continued to connect the Armenians with 'ancient civilisations', suggesting they inherited civilisation from Urartu or the neighbouring Assyrian or Persian kingdoms. Even Lynch, who had attempted to disentangle the different peoples who had inhabited the region, could not detach the Armenians from the idea of 'civilisation' suggesting that, 'To this extent they may inherit the blood of that ancient people which gave to Armenia a degree of civilisation which in many ways it has not been privileged since to enjoy.'[77]

In the majority of British texts, the idea of Armenia as a cradle of civilisation was based on a conflation of biblical myths, racial theories, linguistics and archaeology. The comments of Lord Warkworth in his accounts of his travels in Turkey, *Notes from a Diary in Asiatic Turkey*, capture the essence of popular British approaches: 'a people of Aryan stock allied to the Medes, their origin is lost in the mists of antiquity, though native tradition traces their descent from the two sons of Noah, Shem and Japheth'.[78] Nonetheless, the associations of Armenia with the 'ancient world' were readily employed by Armenophiles to inform their audiences of the achievements of the Armenians. Garabed Hagopian reminded the AAA of the 'mental calibre and martial valour the researches of such men as Dr. Mortman, Sir Henry Layard and others have demonstrated in the entombed treasures of the fallen cities of Armenia, Ani and Dickranaguerd'.[79]

Just as the complexities of Armenian origins could be distilled for the public into the notion of Armenia as an ancient nation, the remainder of the Armenian past was also subject to processes of selection, simplification and manipulation. The worth of studying Armenian history was a matter of some contention. In 1854 Robert Curzon declared that 'the general history of Armenia contains but little that is of interest'.[80] As the 'Armenian question' progressed views like Curzon's became increasingly rare as a consensus that Armenian history was understudied emerged. By the 1890s Alexander MacDonald's remarks that Armenia had 'a history more remarkable than that of the principalities and kingdoms of modern Europe' were by no means uncommon.[81]

British knowledge of the later periods of Armenian history even at the end of the nineteenth century was at best 'fragmentary'.[82] The construction of narratives of Armenian history depended upon the availability of texts in European languages. It was also determined by British concerns, preconceptions and readings of British national history. Discourses of British identity shaped the representation of the Armenian past. Armenian history was fitted into 'known' histories of the ancient world. The Armenians were traced through the past via classical texts and inscriptions. A reliance on a narrow selection of classical texts, such as Xenephon's *Anabasis*, to 'verify' Armenian versions of the past was typical. These texts were not only used to 'map' the Armenians but were treated as an authority on Armenian characteristics and society. They were used as a prism through which to interpret nineteenth-century Armenia, as it was assumed that little had changed since that time.

The availability of texts was not the only factor shaping British conceptions of Armenian history: contemporary social, cultural and political preoccupations also helped determine which periods were worthy of attention. A great deal of attention was focused upon the periods during which the Armenians had greatest political power, such as the empire of Tigranes the Great, c. 95–55 BC, and the medieval kingdoms at Ani, Van and Cilicia. This focus on Armenian 'golden ages' served to demonstrate the degradation of the Armenians under Ottoman rule and to highlight their potential for national development in the future.

Christianity was as much a theme in British writings on the Armenian past as 'the nation'. Armenian history was rich in religious associations, occupying an important place in Christian history. Legends of the Armenian conversion to Christianity by Gregory the Illuminator in the fourth century were repeatedly recounted by British travellers, especially those who visited Etchmiadzin, the seat of the Patriarch. British Armenophiles also admired Armenia's status as the first nation to convert to Christianity. This helped to reinforce the idea that the Armenians were in the forefront of not only religious progress but also the general progress towards civilisation that this embodied.[83]

Conversion was seen as the starting point in a remarkable example of Christian strength and survival in a hostile environment. In this context of 'survival' racial and religious characteristics overlapped. Armenia was idealised as an outpost of Christianity, the 'last defence' of the Christian faith. It was believed that to survive under these circumstances, the Armenians had made great sacrifices. Thus even before the massacres of the late nineteenth century the language of sacrifice and martyrdom was applied to Armenia:

> There is something grand in the sacrifice that the ignorant and stout-hearted Asiatics made in the cause of religion. Nowhere was persecution so long and cruel, martyrdom so terrible, self-denial so complete, as among the people of the land where the human race is fabled to have had its origin.[84]

British scholars and travellers alike frequently made the assumption that successive incursions of Islamic peoples into the region from the medieval period onwards brought about a decline of Armenian civilisation and culture. Later periods of Armenian history were therefore dismissed as periods of conquest and destruction by the Persians, Arabs, Mongols and eventually the Ottomans. These periods were regarded as long stretches of empty time, significant only in that the Armenians managed to survive and preserve their faith.[85] However the medieval Armenian kingdoms such as the Bagratid Kingdom at Ani, the Arsruni Kingdom at Van and the later Kingdom of Cilicia were considered worthy of British attention. In the case of Cilicia, this was principally due to the part it played in the Crusades, but there was also interest in the religious art and architecture which developed in the region. Illuminated manuscripts began to be collected not only by Armenians, but also by Europeans. European travellers often commented on the collections of manuscripts held at Etchmiadzin and admired the translation and publishing of the Mekhitarists.[86]

The study of Armenian manuscripts was a specialised area and medieval Armenian architecture had more appeal for most visitors to Armenia than illuminated manuscripts, literature or historical epics. In particular, the ruins of the city of Ani captured the imaginations of numerous British travellers. Ani was located in a remote region, on the borders of the Russian and Ottoman Empires. The Russo-Turkish wars had drawn attention to the region, bringing diplomats and travellers alike to the ruined city. Like Van, Ani had a romantic appeal for travellers, with the ruins of the city viewed as part of the wild, untamed landscape. Over the course of the nineteenth century Ani, like Ararat, became a well-known site on travel routes through Armenia.[87]

The appeal of Ani went beyond its romantic appearance. The city, known as the city of a thousand churches, also assumed significance as a Christian site, standing alone in what appeared to be a wilderness of Islam. By the late nineteenth century Ani had also become firmly associated with the past achievements of the Armenian nation. In 1885, images of the city were published in the English journal, *The Graphic*, provided by Garabed Hagopian, the London-based diaspora activist.[88] Publicity like this played an important role in the representation of Armenia as a site of civilisation and Christianity. The idea of Ani as a monument of Christianity was reflected in perceptions of Armenian religious architecture more generally: 'It was truly refreshing to come upon such very beautiful relics of Christian Art in so wild a country.'[89]

In 1850 Layard had expressed admiration for Armenian architecture, drawing the conclusion that 'the connection between eastern and western architecture was well worthy of study and cannot be better illustrated than by the early Christian ruins of Armenia.'[90] Around half a century later, in his 1902 history of Armenia, Lynch provided the most in-depth British descriptions and interpretations of Armenian architecture. He took a particular interest in the ruins of Ani, providing long descriptions of its historical and architectural development, tracing the evolution of architectural styles. Like others before him he was particularly impressed by the cathedral at Ani: 'Although of small proportions, if judged by European standards, it is nevertheless a stately building. It bears the imprint of that undefinable quality, beauty, and can scarcely fail to arouse a thrill of delight in the spectator.'[91] Like Layard, he, measured Armenian architecture against a 'western' yardstick:

> In no case do we discover any trace of barbarism; the designs are sober and full of grace, the execution is beyond praise. The impression that we take away from our survey of these various merits is that we have been introduced to a monument of the highest artistic merit, denoting a standard of culture which was far in advance of the contemporary standards in the West.[92]

His surprise at the architectural standard of the Cathedral at Ani reflects the way that whilst aspects of Armenian culture and society were often admired by the British, the Armenians were still not accepted as part of the same cultural world as Western Europe. High architectural standards in Armenia were treated as an anomaly rather than a 'natural' ability. Although Ani was a potent symbol of the bonds of Christianity and civilisation, responses to the city were not without their ambiguities. Reactions to Ani provide insight into the ways in which Armenia was conceptualised as 'different', not completely accepted as part of the Christian, civilised world. As such they provide a useful starting point from which to draw out some of the ways in which this difference was constructed and explained.

Ambivalence, distancing and difference

It is helpful at this point to return to the work of Lynch, whose opinions are particularly telling. He suggested that although Ani represented a pinnacle of medieval architectural development, this 'golden age' of artistic achievement was over: 'Years upon years have elapsed since district and city throbbed with the pulse of human life.'[93] His words echoed those of other writers, who viewed Armenia as the scene of departed greatness. In James Creagh's words, 'solitary ruins, silent and deserted, speak of past greatness; and the wonderful remains of the dead city of Ani, in the plain of Kars, is an imperishable monument of the wealth, address and enterprise of fallen grandeur'.[94] Ani provided perhaps the most vivid demonstration of the contrast between the bleakness of the present and the glories of the past. That the cultural, political and religious achievements of the past were strikingly absent from the present led to disappointment and disillusion.

For those who encountered the Armenians in the Russian or Turkish provinces the 'otherness' of the Armenians was demonstrated on a daily basis by the difficulties and indignities of travel. Travel in Armenia appeared to be no less fraught with the 'tedious arrangements of eastern travel' than anywhere else.[95] Unreliable guides, shady dealings and the dirt and discomfort of lodgings, familiar features of Victorian travel accounts, pepper Armenian travel narratives. The risks posed by travel in Armenia also feature heavily in these narratives, as do the exciting 'adventures' the authors undertake and grave dangers they overcome.

The 'otherness' of Armenia is also made apparent in the abundant descriptions of mundane details of everyday life in the region. Standards of cleanliness and hygiene, for example, played a key role in marking out a lack of civilisation. In this respect the peasantry of Armenia was subject to the worst kind of criticism. Blunt described peasant women as 'without possessing the redeeming point of cleanliness'.[96] Their homes were also thought unhygienic. Mrs William Ramsay's description of her stay in an Armenian home was typical. At first sight she thought her accommodation clean and comfortable, 'lined with wood and furnished with pretty carpets'. Her opinions changed somewhat however when she was awoken by biting insects in her bed.[97] Her account suggests that even superficial cleanliness could not disguise the fact that Armenian standards were never quite the same as those 'at home'. For this reason travellers were thankful for the presence of missionaries and consuls in Armenia. Not only were they treated as a much more reliable source of information than the local population, but they could also provide welcome home comforts – islands of civilisation in the wilderness.[98]

Many travellers held an even worse opinion than Mrs Ramsay regarding Armenian domestic arrangements, discovering that Armenian homes did not have the accoutrements to make them comfortable for the western traveller. The practice of housing humans and livestock under the same roof was universally regarded as distasteful. Reactions to Armenian housing, in rural areas at least, fluctuated between curiosity and disgust, and a description of the 'underground' homes of the Armenian peasants came to be a familiar anecdote.[99] It reinforced the idea of the Armenians belonging to nature rather than the modern world. It created an image of primitiveness, underscoring the difference between Armenia and the Britain they thought of as socially and technologically progressive.

The Armenia encountered by British travellers on an everyday basis merged into a generic image of the 'East' where orientalist stereotypes abounded. The comments of the Reverend George Hepworth illustrate this viewpoint particularly effectively. He observed that in rural areas the Armenians were 'As low in many respects as either the Turks or the Kurds . . . you cannot tell an Armenian from a Kurdish village by anything that meets the eye of the traveller.' At this level few distinctions were drawn between Armenians, Turks or other peoples of the Ottoman Empire.[100]

Despite this blurring of boundaries, the fact that the Armenians were Christians distinguished them from the surrounding populations. Early conversion and the survival of their faith through times of adversity were regarded as a demonstration of the promise of the Armenians, of their intrinsic good and capacity for progress. Christianity was a focus for Armenophile propaganda and assisting the Armenians was portrayed as a specifically Christian duty.

Nevertheless, the Armenian Church was not treated as the equal of its British counterpart. The majority regarded it as deeply flawed and in serious need of reform. Just as admirers of the Armenian past were disheartened by the present condition of the Armenian people, the condition of the Armenian Church did not always meet the standards of religious practice expected by many British observers. Assessments of the Armenian Church were complex, as although the Armenians as a whole were characterised as 'Christian brothers' there were deep religious divisions within the Armenian community.[101] Armenian Protestants, converted by American missionaries, were admired as the bearers of an 'advanced' form of Christianity. Armenian Roman Catholics met with a more mixed response.

The Armenian Apostolic or Orthodox Church occupied a still more ambivalent position in the British imagination. It was regarded as an ancient and authentic church, yet its standards were thought to have been eroded. Aspects of Armenian religious doctrine were thought incorrect and religious practice assumed to be lax. Armenia may have been a sacred site but its religious institutions were thought of as backward and inferior.

. The main charge levelled at the Armenian Church by British writers was that of 'superstition', shorthand for a reliance on ritual or mysticism and inadequate knowledge of the Bible. Armenian religious rituals, just like the conversion myths, were regarded as curiosities rather than as having any intrinsic spiritual value. Unusual ceremonies, such as those associated with birth and death, were described in detail by a number of British writers, a practice which created the image of Armenian belief as primitive or backward, likening it to belief systems encountered in other 'less civilised' parts of the world.[102] The existence of these religious practices was often regarded as a continuation of pre-conversion 'pagan' practices. Lucy Garnett suggested that 'it is less easy than in the case of the Greeks to ascertain to what extent the church feasts of the Armenians are survivals of pagan festivals'.[103] This implied that Armenia was not fully Christianised and underlined the continuing need for missionary work.

British observers also criticised more 'orthodox' practices and ceremonies. Marriage ceremonies, for example, were regarded as entertaining spectacles to be studied for what they could reveal about another culture or enjoyed as part of the local scenery. They were rarely treated as serious religious services.[104] Other Orthodox rituals were deemed outdated or improper. Even Bryce, a staunch supporter of the Armenian cause, found fault with the religious practices he encountered at Etchmiadzin. Upon seeing a relic of the hand of St Gregory the Illuminator used in the ceremony of the consecration of the patriarch, he was startled to find such a practice 'in full force in an important and respectable branch of the Christian Church. In the middle ages nothing would have seemed more natural or impressive. In the nineteenth century it looks a little different.'[105]

The condition of the clergy also caused great consternation. Although visitors to Etchmiadzin expressed great respect for the Catholicos and the Bishops, the lack of education and poverty amongst the lower clergy concerned them. Bryce, for example, expressed his disappointment about the Armenian monastic orders, who had, he says 'quite shocked Roman Catholic travellers by enforcing no rule of silence'.[106] Concern about the lack of education within the clergy related to a broader concern for educational standards in Armenia. Education through the Church was regarded as perhaps the only way to improve standards and bring about 'progress' in Armenia. Even the most ardent Armenophiles thought religious change a matter of urgency.

Just as domestic arrangements and religious practice came under the scrutiny of British observers, the examination of the situation of Armenian women represented another means by which standards of civilisation in Armenian were evaluated. This interest in Armenian women was not unusual. During the nineteenth and early twentieth centuries the observation and description of 'native' women occupied a prominent place in travel writing. As Reina Lewis points out, 'evocative and detailed description of orientalised women was an expected trope of material about the Orient.'[107] The feminising of the 'East' and the characterisation of the Ottoman Empire in particular as an exotic site of sexual adventure and freedom is a well-documented aspect of orientalist discourse: 'The West feminised the East and eroticised it. Like the female body in the West, the Orient served as the site of mixed feelings, attraction and repulsion; intimacy and a sense of difference.' Recent scholarship has however stressed the complexities of the relationship between gender and orientalism, suggesting that the orient should not simply be seen as a site of male fantasy and power.[108]

Thus Armenian women featured in British writings on Armenia in a variety of ways. Though women were rarely the primary concern of British travellers, few failed to devote at least a few paragraphs to the appearance, condition and roles of the women that they observed.[109] The interest in the 'condition' of Armenian women reflected the desire to investigate the extent of hardship and suffering amongst the Armenian population. The condition of women acted as an index for the condition of Armenia. Such debates over the condition of Armenian women were not conducted in isolation but shaped by parallel conflicts and debates regarding the position of women in British society. For example, Mills and Lewis suggest that European women's representations of the Ottoman harem 'tended to be determined by their own concerns about European gender relations'.[110]

The concern expressed for the condition of Armenian women did not put paid to representations of these women as exotic sexualised figures. The beauty of Armenian girls was a frequent point of reference for British writers, both male and female, who represented these women within pre-existing conventions of oriental beauty. Lucy Garnett described the 'languorous expression of their dark, almond shaped eyes'.[111] The journalist

E. A. Brayley Hodgetts, in his account of his investigative travels in Armenia, meanwhile acknowledged the diversity of Armenian women but continued to rely upon stereotypes of oriental beauty:

> It is a common belief that all Armenian women are dark, languorous and Oriental looking, but this idea is erroneous, there is a fair type as well as a dark and I can only say that the great ladies, young, beautiful and graceful, whom I saw collected at this ball, were fairly dazzling.[112]

Such descriptions, however sympathetic, relied on an objectification of Armenian women and their treatment as passive features of the oriental 'scenery', existing primarily to satisfy the curiosity of European observers.

Detailed physical descriptions of Armenian women also served to distinguish them from European women. In a period when it was believed that racial difference could be identified through physiognomy, mention of dark skin, dark eyes and exotic features contributed to the racialising of difference between Armenians and British. This process of differentiation relied not only upon physical appearance but was thought to be reflected in clothing through the 'national' or 'traditional' costumes which were also described at length. Henry Barkley claimed Armenian peasant women were clothed in 'loose baggy trousers, tied in at the ankle; round the waist is a coloured shawl in two or three loose folds, a linen shirt, a short loose jacket, the head tied up in a rag, and the hair hanging down their backs in five or six plaits. As for shoes they scarcely wear them.'[113] Isabella Bishop presented an equally exotic and somewhat patronising picture of Armenian dress, 'A white band bound across the chin up to the lips suggests a broken jaw, and the tout ensemble of the various wrappings of the head a perennial toothache.' She observed that fashion in Armenia was 'unchanging', adding to the image of rural Armenia as backward and timeless.[114]

Textual descriptions of Armenian dress were often accompanied by photographs or drawings of women in 'native' dress which provided a vivid demonstration of 'otherness'. Fascination with 'native' costume was not restricted to the Armenians. Photographic studios existed which could provide costumes matched to numerous ethnic or racial types. Sarah Graham-Brown has explained that as the societies of the Middle East were thought to be in a 'time warp', photographing native costume was a way of capturing or preserving these 'pristine' societies.[115] Interest in 'native' dress was not restricted to women: photographs of male Armenians did feature but the emphasis was different. Whilst the men were usually named individuals or fulfilling a certain role, for example a guide or guard, women were unnamed, serving only as representatives of a 'type' or evidence of the exotic and primitive.[116]

In these ways images of Armenian women served as a way of distancing the Armenians. In terms of appearance they were presented as exotic and remote. Yet representations of Armenian women did not only function as a demonstration of 'otherness'. The representation of Armenian women in British texts differed from that of Turkish and Islamic women in a number of ways, all of which suggested that the Armenians had more in common with British women than their neighbours. Armenian women were represented as different in 'character' or 'nature' from Turkish women and their role and position within society was conceived of as quite different.

The lives of the women of the Ottoman Empire had provoked curiosity amongst European travellers throughout the nineteenth century. In particular, the development of 'harem literature' as increasing numbers of female European travellers were able to gain access to the private quarters of Turkish women, spurred on interest into the conditions in which they lived. European responses to the harem were complex and varied: many Victorian female writers desexualised the space and recast the harem as a middle-class home.[117] Nonetheless, the harem retained its sexual and oppressive connotations as part of the 'well established Western fantasy of Ottoman depravity'.[118]

Armenian women were not viewed as part of the world of the oriental harem either as a site of sexual possibility and adventure, or as a domestic space. The harem was closely associated with the practice of polygamy and, as Christians, Armenian women were thought to have escaped this form of oppression.[119] Nevertheless, representations of Armenians, who lived as part of Ottoman society, could not fail to engage with this central trope of orientalist discourse. For nineteenth-century critics of the Ottoman Empire, the harem could evoke all that was amiss with Ottoman society:

> It came to be regarded as a microcosmic Middle East, apotheosising the two characteristics perceived as essentially Oriental: sensuality and violence . . . From the enlightenment onwards the harem came to be not merely a psychosexual symbol, but a metaphor for injustice in civil society and the state and arbitrary government.[120]

In the context of Armenophile writing, the harem acquired specific meanings. It was utilised by supporters of the Armenians as a contrast, exemplifying everything that the Armenians were not. Armenian women were contrasted with the sexualised inhabitants of harems, as pure, innocent Christian women with high moral standards. Life in a harem was represented as a dire threat to vulnerable Armenian women at risk of Turkish 'lustfulness', rather than a standard life experience. Hodgetts' remark, 'I never heard of or saw, an Armenian woman of the unfortunate class' is typical.[121] Hodgetts also touched upon another important aspect of the image of Armenian women, contrasting them with the popular image of the harem as a site of languor and idleness, stifling to its inhabitants, by observing that they 'cannot keep idle for a single minute'.[122]

The kind of attention accorded the harem reflects the way that the treatment of women was thought to embody fundamental differences between East and West. The treatment of women, and particularly practices such as veiling, polygamy and seclusion, was widely regarded as a measure of civilisation and progress.[123] The conditions of Turkish women, for Armenophiles who believed themselves to be progressive, were indicative of the despotic nature of the Ottoman government. Bryce observed: 'Nothing strikes a Western with more disgust than the way he sees women treated in Mohammedan countries. It is not so much the enforced seclusion that revolts you as the tacit assumption that women are inferior creatures altogether.'[124] For Bryce the veil symbolised wider attitudes to women.[125] He observed that Armenian women were, like Muslim women, veiled but suggested this was in the spirit of safety rather than oppression. In fact Bryce argued that the attitude to women amongst Armenians was 'the most fundamental difference that separates them from the Muslims, probably it is this which, more than anything makes them progressive while the others remain stagnant'.[126]

Bryce's conclusions were not universally shared. Representations of the female population were typically varied, reflecting the fact that practices varied over time, from place to place and amongst different sectors of Armenian society. Layard claimed that Armenian women were 'said to be handsome, but even more rigidly concealed than the Mohammedan ladies'.[127] Barkley on the other hand thought the situation of the Armenian and Turkish women was similar. 'Armenians have greatly adopted the manners of the Turks. The women live apart from the men in rooms of their own during the day; they cover their faces in the street when they go out and wear a cloak like that of the Turkish women.'[128]

The differing opinions on the actual position of Armenian women in Ottoman society were accompanied by equally varied opinions on how their position could, or should, be improved. Armenophiles interpreted the oppression of Armenian women as a function of the flaws in

Ottoman, rather than Armenian, society. Armenian women tended to be portrayed as victims of Ottoman oppression, an image which would be elaborated upon when the oppression of the Armenians spilled over into atrocity and massacre. When this occurred doubts about the 'otherness' of Armenian women were set aside and they were recast as innocent Christians subjected to the horrors of exploitation at the hands of the 'lustful Turk'.

Civilisation, progress and degeneration

> There is no place in Europe, except Constantinople and probably few places in the world, where one feels so in the middle, so to speak, of so many cross currents, so many diverse associations of the past and possibilities for the future.[129]

The observations of James Bryce highlight the disorientation which the situation in Armenia caused for many European travellers. The realisation that Armenia was 'in the middle' was only the beginning. Understanding how this situation had arisen and its implications for the future was even more challenging. Untangling the complexities of the Armenian situation presented a puzzle that British observers were keen to resolve. Though Armenia was commonly thought to be 'geographically' in Asia, as a site of Christianity and 'civilisation' it clearly did not fulfil orientalist stereotypes of 'the East'.

Armenians inhabited the regions thought to represent the meeting point or crossroads of East and West. This region could be viewed in a positive light as a site of cultural or economic exchange. More often than not, however, it was perceived of not as a bridge or connection but instead as a cultural and religious boundary or even as a site of conflict where East and West clashed.[130] The region was therefore thought to be threatening, and especially prone to violence and unrest. In turn this meant it was regarded as a place where the intervention of Europe in order to ensure stability or security was thought desirable or even inevitable.

Geographical explanations accounting for the predicament of Armenia in terms of its location on the borders of East and West were incorporated into broad historical interpretations that negotiated the distance and sameness of Armenia through the concepts of progress, time and civilisation. This involved a general consensus that the distant past of Armenia played an important role in the development of 'civilisation'. This emphasis on Armenia's distant past had a dual significance. It simultaneously created bonds between Armenia and Britain as sites of 'civilisation', whilst distancing Armenia from Britain by drawing attention away from the 'real' Armenia into the distant past.

In British travel writing Armenia was represented as a historical site, a place where events of universal significance had, but no longer, occurred. Visitors to Armenia were acutely aware that they were journeying through a site of their 'own' history. The words of George Hepworth are telling: 'There is hardly a village which does not contain relics of the past.'[131] Alexander MacDonald shared these sentiments:

> In fact, turn our steps north, south, East or West, in this ancient land, we tread, as it were, on history stratified. Here it was that the confluent streams of old world humanity mingled and contended for Empire, and as the results of their conflicts influenced potentially the growth of that civilization which now blesses countries far distant from it.[132]

By repeatedly drawing attention to the distant past in this way, Armenia was made to appear 'timeless', with no sense of change or development. Johannes Fabian's exploration of the way that time is used as a 'key category with which we conceptualise relationships between us (or our theoretical constructs) and our objects (the other)' illuminates the case of Armenia.[133] 'Freezing' Armenia in its distant past was a powerful means of creating difference. Armenia was removed from the European trajectory of progress and development, languishing in the lower levels of development, failing to progress through history and attain the heights of European civilisation.

The image of Armenia as a place where civilisation no longer resided became commonplace. Nonetheless, it did not fully answer the question of how or why Armenia had failed to follow the same trajectory of development of the European world. In a sense this question was answered through an overarching belief that civilisation 'naturally' passed from East to West. After all, the Near East was home to the remains of numerous ancient civilisations which had faded into obscurity. As the archaeologist Hogarth observed, 'The Anatolian was living in great cities when we were setting up shapeless monoliths on Salisbury Plain.'[134]

However, many of the British individuals who encountered Armenia subscribed to a more complex interpretation of its lack of development. This interpretation was closely allied to their reading of the contemporary condition of the Ottoman Empire. It was based on the premise that barbarian invasions from the East had brought about decline, halting progress and development in all aspects of Armenian society and culture. Opinions on the dating of this 'decline' varied. Lynch argued that 'the natural development of the Armenian people was suddenly arrested by the Seljuk conquest'.[135] For him, the ruins of Ani were a powerful visual symbol of arrested development which reflected the general paralysis of Armenian society. They were also impressive evidence of the 'barbaric' nature of the Turks and a reminder that they were an alien and damaging presence in the region.

The current situation in Armenia was regarded as proof that decline continued and the 'Armenian question' as the inevitable product of a decline which set in centuries ago. The 'flaws' encountered in modern Armenians were in turn viewed as yet another a symptom of this decline. Armenophiles argued that Ottoman rule had caused the Armenian people to become weak, submissive, greedy and unscrupulous: 'Hundreds of years of oppression have stamped out all manly feeling, and made them what they are, a people fit for slavery, who's noblest ambition is to cheat and outwit their masters.' It was implied that not only had Turkish rule halted the progress of a promising nation, but that the Armenians had degenerated under it.[136]

Degeneration was thought to be a predictable effect of Turkish government. In fact, it was argued that it had already been observed earlier in the century in Ottoman-ruled Greece, an area long regarded as 'polluted by the taint of Turkish culture'.[137] Degeneration at the hands of the Ottomans or the idea of an Ottoman 'taint' was a familiar concept for British supporters of the Armenians. It allowed the Armenians to have a great deal in common with Britain but explained the vast differences in the present condition of the Armenians and the British.

'Degeneration' was also a prominent theme in late nineteenth-century culture, used to frame anxieties not only about distant peoples living beyond Britain but also social problems within the country's borders. It was not surprising then for the predicament of the Armenians to be framed in such terms:

> Degeneration in the second half of the nineteenth century served not only to characterise other races (for instance that other races had degenerated from the ideal physique of the white races) but also to pose a vision of internal dangers and crises within Europe. Crime, suicide, alcoholism and prostitution were understood as 'social pathologies' endangering the European races, constituting a degenerative process within them.[138]

Degeneration was the flipside of the evolutionary thought which had become prevalent in nineteenth-century understandings of society and culture. In the second half of the century theories of socio-cultural evolution developed by scholars such as Edward Tylor elaborated a scale of human development progressing in stages from savagery to civilisation. 'Civilised' societies such as Britain were imagined to be at the top of this scale whilst cultural variation was explained in terms of stages of development along it. According to George Stocking, 'social evolution was a process by which a multiplicity of human groups developed along lines which moved in general towards the social and cultural forms of Western Europe'.[139] Whilst most of those interested in Armenia were not interested in theorising development to this degree, they were more than ready to employ the vocabulary of this approach.

In general it was assumed that societies would progress towards civilisation, though not all would attain the same standards. Degeneration was thought to be an uncommon localised phenomenon. William Ramsay remarked on the uniqueness of conditions in the Ottoman Empire:

> Gradually the Christians in most places acquiesced, as we have seen, in the Oriental spirit and the Oriental religion of the dominant race. It is a remarkable instance of degeneration from civilised to barbarian society and one which it would be instructive to study in detail.[140]

Belief that the Armenians had degenerated was clear from the language used to describe and classify them. Fanny Blunt described them as, 'primitive, semi-civilised' whilst Hepworth observed they were 'practically savages and live the life of savages . . . As thoroughly primitive in their habits as the cave dwellers of the earliest historic days'.[141] This language associated them with the 'lower' stages of civilisation.[142]

The idea of degeneration also provided a critique of Ottoman rule. The degeneration which had occurred under the Ottomans could be contrasted with the 'civilising mission' of British imperialism, improving the peoples at lower levels. For later writers especially, Armenian 'backwardness' was more of an indictment of Turkish rule than a direct criticism of the Armenian people. It was argued that, given the right conditions, the Armenian people could and would make rapid progress. In order to illustrate this, British Armenophiles pointed to the achievements of Armenians in the diaspora in Europe and under Russian rule. Frances Seymour Stevenson told the AAA that the British should be familiar with the capabilities of the diaspora Armenians who had 'proved their capacity in the political as well as the commercial walks of life'.[143]

The improved conditions of Armenians encountered in Russian-ruled Transcaucasia was also regarded as evidence of Armenian 'progress'. Though there was disagreement over the conditions of Armenians in

Russia, British observers generally agreed that more stable and peaceful conditions had allowed the Armenians to develop and play an important role in society.[144] The journalist W. T. Stead contrasted the situation of the Armenians in Russia and Turkey in typically dramatic terms:

> On one side of the frontier there peace reigns, and prosperity, tranquillity is assured and law and order is as well observed as in any civilised country. On the other side we find rapine, outrage, massacre, and all the hideous concomitants of a civil war in which all the fighting is on one side.[145]

Though few others claimed the differences were so extreme, there was a sense that Russian rule had been beneficial for the Armenians. Lynch termed it 'deliverance from the licence and anarchy of former years'.[146] Even the Armenophiles (usually less likely that their Tory peers to see Russia as a threat to Britain) portrayed Russia as only the lesser of two evils. Hodgetts admired Russia's civilising mission in the region but was concerned about Russia 'carrying this mission too far'.[147]

Even in the Ottoman Empire, British observers described glimpses of Armenian development. Many attested to the important role played by the Armenians in finance and trade, describing the European lifestyles of the Armenian inhabitants of Constantinople and other cities of the Ottoman Empire. The educated, city-dwelling Armenians were carefully distinguished from the more numerous Armenian peasants of Eastern Anatolia: 'While in point of culture the Armenians of the Aegean would compare not unfavourably with Europeans, the dwellers in the remote fatherland have advanced but slowly.'[148] The 'advanced' Armenians were regarded as having succeeded against the odds. However, their European lifestyles also inspired doubts in British observers, who were quick to point out the problems of the rapid adoption of European habits. Fanny Blunt complained of a lowering of standards of morality, as the Armenians often 'abuse the freedom of European manners'.[149] Thus, although the poverty and ignorance of the Armenian peasantry was lamented, in a sense they were regarded as 'authentic' Armenians, rooted in the soil of their homeland, unlike the educated, cosmopolitan and morally suspect elite.

Doubts about the 'habits' of westernised Armenians were one expression of the belief that the Armenian development must be guided by British supervision. Michael Herzfeld's observations about European attitudes to Greece are telling:

> Even when Eurocentric observers do acknowledge the existence of mental capacities, the rhetoric of tolerance founders on the assumption that these

capacities are in some sense latent in an ethnic population – that they are given to passive subjects by God, but stimulated into active form by European culture and language alone.[150]

As in the case of the Greeks, whilst British observers expressed sympathies for the Armenians they remained convinced of their own cultural superiority. Their relationship with the Armenians was not premised upon equality but upon the idea that Britain's position as a civilised nation and an imperial power entailed a duty towards them. This was why the claims of Armenian nationalists were so often disregarded or disparaged by British observers. In their eyes Armenian independence depended on the slow growth of civilisation, occurring at a pace determined by Britain, not nationalist 'agitators'.[151] For this reason many British Armenophiles advocated the creation of a Christian governorship in Armenia. Canon MacColl suggested that:

> The precedent of Lebanon must, therefore, be followed – I trust with more generosity towards the Christians. A constitution must be drawn up for Armenia by someone acting on behalf of the Great powers or those of them who have already intervened in this matter; and that constitution must insist, as a minimum, on the appointment of a Christian Governor of Armenia, provided with some sort of force to maintain order; the Governor to be appointed direct by the powers or subject to their approval, and irremovable without their sanction.

The idea that Armenian development must be determined by the 'civilised' powers was echoed in the work of missionaries. The missionaries were not in the Ottoman Empire to convert Armenians but to bring a 'higher conception of what constituted Christian life'.[152] Their work extended into education and employment. Barkley explained that the missionaries were engaged in 'teaching the gospel to the natives of these parts, educating them and trying to raise them to a higher state of civilization'.[153] Their 'achievements' with the Armenian people provided another example of the progress the Armenians could make under a guiding hand.

This kind of 'progress' was demonstrated in the images of Armenian women which were included not only in travel accounts but also in the various publications of humanitarian and missionary organisations, such as the *Friend of Armenia*. Just as images of women in native dress could represent 'otherness', so adoption of western dress represented a progression towards civilisation. Neat rows of Armenian women and children dressed in western work or school uniform provided a visual demonstration of the adoption not only of the Christian faith, but also the morality and work ethic supposedly inculcated by the missionaries.

The Armenian massacres

Whilst British Armenophiles attempted to inform the British population about the fate of the Armenians and European governments wrangled over the implementation of reforms in the Ottoman Empire, the situation of the Armenians grew steadily worse.[154] The persecution of Armenians continued, particularly in the distant eastern provinces of the empire. Under the rule of Sultan Abdulhamid the situation became worse due to the settlement of Muslim refugees from Europe in Armenian territories and the creation of the irregular Kurdish 'Hamidiye' corps in 1891. Conflicts between Armenians and Kurds were manipulated by the Ottoman authorities, often resulting in attacks on Armenian villages. Armenians were forced to provide shelter for the Kurds in the winter and were subject to repeated attacks from marauding Kurdish tribes. As Armenians were forbidden to bear arms under Ottoman law they were unable to protect themselves from these attacks. To make matters worse, as Christian testimony was not accepted in the Ottoman courts, it was virtually impossible for Armenians to seek justice.[155]

In summer 1894 increasing oppression of the Armenians erupted into widespread massacres. The massacres were initially triggered by an uprising in the district of Sassoun over the payment of extraordinary taxes. This resulted in the massacre of the Armenian population of the region. The initial violence was followed by widespread massacres in the second half of 1895 and the summer of 1896.[156] The massacres once again thrust the Armenians into the European spotlight and European diplomats again turned their attention to the resolution of the 'Armenian crisis'. Protests by British consuls forced the Ottoman authorities to hold an investigation into events at Sassoun but the results were not considered satisfactory and a further European investigation was held.[157]

British Armenophiles and the massacres

In Britain the fate of the Armenians began to capture the public imagination more than ever before as graphic accounts of the massacres appeared in the press and the accounts of American missionaries. Reactions to the massacres were, according to Roy Douglas, 'violent and immediate, a thrill of horror ran through the land, without distinction of party or social class'.[158] The plight of the Armenians was swiftly politicised. The campaign on behalf of the Armenians was, according to Shannon, 'an agitation of moral outrage in Britain reminiscent of Bulgaria and 1876'.[159]

Gladstone became the figurehead of the Armenian cause. His interventions immediately provided a link between the fate of the Armenians and that of the Bulgarians twenty years previously. This connection detracted from the particularities of the Armenian people that had been elaborated upon in Armenophile discourse over the past two decades, submerging them in a catch-all category of 'suffering Christians'. Though effective in terms of eliciting sympathy for their cause, this rendered the Armenians passive victims, shifting attention from their own articulation of the situation and failing to recognise their specific needs.

Gladstone spoke at Chester in August 1895 on the subject of the Armenian massacres, expressing his support for Armenia in uncompromising terms. The rhetoric was near-identical to that utilised in his *Bulgarian Horrors* pamphlet twenty years previously, its fundamental premise being that Ottoman rule over Christian minorities must be brought to an end: 'I do not hesitate to say that much the cleanest way of dealing with this subject, if we could have done it, would have been to tell the Turk to march out of Armenia.'[160] Gladstone also wrote to the *Daily Chronicle* in September 1895 and his association with the Armenian cause was ensured by his devoting his last speech to the subject, breaking with consensus by suggesting that Britain should act unilaterally and cut diplomatic ties with the Ottoman Empire.

The presence of Gladstone was not the only similarity of the Armenian campaign to the Bulgarian agitation. Several other leading politicians, churchmen, scholars and journalists, including W. T. Stead, Canon MacColl and the Duke of Argyll re-emerged to support a cause regarded as akin to that of the Bulgarians. The Armenian cause was not only linked to the Bulgarian agitation by membership. The Bulgarian campaign effectively paved the way for the Armenian 'agitation' by engaging the British public with questions of foreign policy and transforming the fate of minorities in the Ottoman Empire into a matter of public concern.

Despite these similarities the situation in 1895 was very different from that of 1876, in both domestic and international terms. When the Armenian massacres began a Liberal government under Rosebery was in power. During the previous two decades several prominent Liberals had championed the Armenian cause and when news of the massacres emerged, Liberal expressions of support intensified. Despite this, the international political situation and the necessity of protecting British interests meant that multilateral intervention on behalf of the Armenians was impossible. Unilateral intervention was thought to be an unacceptable alternative. When the Liberals were replaced by a Tory government in July 1895 it seemed that Armenia had once again become an opposition cause.

Even so, the Liberal Party was far from united over the best course of action. Dissent with the ever-powerful Gladstone over how to proceed contributed to the decision of the Liberal leader to resign in October 1896.[161] By this time sections of the Liberal Party were clearly disillusioned with the British failure to put a stop to the massacres and protect the Armenians. G. W. E. Russell and P. W. Clayden of the *Daily News* therefore launched the Liberal 'forward movement' which advocated a more forceful, party-based response to the massacres. Their position had limited appeal and certainly little effect.[162]

The position of the Tories had also changed. Although there were still powerful Turcophile elements in the Government there appears to have been much more readiness to acknowledge the shortcomings of Ottoman rule and recognise the urgency of the Armenian situation. Salisbury made valiant attempts to enlist the co-operation of Russia, Germany and France in intervention in the Ottoman Empire.[163] Rivalries and differing political agendas in the region ensured this did not come to fruition. In his desire to resolve the crisis Salisbury even entertained the possibility of unilateral intervention, but this also failed as he could not gain the necessary political or military backing. Unilateral intervention was thought to be too aggressive and risky an approach, potentially threatening the precarious balance of power in the region.[164] Ultimately great power rivalries rather than domestic party politics prevented intervention. By February 1897 the issue of Armenian reforms had slipped from the international agenda.

Even though the government failed to take decisive action, vociferous public support was expressed for the Armenians, albeit not on the scale of the Bulgarian agitation. The fate of the Armenians preoccupied the Liberal press and periodicals throughout the mid-1890s.[165] Press coverage was augmented by the publication of numerous pamphlets and books. These writings covered everything from the contemporary political situation to ancient history. Though the contemporary condition of the people was the primary focus of these texts, they also included a vast amount of historical information in order to render the Armenian cause interesting and relevant to the British public. Thus the texts of the 1890s synthesised 'scholarly' information and the insights of travellers from earlier periods in order to meet a demand for information from British audiences.[166] Armenian history, literature and culture were put to work in these texts in such a way as to tell the population why the Armenians should gain public sympathy.

The dissemination of information about the Armenians was accompanied by political protests and the growth of philanthropic activities. The massacres added urgency to the work of Armenophile organisations, which intensified their campaigns. A national protest was held at St James' Hall in May 1895 and was addressed by 'authorities' on the Ottoman Empire and its minorities including (once again) the Duke of Argyll and Canon Malcolm MacColl. The resolutions of this public meeting referred to Article 61 of the Berlin Treaty as a concrete legal expression of Britain's responsibility for the Armenian Christians. This was clearly designed to appeal to those unconvinced by abstract talk of shared civilisation or Christian brotherhood.[167] Article 61 would later feature on the front page of the publications of the Friends of Armenia as a rallying cry for the Armenophile movement.[168] At the same time Armenophile organisations provided humanitarian aid for survivors of the massacres which was channelled through missionary organisations and consular officials. This continued on a small scale even after the crisis had abated. Two decades later the massacres and deportations of the Armenians during the First World War would stretch the provision of aid to the Armenians to its very limits.

Representing atrocity

The body of information provided by scholars, travellers, missionaries and diplomats over the course of the nineteenth century meant that in the face of the crises of the 1890s Armenophile organisations had at their disposal a powerful set of images of the Armenians. These were deployed in a number of ways. To demonstrate that the Armenians deserved British support, and to dispel any notions that the Armenians were to blame for their fate, Armenophiles drew upon two main themes, Christianity and civilisation.[169] The Armenians were rarely mentioned without reference to their Christian faith or the use of religious language or imagery which would immediately strike a chord with British audiences.

British Armenophiles such as Bryce were careful not to characterise the conflict between the Armenians and the Turks simply as a religious conflict, preferring to highlight the ill effects of Ottoman rule on Christians and Muslims alike. Frederic Harrison described the Ottoman Empire as 'oppressive to all who live under it'.[170] However, in the frenzied reporting of the massacres, this caution was exercised far less rigorously.[171] Even if the massacres were not directly blamed upon Islam, the language used to describe their effects highlighted the religious dimension; faith became an important marker of difference. As understandings of race, religion and culture were frequently conflated and confused, religious fanaticism was portrayed as one of a number of factors that made the Turks 'barbaric'.

The idea of Armenian 'civilisation' was more nebulous; the term had a multitude of different meanings. In this context it served to identify the Armenians as part of Europe and contrast them with the 'barbaric' Ottomans. Reinforcing this difference meant that the massacres could not easily be dismissed as endemic ethnic conflict in a violent region or as distant eastern barbarians slaughtering each other. Instead it meant that the boundaries between 'East' and 'West' were redrawn, with Armenia safely incorporated into the civilised world of Western Europe.

This treatment of the massacres was of course only possible because of the extensive attention that had been paid to Armenian 'civilisation' in travelogues, scholarly works and other texts over the previous decades. Such an interpretation of the massacres helped ensure that the notion of 'civilisation' remained at the core of British interest in Armenia in subsequent years.

Other characteristics or features which had been commonly attributed to the Armenians remained noticeably absent or were actively refuted; negative stereotypes of Armenians were set aside, allowing for an emphasis on need. Claims that Armenian nationalists were 'troublemakers' and therefore responsible for their own fate were also dismissed; instead their status as innocent victims became the focus. Reservations about the 'otherness' of the Armenians which had previously formed a common thread in British representations were cast aside in new images of Armenian victimhood. The mundane details of Armenian life with all of its dirt, ignorance and superstition which had so disappointed British travellers were now deemed irrelevant. Such ambivalences or negativity towards the Armenians were replaced by a focus upon commonalities with the British people, in the hope of fostering a sense of empathy and responsibility.

In opposition to the image of Armenians as innocent victims the Turks were portrayed as the embodiment of barbarism. Longstanding orientalist stereotypes of the Turks as the barbaric, lustful and fanatically religious perpetrators of atrocity once again came to the fore.[172] Accounts of the massacres associated the Turks with particular acts of violence, including rape, mutilation and the murder of innocent women and children. They depicted the Turks as sadistic, delighting in violence, and provided grim accounts of the tortures they had devised for their victims.

In this respect the depiction of the Armenian massacres recalled that of the Bulgarian horrors twenty years previously when the popular press, led by W. T. Stead at the *Northern Echo*, had provided graphic accounts of Turkish atrocity.[173] Stead's sensationalist and crusading approach to journalism, designed to appeal to a mass audience, provided the backdrop for the extensive coverage of atrocity such as the Armenian massacres.[174] The 'new journalism' associated with Stead played a key role in creating the context in which atrocity stories, and the moral crusades that they were associated with, could thrive. After the demise of the Bulgarian agitation the press turned its attention to a series of other causes, at home and abroad.[175]

Unsurprisingly, Stead turned his attention to the Armenian massacres, authoring a pamphlet, *The Haunting Horrors in Armenia*, a dramatic demand for Britain to fulfil its 'duty' and intervene on behalf of the Armenians: 'Both morally and legally we have not only every justification to intervene, we are guilty of a shameful shirking of an imperative duty if we do not interfere.'[176] Stead's pamphlet quoted extensively from reports of the massacres produced by E. J. Dillon. Dillon had managed to bypass the Sultan's ban on foreign journalists and travelled to Armenia in disguise on behalf of the *Daily Telegraph*. Two of his extended reports in the *Contemporary Review* were equally as inflammatory as anything produced by Stead, describing Armenians:

> Hung up by their heels, the hair of their heads and bodies being plucked out one by one, their bodies branded with red hot irons and defiled in beastly ways that can neither be described not hinted at in England. Their wives dishonoured in their presence and their daughters outraged before their eyes.[177]

Such graphic depiction of violence was a new departure in British images of the Armenians. The Daily Graphic also published a series of illustrated articles, *The Valley of the Shadow of Death*, a macabre combination of travelogue and atrocity journalism describing a journey through Armenia in the aftermath of the massacres. The reports described the fate of the population in the aftermath of the massacres and the devastation they had wrought on the landscape and upon Armenian livelihoods by destroying Armenian homes, farms, shops and churches.[178] The journey to Armenia was presented as an adventurous quest for authentic information about the massacres and the adoption of the narrative style of travel writing made the site of the massacres appear distant, unknown and troubling.

The sensationalist treatment of the massacres in the British press emphasised violence against women. W. J. Wintle was amongst the writers who provided lurid details of attacks on women and children, describing Turks 'ripping open pregnant women, tearing children to pieces by main force'.[179] Extended references to this kind of violence were designed to shock the reader. They also related to preconceptions about Turkish treatment of women, based on popular sexualised images of the harem, polygamy and slavery. The image of Turkish men preying upon Armenian girls was a familiar part of Armenophile discourse.[180] Armenian women were represented as devout, innocent Christians under constant threat of abduction, 'outrage' and slavery in a Turkish harem. Reports of women who committed suicide in order to 'protect their honour' abounded. These women were praised for their actions and portrayed as martyrs for their faith.[181]

British Armenophiles tried to ensure that the massacres of the 1890s were not thought of as an isolated event, but an escalation of oppression encountered on a daily basis by the Armenians, 'to show that the persecution of the Armenians is neither a new thing nor a mere outbreak of spasmodic fanaticism'.[182] Atrocity and massacre were presented as the direct consequence of Ottoman rule over a Christian population. This line of argument harked back to Gladstone's influential condemnation of Ottoman government.[183] He had argued that the Turks had no place in Europe, their rule was illegitimate and in decline, expressing his views in terms of a clash of civilisation and barbarism. The Turks, he suggested, were characterised by 'unbounded savagery' whilst Europe was portrayed as 'civilisation which has been affronted or shamed'.[184] This implied that the protection of the Armenians, and the solution of the Armenian question, could not be resolved without the dismantling of Ottoman rule over the Armenian population.

Conclusions: the rise and fall of the Armenian cause?

After the drama of the Armenian massacres passed, British Armenophiles struggled to maintain public interest in the Armenians. The fate of the Armenians remained distant and different enough to slip from the British public eye. In the following years the public found their attention diverted to other issues, for example the Boer War at the turn of the century. Some of the Armenophiles themselves became drawn into these issues. The involvement of several Liberals with the pro-Boer movement is a key example.

Nonetheless the Armenophile organisations continued their work. The Friends of Armenia supported American missionaries who were active in the region, helping to fund schools, churches and medical care. The diaspora also continued to support the Ottoman Armenians through charity and publicity work. Over the next two decades many of the politicians who had been involved in the Armenophile movement became involved in related but by then more pressing causes, such as the conflict in Macedonia.[185]

The massacres represented a dramatic incursion of Armenian affairs into British politics and society. The outcry that they caused was closely related to the image of Armenia that had been created over the past few decades through the work of scholars, travellers and Armenophile activists. The Armenians had provoked a complex response from these British observers. As Christians living in the 'cradle of civilisation' they were regarded as 'special', worthy of study and protection. This idealised image was not however easily reconciled with disappointment with the standards of living in modern Armenia.

In the context of the 'eastern question', this situation was interpreted in a particular way. The contradictions of the Armenian situation were incorporated into a critique of Ottoman rule. The implication of this interpretation was to reinforce British identities as civilising and benevolent. Thus representing even an ambiguous 'other' could be supportive of hegemonic British identities. Images of the Armenians centred on the interrelated concepts of civilisation and barbarism, and progress and degeneration. These concepts were used to negotiate the 'in-between' position of the Armenians. Through these concepts a close relationship of the Armenians to Western Europe was posited, allowing them to be demarcated from their Turkish neighbours. The Armenians thus became an example of civilisation and barbarism in uniquely close proximity, and the violence which occurred in the 1890s a demonstration of their irreconcilable oppositions.

However, the ambiguous images of Armenia left space for British observers to distance themselves from people and place. 'Degeneration' was invoked to highlight the difference between Armenian peasants and British middle-class travellers. This sense of distance also allowed the Armenians to slip from the public eye when times of crises passed. In times of peace the diaspora and the Armenophiles struggled to make the Armenians relevant to the British population.

Through the Balkan crises these individuals would eventually be drawn back into the 'Armenian question' in the years prior to the First World War. Armenia became a pressing issue once again after it became clear that the Young Turk regime established in 1908 would not deliver the hoped-for improvements in the condition of the Armenians. Massacres in Adana attracted the attention of the British public and after the Balkan wars there were once again international attempts to formulate a reform scheme for Armenia.[186] In 1913 the British Armenia Committee (BAC) was created. An offshoot of the Balkan Committee, it functioned as a pressure group not unlike the AAA of twenty years before.

Immediately prior to the outbreak of war it appeared that a solution to the 'Armenian question' had eventually been found and a reform scheme for the region was agreed upon. The Balkan wars had spurred on this attempt to reform the Armenian provinces of the Ottoman Empire. Appeals for reform were encouraged by the Catholicos, Gevorg V, who petitioned the Russians for help. Meanwhile he called upon Boghos Nubar to use his European contacts to advance the Armenian cause. Armenian leaders in the Ottoman Empire also began to prepare Armenian population statistics and draft reforms. After some wrangling between the powers, the reforms were accepted by the Ottoman government in February 1914.[187] The outbreak of war put paid to this. The Ottoman Empire entered the war against the Allies in October 1914 and the following summer Ottoman authorities began the process of deporting and massacring the Armenian population.

Notes

1 Somakian, *Empires in Conflict*, p. 7.
2 The Armenians sent a delegation to Berlin but were not allowed to join the conference. George, *Merchants in Exile*, p. 34.
3 Quoted in Somakian, *Empires in Conflict*, p. 10.
4 Military consuls were withdrawn in 1882.
5 A. J. Kirakosian, ed., *The Armenian Massacres, 1894–1896: U. S. Media Testimony* (Detroit: Wayne State University Press, 2004), p. 23. The Berlin Treaty stimulated debate about the Armenians. The pamphlet, *The Conference and the Armenians* (London: R. Clay, Sons and Taylor, 1878) drew attention to the consequences of the treaties asking, 'Why should not the Armenians also have their liberty and autonomy?'
6 *Armenia: England's Responsibility* (London: International Association of the Friends of Armenia, Information Bureau, No. 12) argued that 'England has incurred, if not an exclusive responsibility, yet certainly a primary and special

responsibility' for the Armenians. Pamphlet included in Oxford, Bodleian Library, Viscount Bryce Papers, Mss. Bryce 210, fol. 6.

7   On the make-up of the agitation see Saab, *Reluctant Icon*, and Shannon, *Gladstone and the Bulgarian Agitation.*

8   Stevenson, *The Case for the Armenians.*

9   The AAA was founded in 1891 with Bryce as President.

10 'They were, nevertheless, encouraged by alternate Russian and British pressure for reforms, and by the end of the Tanzimat had begun to appeal to these powers in desperation, having lost their initial faith in the Ottoman reform agenda.' Bloxham, *Great Game of Genocide*, p. 38.

11 Suny, *Looking Toward Ararat*, p. 24.

12 Prominent members of the British diaspora community included Garabed Hagopian, lecturer in Armenian history and teacher of oriental languages and Minas Tcheraz, Professor of Armenian at King's College, 'unofficial agent of the Constantinople patriarchate' and later founder of the journal *Armenia*. In 1893 they joined the AAA. George, *Merchants in Exite*, pp. 52–69.

13 Hagopian provided Bryce with the article *The Cry of Armenia* from the Armenians at Van in 1888. Mss Bryce 193, fol. 53.

14 Interest in the condition of the Armenians was part of an interest in the 'common people' of the Ottoman Empire which, according to Billie Melman, increased through the century. Melman suggests this was 'traceable to contemporary ethnographic studies of the lower classes in Britain itself and of the "condition of England question".' Melman, *Women's Orients: English Women and the Middle East, 1718–1918* (London: Macmillan, 1995) 2nd edition. Concern for the Armenians was often paralleled by concern for those thought to be oppressed at 'home'. Buxton, Charles Masterman and G. P. Gooch all played an active role involved in social reform campaigns at home, as well as the Armenian cause. See C. F. G. Masterman, ed., *The Heart of the Empire: Discussions of Problems of Modern City Life in England.* (London: T. Fisher Unwin, 1901).

15 See Anne Redgate, *The Armenians* (Oxford: Blackwell, 1998), pp. 256–259.

16 *The Cry of Armenia* described Armenians as 'That historic people who has a glorious past, and who has from the beginning stood as a champion of civilisation and Christianity, especially in the period of the crusaders.'

17 Walker, *Visions of Ararat*, p. 16.

18 M. Chamichian, *History of Armenia from BC 2247 to the year of Christ 1780 or 1229 of the Armenian Era*, 3 vols, trans. Johannes Advall (Calcutta: Bishop's College Press, 1829) was utilised by numerous scholars and travellers including H. F. B. Lynch in *Armenia: Travels and Studies*, 2 vols (London: Longmans, Green & Co, 1901). In the introduction to *Les Ruines d'Ani*, the French scholar Marie Félicite de Brosset described a resurgence of interest in Armenia in the mid-nineteenth century, listing translations and scholarship on literature, history and archaeology. De Brosset, *Les Ruines d'Ani: Capital*

de *L'Arménie sous les Rois Bagratides, aux Xe et XIe S: Histoire et Description* (St Petersburg: Imprimerie de l'Académie Impériale des Sciences, 1860). See G. Bouatchidze, *La Vie de Marie Brosset* (Paris: Editions du Petit Véhicule, 1996).

19 Jean Antoine de Saint-Martin, *Mémoires Historiques et Géographiques sur L'Arménie*, 2 vols (Paris, 1819). Saint-Martin was inspired by the legend of Van in Khorenatsi's *History of Armenia*. The expedition to excavate the city was led by the German Professor Schulz. His work was abruptly cut short by his murder, but before this he recorded a number of rock-cut inscriptions which were published in Paris in the Journal of the *Société Asiatique* in 1840.

20 See K. E. Abbot, 'Notes of a Tour in Armenia in 1837', *JRGS*, Vol. 12 (1842), pp. 207–220, J. Brant, 'Journey Through a Part of Armenia and Asia Minor in the Year 1835', *JRGS*, Vol. 6 (1836), pp. 187–223, J. Shiel, 'Notes on a Journey from Tabriz, Through Kurdistan, Via Van, Bitlis Se'eert and Erbul to Suleimanyeh in July and August 1836', *JRGS*, Vol. 8 (1838), pp. 54–101. James Ryan highlights the importance of the Royal Geographical Society (RGS) (formed in 1830) in creating an image of the world for the British public 'The RGS occupied a pivotal position between the British scientific establishment and the imperial government and between the elite world of imperial concerns and the wider public sphere.' Ryan, *Picturing Empire: Photography and the Visualisation of the British Empire* (London: Reaktion, 1997), p. 22. On the RGS see Driver, *Geography Militant*, chapter 2.

21 B. Korte, *British Travel Writing: From Pilgrimage to the Postcolonial* (London: Macmillan, 2000), p. 90.

22 Abbot, 'Notes of a Tour', p. 216, W. Hamilton, 'Extracts from Notes Made on a Journey in Asia Minor 1836', *JRGS*, Vol. 7 (1837).

23 W. Hamilton, 'Observations on the Position of Tavium', *JRGS*, Vol. 7 (1837), pp. 74–81. Frequent reference is made to descriptions of Armenia in Xenophon's *Anabasis*. Layard remarks, 'These villages are still such as they were when Xenophon traversed Armenia.' A. H. Layard, *Discoveries in the Ruins of Nineveh and Babylon, with Travels in Armenia* (London: John Murray, 1853), p. 14.

24 This echoes Roland Barthes in *The Blue Guide*, 'Just as hilliness is overstressed to such an extent as to eliminate all other types of scenery, the human life of a country disappears to the exclusive benefit of its monuments.' Barthes, *Mythologies* (London: Vintage, 2000) first published 1957, p. 75.

25 Bryce, *Transcaucasia*.

26 The writings of travellers played an important role in generating interest in the Balkan minorities. Georgina Mackenzie and Adelina Irby's *Travels in the Slavonic provinces of Turkey-in-Europe* had brought the 'south Slavs' to the attention of the British public. Todorova, *Imagining the Balkans*, p. 97.

27 The journalist Alexander MacDonald claimed the purpose of his work was,

'not merely to make them acquainted with a region so rich in its historical associations . . . but also with a view of deepening their interest in the unsatisfactory, if not painful, condition of its people'. A. MacDonald, *The Land of Ararat or Up the Roof of the World* (London: Eden, Remmington and Co., 1893), p. 323.

28 Isabella Bishop, *Journeys in Persia and Kurdistan*, 2 vols (London: John Murray, 1891), p. 331. On gender and travel writing, see Mills, *Discourses of Difference.*

29 W. F. Ainsworth, *Travels and Researches in Asia Minor, Mesopotamia, Chaldea and Armenia* (London: John W. Parker, 1842), p. 393.

30 Bryce, *Transcaucasia*, p. 2.

31 MacDonald, *Land of Ararat*, p. 10.

32 A minority of British observers believed that colonialism was the only solution to Ottoman decline. D. G. Hogarth comments, 'perhaps some day European colonists may return from the lands of fever and flu where their second generation hardly holds its own and their third fails, to take up this portion of their legitimate heritage'. Hogarth, *The Wandering Scholar in the Levant* (London: John Murray, 1896), p. 89.

33 See Benedict Anderson, *Imagined Communities* (London: Verso, 1991) revised edition, pp. 174–175 on the colonial practices of mapping and the imagining of nations.

34 NA FO 881/6621, Report on the population of Asia Minor, Colonel W. Everett, 11 May 1895.

35 NA FO 424/181, 237, Memorandum from Lynch outlining a scheme for better government in Asia Minor, March 1895.

36 Although nineteenth-century nationalist discourse portrayed nations as natural divisions of society, recent scholarship has stressed that they are modern constructions. See E. Hobsbawm, *Nations and Nationalism since 1780: Programme, Myth, Reality* (Cambridge: Cambridge University Press, 1990), Anderson, *Imagined Communities.* For an overview, see G. Eley and R. Suny, 'Introduction: From the Moment of Social History to the Work of Social Representation', in G. Eley and R. Suny, eds, *Becoming National: A Reader* (Oxford: Oxford University Press, 1996).

37 Hobsbawm, 'Mass Producing Traditions' (especially p. 263).

38 Bryce to the AAA, cited in Stevenson, *The Case for the Armenians.*

39 On the continuing role of archaeological monuments in defining the boundaries of Armenia, see Philip Kohl and Gocha R. Tsetskhladze, 'Nationalism, Politics and the Practice of Archaeology in the Caucasus', in P. Kohl and C. Fawcett, eds, *Nationalism, Politics and the Practice of Archaeology* (Cambridge: Cambridge University Press, 1995) and Pavel Dolukhanov, 'Archaeology and Nationalism in Totalitarian and Post Totalitarian Russia', in J. Atkinson, I. Banks and J. O'Sullivan, eds, *Nationalism and Archaeology* (Glasgow: Cruthie Press, 1996).

40 For the perspective of an Armenian nationalist leader see, Avetis Nazarbek, 'Zeitun', *Contemporary Review*, Vol. 69 (1896).

41 Bloxham suggest that 'ordinary' Armenians 'evinced little support for the nationalist's actions': *Great Game of Genocide*, p. 50.

42 See Anaide Ter Minassian, *Nationalism and Socialism in the Armenian Revolutionary Movement* (Cambridge, MA: Zoryan Institute, 1983) and Louise Nalbandian, *The Armenian Revolutionary Movement: The Development of Armenian Political Parties Through the Nineteenth Century* (Berkeley: University of California Press, 1963).

43 Nubar Pasha on the 'Armenian question' in Stevenson, *The Case for the Armenians*, p. 13. Nubar Pasha drew up a reform scheme for the Armenian provinces in the 1878, prior to Berlin. It was republished in 1890 as *A Practical Scheme for the Solution of the Armenian Question* (Manchester: Guardian Printing Works, 1890).

44 Bryce, *Transcaucasia*, p. 408. James Creagh shared his positive attitude, 'Of all the Asiatic races the Armenians are the most national; and as they love their language as well as their country.' Creagh, *Armenians, Koords and Turks*, 2 vols (London: Samuel Tinsley and Co., 1880), p. 277.

45 F. J. Blunt, *The People of Turkey: Twenty Years Residence among Bulgarians, Greeks, Albanians, Turks and Armenians* (London: John Murray, 1878) p. 130.

46 Bishop, *Journeys*, p. 277.

47 Henry Barkley, *A Ride through Asia Minor and Armenia: Giving a Sketch of the Characters, Manners and Customs of both the Mussulman and Christian Inhabitants* (London: John Murray, 1891), p. 154.

48 See Hall, *Cultures of Empire*, pp. 19–20. Hall points out that races were discursively constructed, 'the time of Empire was the time when anatomies of difference were being elaborated, it was the work of culture' (p. 20).

49 MacDonald, *Land of Ararat*, p. 5.

50 Creagh, *Armenians, Koords and Turks*, p.vi.

51 Bishop, *Journeys*, p. 336.

52 W. Ramsay, *Impressions of Turkey during Twelve Years Wanderings* (London: Hodder & Stoughton, 1897), p. 190. Hodgetts refers to these stereotypes, 'a lazy, cunning, dangerous, slippery person, who can be trusted to cheat anyone he meets'. E. A. B. Hodgetts, *Round about Armenia: The Record of a Journey across the Balkans, through Turkey, the Caucasus and Persia in 1895* (London: Sampson & Co., 1896), p. 109. Republished in 1916.

53 On nineteenth-century racial thought see N. Leys Stepan, *The Idea of Race in Science* (London: Macmillan, 1882), E. Barkan, *The Retreat of Scientific Racism* (Cambridge: Cambridge University Press, 1992) and S. Jones, *The Archaeology of Ethnicity* (London: Routledge, 1997), pp. 40–44.

54 George Stocking points out that 'the external forces which nourished a broadly polygenic point of view were, if anything, intensified: the gap between civilized white men and savage black men, and the need to justify

the white man's imperial dominion, were becoming greater than ever before'. Stocking, *Race, Culture and Evolution. Essays in the History of Anthropology* (Chicago: University of Chicago Press, 1968), p. 47.

55 Race remained important after the First World War. In 1928 Fridtjof Nansen, League of Nations High Commissioner for Refugees, addressed the issue of race, utilising physical features, such as skull size, to address the question of racial origins. F. Nansen, *Armenia and the Near East* (New York: Da Capo Press, 1976) reprint of 1928 publication, chapter 10.

56 Blunt, *The People of Turkey*, Preface, pxxi.

57 Bryce, *Transcaucasia*, p. 282.

58 See Suny, *Looking Toward Ararat*, pp. 6–11.

59 Byron was familiar with the Eden legend. He studied Armenian at the Mekhitarist monastery in San Lazzaro, Venice, between 1816 and 1817. In his introduction to an Armenian Grammar he stated, 'If the scriptures are rightly understood; it was in Armenia that paradise was placed.' Despite his celebrity Byron had little impact in bringing the Armenians to the attention of the British public. Walker, *Visions of Ararat*, chapter 4.

60 Ararat was not originally associated with the flood legend. Levon Abrahamian explains that the crusades and later Armenian hopes of salvation from Turkish rule catalysed the association of the mountain (which the Armenians call Masis) with biblical Ararat. As the Armenians 'began to participate in the political scenes of Europe and Russia in the eighteenth century Masis-Ararat became the nation's symbol'. L. Abrahamian and N. Sweezy, eds, *Armenian Folk Arts, Culture and Identity* (Bloomington: Indiana University Press, 2001), p. 38.

61 D. W. Freshfield, *Travels in the Central Caucasus and Bashan including Visits to Ararat and Tabreez and ascents of Kasbeh and Elbruz* (London: Longmans, Green & Co., 1869), p. 121.

62 See J. J. Moscrop, *Measuring Jerusalem. The Palestine Exploration Fund and British Interests in the Holy Land* (London: Leicester University Press, 2000). He explains that 'the parallel was clear and simple. The chosen people of old, the Israelites, had been succeeded by the new chosen people, the English' (p. 2).

63 M. Mazower, 'Travellers and the Oriental City', *Transactions of the Royal Historical Society*, 12 (2002), p. 77.

64 Bryce, *Transcaucasia*, p. 282.

65 M. L. Pratt, *Imperial Eyes: Travel and Transculturation* (London: Routledge, 1992) p. 204.

66 Racial origins could (it was thought) be traced by tracking linguistic change. Archaeology was also utilised as a method of tracing peoples and nations through the past. The development of archaeology was also a part of this desire to trace racial and national origins: 'The rise of nationalism established a vested interest in the study of national origins and histories; preferably histories illustrating the great antiquity and continuity of the nation concerned.' Jones, *The Archaeology of Ethnicity*, p. 19.

67 L. Poliakov, *The Aryan Myth: A History of Racist and Nationalist Ideas in Europe* (London: Sussex University Press, 1971).

68 Lynch, *Armenia*, p. 465.

69 Indo-European origins were often taken for granted. One notable exception, which focused upon Armenian racial origins and the Aryan connection, was John S. Stuart Glennie's attempt to trace the Aryan origins of the Armenian people. Glennie, 'Introduction', in L. Garnett, *The Women of Turkey and their Folklore*, 2 vols (London: David Nutt, 1890).

70 The Urartian Kingdom existed in the regions of the Armenian homeland between the ninth and sixth centuries BC (approximately). See Redgate, *The Armenians*, pp. 29–49, C. Burney and D. M. Lang, *The People of the Hills: Ancient Ararat and Caucasus* (London: Weidenfeld and Nicholson, 1991), D. M. Lang, *Armenia: Cradle of Civilisation* (London: Allen & Unwin, 1980) 3rd edition (corrected), P. Zimansky, *Ancient Ararat: A Handbook of Urartian Studies* (Delmar, NY: Caravan Books, 1998).

71 Layard was the first British scholar to investigate Van. Previously he had published *Nineveh and its Remains* popularising interest in the 'great civilisations' of the Near East. He was British ambassador in Turkey (1877–1880) and an MP. Interest in Van continued: the British Museum later commissioned Layard's assistant Rassam to carry out investigations in the region. At Toprak Kale he investigated another 'palace citadel of the Urartian Kings'; nothing was published from these excavations. Lynch later published images of the artefacts from Van in the British Museum in *Armenia: Travels and Studies*. On the 'rediscovery' of Urartu see Zimansky, *Ancient Ararat*, pp. 286–290.

72 Layard, *Discoveries*, p. 390.

73 Ibid., p. 402.

74 Layard declared Khorenatsi's interpretation of the inscriptions incorrect. 'Modern research has proved them to belong to a far different period than that to which they were assigned by the Armenian antiquary', Layard, *Discoveries*, p. 391.

75 Armenian origins are highly contested. Suny explains that 'Although the link between Urartu and the Armenians took hold in the popular mind, most scholars believed Urartu to have been a distinct pre-Armenian culture . . . Nevertheless a revisionist school of historians in the 1890's proposed that, rather than being migrants into the region, Armenians were the aboriginal inhabitants.' Suny, 'Constructing Primordialism', p. 18.

76 Lynch, *Armenia*, p. 53–72.

77 Ibid., pp. 70–71.

78 H. A. G. Percy, *Notes From a Diary in Asiatic Turkey* (London: E. Arnold, 1898), pp. 93–94. Armenian traditions suggested that they were descended from Haig, son of Japheth.

79 G. Hagopian, 'Appeal to the British Nation', in Stevenson, *The Case for the Armenians*, p. 10.

80 R. Curzon, *Armenia: A Year at Erzeroom, and on the Frontiers of Russia, Turkey and Persia* (London: John Murray, 1854), p. 243.
81 MacDonald, *Land of Ararat*, p. 5.
82 K. Bardakjian, 'Armenia and the Armenians through the Eyes of English Travellers of the Nineteenth Century', in R. Hovannisian, ed., *The Armenian Image in History and Literature* (California: Undena Publications, 1981), p. 140.
83 The conversion was dated to AD 301 under King Tiridates; the conversion legend was recounted by the fifth century Armenian historian Agathangelos.
84 Blunt, *The People of Turkey*, p. 322.
85 Scholarship on medieval Armenia is extensive. For a brief overview see Redgate, *The Armenians*, chapters 7–10, and R. Hovannisian, ed., *The Armenian People from Ancient to Modern Times, vol. 1, The Dynastic Periods* (Basingstoke: Palgrave Macmillan, 2004).)
86 The most significant contribution to scholarship on Armenian manuscripts was made by F. C. Coneybeare who in 1891 translated the Paulican text *The Key of Truth* and catalogued the Armenian texts in the British Museum. Walker, *Visions of Ararat*, chapter 10. Curzon was also a collector. See also F. C. Coneybeare, 'Notes on Some Early Ecclesiastical Practices in Armenia', *Folklore* Vol. 18, No. 4 (December 1907).
87 De Brosset's *Ruines d'Ani* and Charies Texier's *Description de l'Armenie* (Paris, 1842) drew attention to Ani. See also the website *Virtual Ani*, www.virtualani.freeserve.co.uk, and R. Kevorkian, ed., *Ani, Capitale de l'Armenie en l'An Mil* (Paris: Paris Musees, 2001).
88 *Virtual Ani*.
89 Bishop, *Journeys*, p. 389.
90 Layard, *Discoveries*, p. 33. The idea of the diffusion of Armenian architectural styles was given full expression in the work of Josef Strzygowski, *Die Baukunst der Armenier und Europa* in 1918, a 'highly politicized and often offensive work which linked indo-European thought to architecture': Christina Maranci, *Medieval Armenian Architecture: Constructions of Race and Nation* (Leuven: Peeters, 2001), p. 1.
91 Lynch, *Armenia*, p. 371.
92 Ibid.
93 Ibid., p. 335.
94 Creagh, *Armenians, Koords and Turks*, pp. 3–4.
95 Lynch, *Armenia*, p. 369.
96 Blunt, *The People of Turkey*, pp. 132–133.
97 Mrs W. M. Ramsay, *Everyday Life in Turkey* (London: Hodder and Stoughton, 1897), p. 41. Mrs Ramsay was the wife of the archaeologist and classical scholar William Ramsay.
98 Barkley contrasted the homes of missionaries in Kaiseriah with the 'filthy hovels' of the Armenians, *A Ride through Asia Minor*, p. 151.

99 Curzon refers to the Armenians 'hiding at this time of year in their strange holes and burrows'. Curzon, *Armenia: A Year at Erzeroom*, p. 34. Hodgetts described Armenians living in 'mud huts'. Hodgetts, *Round about Armenia*, p. 41. The origin of these ideas lay in the content of Xenophon's *Anabasis*.

100 G. Hepworth, *Through Armenia on Horseback* (London: Ibister and Company, 1898), p. 354.

101 In 1830 a separate Catholic millet was created and in 1850 a Protestant millet was formed.

102 Blunt and Garnett devote considerable attention to rituals surrounding birth and death. See Blunt, *The People of Turkey*, chapter 7 and Garnett, *The Women of Turkey*, chapter 7. Both books focus upon customs and folklore.

103 Garnett, *The Women of Turkey*, p. 255.

104 Blunt and Garnett describe marriage ceremonies; their descriptions are near identical. See Blunt, *The People of Turkey*, chapter 8.

105 Bryce, *Transcaucasia*, p. 304. On reactions to the Armenian Church at home see 'The Armenian Church in Manchester', *The Sphinx* Vol. IV, No. 129 (28 January 1871), which described Armenians, 'chanting or intoning from the books in a strange, weird and altogether Eastern & Asiatic manner'. p. 27.

106 Bryce, *Transcaucasia*, pp. 308–311.

107 R. Lewis, *Re-Thinking Orientalism: Women, Travel and the Oriental Harem* (London: I. B. Tauris, 2004), p. 143.

108 Melman, *Women's Orients*, p. 4. See also Lewis, *Re-Thinking Orientalism* and Mills, *Discourses of Difference*.

109 A few focused on women. Blunt and Garnett offered an ethnographic approach, comparing female populations of the Ottoman Empire. See Garnett, *The Women of Turkey*, vol. 1, chapters 6–10 and Blunt, *The People of Turkey*, chapter 5.

110 R. Lewis and S. Mills, 'Introduction', in Lewis and Mills *Feminist Postcolonial Theory: A Reader*, p. 16.

111 Garnett, *The Women of Turkey*, p. 209.

112 Hodgetts, *Round about Armenia*, p. 145.

113 Barkley, *A Ride through Asia Minor*, p. 87.

114 Bishop, *Journeys*, p. 279.

115 S. Graham-Brown, *Images of Women: The Portrayal of Women in Photography of the Middle East, 1860–1950* (London: Quartet, 1988), p. 53. J. T. Bent said the Armenian women of Julfa presented 'a truly quaint picture of primitive humanity'. Bent, 'Travels among the Armenians', *Contemporary Review*, Vol. 70 (December 1896), p. 703.

116 Ryan considers the way in which photography came to be used as a tool for the identification and classification of racial types in the imperial world. This was the context in which images of Armenians were produced, circulated and received. Ryan, *Picturing Empire*, chapter 6.

117 Melman, *Women's Orients*, p. 162. Lucy Garnett believed Turkish women

were in a good position, that the harem and the veil offered sanctuary and protection. This was in contrast to the view of most Armenophiles. See Lucy Garnett, 'Women under Islam', *The Nineteenth Century*, Vol. 37 (January 1895), pp. 57–70.

118 Lewis, *Re-Thinking Orientalism*, p. 98.

119 Polygamy, like the harem 'had accrued a symbolic importance out of all proportion to its actual practice': Lewis, *Re-Thinking Orientalism*, p. 98.

120 Melman, *Women's Orients*, p. 60.

121 Hodgetts, *Round about Armenia*, p. 138.

122 Ibid., p. 121.

123 Joanna de Groot points out that whether the treatment of women in 'Oriental societies' was responded to in a moralising and judgemental, or voyeuristic and indulgent, way it still contributed to 'the emergence of the most widely accepted stereotypes of the Orient as corrupt and decadent, uniting sexual licence with violent cruelty'. De Groot, 'Sex and Race: The Construction of Language and Image in the Nineteenth Century', in Hall, *Cultures of Empire*, p. 49. For background see 'Introduction' in N. R. Keddie and Beth Baron, eds, *Women in Middle Eastern History: Shifting Boundaries of Sex and Gender* (London: Yale University Press, 1991).

124 Bryce, *Transcaucasia*, p. 397.

125 Lewis and Mills point out, 'The response to the veil is always overdetermined, reliant on a series of gendered, imperial and classed dynamics which respond to the seclusion of women in a variety of ways but which always privilege the veil as a symbol of the hidden order of Oriental society and as proof of its inimical difference from the West.' Lewis and Mills, *Feminist Postcolonial Theory*.

126 Bryce, *Transcaucasia*, p. 376.

127 Layard, *Discoveries*, p. 403.

128 Barkley, *A Ride through Asia Minor*, p. 222.

129 Bryce, *Transcaucasia*, p. 123.

130 Recent scholarship on 'borders' has emphasised their socially constructed nature and their role as sites of transition and exchange as well as barriers or boundaries. See for example M. Baud and W. Van Schendel, 'Toward a Comparative History of Borderlands', *Journal of World History*, Vol. 8, No. 2 (1997).

131 Hepworth, *Through Armenia on Horseback* p. 14.

132 MacDonald, *Land of Ararat*, p. 3.

133 J. Fabian, *Time and the Other: How Anthropology Makes its Object* (New York: Columbia University Press, 2002), p. 189.

134 Hogarth, *Wandering Scholar*, p. 98.

135 Lynch, *Armenia*, p. 380.

136 Barkley, *A Ride through Asia Minor*, p. 111.

137 Herzfeld, *Anthropology through the Looking Glass*, p. 7.

138 D. Pick, *Faces of Degeneration: A European Disorder, c. 1848–1918* (Cambridge: Cambridge University Press, 1989), p. 21. See also J. E. Chamberlain and S. L. Gilman, eds, *Degeneration: The Dark Side of Progress* (New York: Columbia University Press, 1985).

139 Stocking, *Race, Culture and Evolution*, p. 119.

140 Ramsay, *Impressions of Turkey*, p. 103.

141 Blunt, *The People of Turkey*, p. 133, Hepworth, *Through Armenia on Horseback*, p. 211.

142 In Armenia Christianity was thought to have degenerated. J. T. Bent described an 'exceedingly degraded' Church. Bent, 'Travels among the Armenians', p. 699.

143 Stevenson, *The Case for the Armenians*, p. 35.

144 Russian Armenians, though subject to sporadic repression (for example in 1885 Armenian schools were closed and in 1903 Church property was seized), generally enjoyed greater freedom than Ottoman Armenians: 'Caucasian Armenians thus had a relatively more secure life, somewhat easier access to urban life and western developments than did the great mass of Armenians in western Turkey': Suny, *Looking Toward Ararat*, p. 19.

145 W. T. Stead, *The Haunting Horrors in Armenia* (London: 'Review of Reviews', 1896), p. 13.

146 H. F. B. Lynch, 'The 'Armenian question: Part II, in Russia', *Contemporary Review*, Vol. 66 (July 1894), p. 92.

147 Hodgetts, *A Ride through Armenia*, p. 127.

148 Garnett, *The Women of Turkey*, p. 217.

149 Blunt, *The People of Turkey*, p. 133.

150 Herzfeld, *Anthropology through the Looking Glass*, p. 88.

151 Hodgetts believed nationalism was the work of 'agitators' who lacked 'manliness and courage': Hodgetts, *A Ride through Armenia*, p. 111.

152 E. M. Bliss, *Turkey and the Armenian Atrocities* (London: T. Fisher Unwin, 1896), p. 63. Missionaries played a key role in the education of the Armenian population, running colleges including Euphrates College in Harput and American College in Van. The missions were organised by the American Board of Commissions for Foreign Missions in Boston: by the start of the nineteenth century they had 12 mission stations and 270 outstations in Asiatic Turkey run by 145 missionaries and over 800 native workers. See Moranian, 'The Armenian Genocide and American Missionary Relief Efforts'.

153 Barkley, *A Ride through Asia Minor*, p. 150.

154 On Armenian/Ottoman relations prior to the massacres and the relationship between nationalist agitation and the massacres see Bloxham, *Great Game of Genocide*, pp. 49–57.

155 See Hovannisian, 'The Historical Dimension of the Armenian Question', and Somakian, *Empires in Conflict*, chapter 1.

156 Hovannisian suggests that 100–200,000 Armenians died as a result of the

massacres. Hovannisian, 'The Historical Dimension of the Armenian Question', p. 25.

157 For details of the investigation and the reports of the British consuls on the situation of the Armenians in 1895 see NA FO 424/181 – 424/183. Information about the plight of the Armenians reached the British government via consuls in Eastern Anatolia and American missionaries.

158 Douglas, 'Britain and the "Armenian Question"', p. 117.

159 R. Shannon, *Gladstone: Heroic Minister, 1865–1898* (London: Allen Lane, 1999), p. 572.

160 *Mr Gladstone on the Armenian Question*, p. 11.

161 Douglas, 'Britain and the "Armenian Question"', pp. 130–131.

162 See G. W. E. Russell, 'Armenia and the Forward Movement', *Contemporary Review*, Vol. 71 (January 1897) and P .W. Clayden, *Armenia: The Case against Salisbury. A Journalist's Glance Back over Twenty Years* (London: H. Marshall & Son, 1897).

163 Armenophiles claimed Salisbury had 'betrayed' the Armenians at the Berlin Conference. 'The action he took in 1878 condemned him for the future': *Daily Chronicle*, 24 November 1896 (Bibliothèque Nubarian, Paris: Press Cuttings Collection).

164 Marsh, 'Lord Salisbury and the Armenian Massacres'. Marsh claims Salisbury was 'determined to do more than his predecessors had attempted and more than public opinion required to protect the Armenians' (p. 74). See also A. O. Sarkissian, 'Concert Diplomacy and the Armenians 1890–1897', in A. O. Sarkissian, ed., *Studies in Diplomatic History* (London: Longman, 1961), pp. 48–75.

165 The massacres were covered in Liberal-leaning periodicals, including the *Contemporary Review* and *The Nineteenth Century*. Press coverage is detailed in Kirakosian, *The Armenian Massacres 1894–1896: U. S. Media Testimony*. For coverage of the massacres in the British and European press see Bibliothèque Nubarian, Paris, Press Cuttings Collections 1895–96. Some sections of the press (particularly the *Daily News* and *Daily Chronicle*) were more sympathetic than others. William Watson published a collection of poetry on the subject. Watson, *The Purple East: A Series of Sonnets on England's Desertion of Armenia* (London: John Lane, 1896).

166 Examples include MacDonald, *Land of Ararat* and Hodgetts, *Round about Armenia*.

167 See Mss Bryce 209, fol. 36–38, pamphlet from National Protest 7 May 1895 and G. Rolin-Jaequemyns, *Armenia, the Armenians and the Treaties* (London: John Heywood, 1891).

168 The Friends of Armenia focused on relief rather than politics.

169 These themes could be utilised in a number of different ways. The carefully reasoned prose of James Bryce was in complete contrast to the lurid narra-

tives of the journalist Dillon, yet both depicted Armenia in terms of civilisation and Christianity.

170 Harrison, *Cross and Crescent*, p. 709.

171 MacColl was a harsh critic of the Ottomans and his attitude to Islam ambivalent. Whilst claiming, 'I have no antipathy or any sort of ill-will against Musulmans as such, or even against Turks,' he stated in the same work, 'its [Islam's] object [is] to reduce all mankind to a cruel servitude or death'. Rev. Malcom MacColl, *England's Responsibility towards Armenia* (London: Longmans, Greene & Co., 1895), p. 7, p. 63. Missionary accounts of the massacres emphasised the 'problem' of Islam. E. M. Bliss claimed that the Turks had 'been taught by their priests to look upon the Christians as dogs': Bliss, *Turkey and the Armenian Atrocities*, p. 555. He hoped missionary work could 'disinfect the land of the scimitar from its awful taint' (p. 4).

172 See Wheatcroft, *Infidels* on the development of images of the Ottomans over the nineteenth century and their pre-nineteenth-century roots.

173 On the reporting of the Bulgarian atrocities see Wheatcroft, *Infidels*, p. 261 and Hupchick, *Constantinople to Communism*, p. 264.

174 Stead's later work *The Maiden Tribute to Modern Babylon* also had some parallels. This report into rape and white slavery in London had much in common with descriptions of rape, polygamy and 'harems' in images of the Ottoman Empire. There is an interesting interplay between the use of orientalist stereotypes to describe perpetrators and victims of these crimes 'at home' and abroad. J. Walkowitz, *City of Dreadful Delight, Narratives of Sexual Danger in Late-Victorian London* (London: Virago, 1992), p. 29.

175 Kevin Grant has highlighted the importance of the press. 'Humanitarian activists would further benefit from the proliferation of newspapers, illustrated magazines and especially the sensationalist press in Britain after the 1890's': Grant, *Civilized Savagery*, p. 36.

176 Stead, *Haunting Horrors*, p. 21.

177 E. J. Dillon, 'The Condition of Armenia', *Contemporary Review*, Vol. 68 (August 1895).

178 *Daily Graphic*, Vols. 23–28 (1897) (Bibliothèque Nubarian, Paris: Press Cuttings Collection)

179 W. J. Wintle, *Armenia and Its Sorrows* (London: Andrew Melrose, 1896), p. 71.

180 See the extract from Gladstone's letter to the *Daily News*, 27 August 1889, which told the story of Ghiulisar, an Armenian girl abducted by the notorious Moussa Bey. Mss Bryce 193, fol. 159, pamphlet entitled *The Turkish Cruelties in Armenia*.

181 The story of the women of Sassoun who jumped from a precipice in order to escape the Turks was recounted in numerous pamphlets and books including Wintle, *Armenia*, chapter 6.

182 Wintle, *Armenia*, p. 53.

183 Roessel points out that 'Gladstone's logic was firmly rooted in the perceived

differences between Europe and Asia, which had been prevalent in Europe since the enlightenment. His use of oriental words to enumerate the different Ottoman officials underscored their unsuitability to administer a part of Europe.' Roessel, *In Byron's Shadow*, p. 132.

184 Gladstone, *Bulgarian Horrors*, pp. 55–62.

185 In response to events in Macedonia the Balkan Committee was formed in 1903. It included longstanding supporters of the minorities in the Ottoman Empire such as Bryce, who were joined by a newer generation including Charles Masterman and Noel Buxton. 'A generation imbued with moral and humanitarian principles and inspired by Gladstonian Liberalism [which] took up the "Armenian question" in the early twentieth century': A. Nassibian, *Britain and the Armenian Question* (London: Croom Helm, 1984), p. 36.

186 For the response to the Adana massacres see *The Friend of Armenia* Vols. 38–41.

187 R. Hovannisian, *Armenia on the Road to Independence* (Berkeley and Los Angeles: University of California Press, 1967), pp. 33–34 and see D. Bloxham, 'Determinants of the Armenian Genocide', in Hovannisian, *Looking Backward, Moving Forward*, p. 33. The reform plan provided for two inspectors in the Eastern Vilayets, see Roderic H. Davison, 'The Armenian Crisis (1912–1914)', *American Historical Review*, 53 (April 1948).

3

'The murder of a nation': representing the Armenian genocide of 1915

Introduction

In the early summer of 1915 emerging reports of deportations and massacres in the Ottoman Empire generated renewed British interest in the fate of the Armenians. As evidence of the terrible events that had occurred gradually came to light it provoked an international outcry. The Armenian diaspora, the British government and Armenophile organisations united in expressions of outrage and immediately began the work of mobilising public support for the Armenians.

In this chapter I investigate British responses to the Armenian massacres of 1915, examining the ways in which Armenia, and the Armenians, gained new significance in Britain in the context of world war. The first part of the chapter focuses upon the discovery of the fate of the Armenian people and the dissemination of this information amongst the British public. The following parts examine in detail British representations of the massacres and deportations.

The reporting of atrocities and massacres in the Ottoman Empire during the late nineteenth century had made the notion of Armenia as a site of violence, and the Armenians as victims, familiar to the British public. Violence and atrocity had come to be regarded as endemic in the Ottoman Empire. As the 'eastern question' had evolved, the management or containment of this violence had come to be perceived as a British responsibility.

Despite this characterisation of Armenia as a site of violence the scale and nature of the massacres of the Armenians in 1915 was deeply shocking to the British public. The extensive programme of massacres and deportations was recognised to be of a different order to previous 'atrocities' and was widely regarded as a systematic attempt to finally destroy or, according to contemporary terminology, 'exterminate' the Ottoman Armenian population.

The next part of this chapter examines 'new' elements in the representation of the fate of the Armenians, and their relationship to pre-existing perceptions of the Armenians and discourses of Ottoman atrocity and violence. The 1915 massacres occurred during wartime and were committed by an enemy rather than an ally of Britain. This set of circumstances meant the massacres were imbued with new meanings. The fate of the Armenians was no longer only of interest to a minority of British individuals but, as an enemy atrocity, assumed significance on a national scale.

Some historians have regarded British responses to the Armenian massacres in terms of self-interested and cynical exploitation of Armenian sufferings for propaganda, followed by 'abandonment' in the post-war period.[1] It is clearly true that the Armenian massacres were utilised in British propaganda campaigns, and that wartime promises to the Armenians were not fulfilled. However, simply acknowledging that the massacres were utilised as propaganda does not provide an adequate analysis of the British representation of and response to the Armenian genocide.

Images of the Armenian massacres were not only a matter of 'official' propaganda, directed by the government; a wide variety of charitable organisations and pro-Armenian pressure groups also attempted to draw attention to the fate of the Armenians. These bodies constructed a sympathetic image of Armenia as worthy of political and humanitarian support. In order to do so they drew upon pre-existing notions of the region as a site of Christianity and culture. These sympathetic images of Armenia were utilised in representations of the massacres which expressed beliefs about the war, the enemy and British identities. In these images a sharp contrast was made between civilised Britain, protecting innocent people, and a barbaric, amoral enemy which massacred its own population without mercy.

In addition to helping to define the enemy and thus give meaning to the war, representations of the Armenian massacres also provided a space where questions about the future of the region could be aired. The changes in geopolitics wrought by the war meant that the representation of the Armenian massacres came to be bound up with new concerns centred upon the idea of national self-determination. The massacres were widely perceived as an act of violence against 'the nation', bringing to the fore broader concerns about the future national security and development of the Armenians. What emerged very clearly was the desire on the part of British parties to redefine and even reclaim Armenia as a part of civilised Europe.

The Armenian massacres and the British public

The Ottoman authorities began to deport and massacre the Armenian population in April 1915. Upon discovering what was taking place, Allied governments acted quickly, responding to initial reports with a joint declaration:

> In view of this new crime of Turkey against humanity and civilization, the Allied governments make known publicly to the Sublime Porte that they will hold all members of the Turkish government, as well as those officials who have participated in these massacres, personally responsible.[2]

The declaration had no effect upon the progress of the deportations and massacres, which continued apace over the summer.[3] Attempts at intervention made slow progress. The war had rendered British contact with the interior of the Ottoman Empire minimal.[4] Travel, trade and diplomatic relations had come to an abrupt halt. Reports of the massacres arrived in piecemeal fashion, via personal contacts and informal Armenophile networks. Those concerned had to rely on information gathered by remaining diplomats, the diaspora, Armenian refugees and American missionaries.[5] Nonetheless, according to Akaby Nassibian, by autumn 1915 there could be no doubt in the minds of Allied governments about the scale of what had occurred.[6] By October the fate of the Armenians was accorded serious attention. With the help of Armenophile protests, the massacres became the subject of parliamentary debates and attracted in-depth press coverage.

Armenia as a national cause

Longstanding supporters of the Armenians played a key role in bringing the fate of the Armenians to light. Even though interest in the fate of the Armenians had waned since the crises of the 1890s, Armenophile activists and humanitarians had continued their campaigns, maintaining contacts with Armenians in the Ottoman Empire. The war disrupted their information channels, but they were still the best placed to obtain news, often from the missionary organisations they continued to support.[7]

The war also prompted the formation of new Armenophile bodies such as the Armenophile campaigner Emily Robinson's Armenian Red Cross and Refugee Fund.[8] Other organisations such as the BAC re-directed and intensified their efforts.[9] These organisations took on a variety of different roles. The Armenian Red Cross and Refugee Fund concentrated on raising funds for humanitarian relief whereas the BAC acted as an elite pressure group, petitioning MPs and drawing the attention of the press to the fate of the Armenians. They also worked with the diaspora and were in close contact with the Armenian National Delegation in Paris (ANDP) led by Boghos Nubar Pasha.[10] The ANDP became the self-appointed leaders of the Armenian population for the duration of the war, campaigning for the recognition of Armenian national rights.

Whilst Nubar Pasha led the Armenophile movement in Paris, James Bryce was the figurehead of the British movement. Since the publication of *Transcaucasia and Ararat*, Bryce had been at the heart of the British Armenophile movement. In 1915 he began another intensive campaign on behalf of the Armenians. Bryce had an impressive range of contacts with Armenophiles and Armenians. As such he was particularly well positioned to access information about the massacres.[11] He was widely regarded as an 'expert' on the subject of Armenia and his opinions were often sought for prefaces to pamphlets and books.[12] He therefore played a central role in shaping British understandings of the Armenians and their fate. On 6 October 1915, Bryce addressed a House of Lords debate, recounting what he had learned about the massacres and deportations:

> No provisions were given them by the Turkish government. In many cases the women were stripped naked and made to travel in that condition. Many of the women went mad and threw away their children, being unable to carry them any further. The Caravan route was marked by a line of corpses, and comparatively few seem to have arrived at the destination that was stated for them.[13]

Bryce's information was regarded by the British government and public as reliable, in contrast to the press reports that were widely thought to be prone to exaggeration, sensationalism and misinformation. His brief but shocking report to parliament included the sets of images that embodied the horror of the Armenian genocide for the British population. These images, of suffering women and children, sadistic Turks and Kurds and the relentless presence of Armenian corpses were reiterated in more elaborate and detailed forms over the course of the war.

Bryce's speech marked an important stage in the transformation of the 'Armenian question' into a 'national' cause. A flurry of articles in the British press which followed described the massacres in graphic terms and alerted wider audiences to them. As in the case of the massacres of the 1890s, most reporters did not shy away from providing lurid details of murder, rape and mutilation. All expressed shock at the unprecedented scale of the massacres. The *Manchester Guardian* was not alone in its expressions of horror at the sheer numbers of bodies littering the Armenian landscape: 'The roads and waters of Armenia form one vast charnel house.'[14] *The Times* also offered detailed and lurid accounts of 'Men shot down in cold blood, crucified, mutilated, or dragged off for labour battalions, children carried off and forcibly converted to Islam, of women violated and enslaved in the interior.'[15]

These reports provided a vivid picture of the fate of the Armenians, adding to the sense of public outrage. However, they formed only one dimension of the public image of the massacres. Armenophiles and humanitarian organisations also attempted to inform the public about the massacres, publishing books and pamphlets. Information from all of these sources shared a common theme, claiming Britain had a special moral duty towards the Armenians and was obliged to protect them. Their arguments were based upon the notion of bonds of Christianity and civilisation between Britain and Armenia. Supporters of the Armenians also referred to the argument that the Berlin Treaty had created a legal responsibility for the Armenians.[16] 'Duty' and 'responsibility' were envisioned in terms of both alleviating immediate suffering and ensuring the security of the Armenian people in the longer term.

The British government, despite its failure to take an effective stance on Armenia in the past, was less hesitant in 1915. It played a vital role in transforming the fate of the Armenians from a minor, if contentious, matter in party politics, into a national concern. A national appeal, the Armenian Refugees (Lord Mayor's) Fund (LMF), was set up in October 1915 as the existing Armenophile organisations proved unable to cope with the new demands placed on them. This public fund was inaugurated with a meeting at Mansion House at which various public figures expressed their support for the Armenians.

Throughout the war, government ministers and MPs made numerous public professions of commitment to protecting the Armenians and condemnations of the Turkish government. They did not restrict themselves to humanitarian concerns but also began to engage with political questions of the future of Armenia. At the Guildhall in November 1916, the

Prime Minister promised the war would be followed by 'an era of liberty and redemption for this ancient people'.[17] This statement was typically vague, and indeed the sincerity of the British government's pronunciations on Armenia has subsequently been called into question.[18] In the early stages of the war, however, expressing support for the Armenians was clearly thought unproblematic, fitting well with British 'official' war aims. It provided added legitimacy to claims that Britain was engaged in a just and moral cause, not an aggressive imperialist war.

This is not to suggest that the stance taken by the government came about simply as an 'instinctive' or purely altruistic response to human suffering. The sympathetic treatment of the Armenians was related to wartime diplomacy and geopolitical agendas. The outbreak of war had overturned traditional British policy towards the Ottoman Empire: 'A denial of Turkey's right to territorial integrity of its Empire represented a major change from Britain's pre-war policy'.[19] In the past Britain had been reluctant to threaten the precarious stability of the Ottoman Empire and because of this had never managed to intervene effectively on behalf of the Armenians. By 1915 the last vestiges of British support for the Ottoman Empire had vanished. The British government no longer wished to preserve the Ottoman Empire, but rather to destroy it as swiftly as possible. This aim was shared by France and Russia. So, for the time being at least, rivalry between the powers was no longer a barrier to action.

Documenting the massacres: Toynbee and *The Treatment of the Armenians*

The British government took every opportunity to express their support for the Armenians and condemn the Ottoman government. Politicians involved in the Armenian cause for many years suddenly found their cause incorporated into the government's 'official' agenda. Protection and justice for the Armenians thus became bound up with British war aims and the subject of war propaganda. Official pamphlets concerning the fate of the Armenians were written and distributed by the newly created Propaganda Bureau at Wellington House.[20]

The attention paid to the Armenians by the Propaganda Bureau may have related to the fact that the Armenians had traditionally been a Liberal concern. The Bureau was headed by the Liberal MP Charles Masterman, who had a longstanding interest in the 'eastern question', having been a member of the Balkan Committee, an organisation concerned with the liberty and protection of the Balkan nationalities in the Ottoman Empire. He moved in Liberal circles, was a friend of the Buxtons, long-term advocates of the Armenian cause, and was in contact with numerous other who shared their interest in the Armenians' fate.

Pamphlets produced under the auspices of the Propaganda Bureau included *Armenian Atrocities: The Murder of a Nation* and *The Murderous Tyranny of the Turks*. It was not until December 1916 however that the British government published its most significant expression of support for the Armenians, the Foreign Office 'blue book', *The Treatment of the Armenians in the Ottoman Empire*. This volume, prepared by Bryce and the historian Arnold Toynbee, was intended to provide a comprehensive, region-by-region account of the massacres.[21] The impetus behind the production of this volume was made clear by Toynbee in a letter to James Barton, the Director of the NER humanitarian agency:

> So far we have confined ourselves to publishing pamphlets or communicating extracts to the press; and that is probably the best way of making public what happened and rousing interest on the subject. But we feel that, if this public opinion is to produce any definite effect – that is, if it is to issue in a constructive programme for the future of Armenian Vilayets in the general settlement after the war – we ought to have ready a clear statement of the case for a radical alteration of the present state of things – at least in so far as the case is grounded on the culminating acts of the Ottoman government during the past year.[22]

The final version of *The Treatment of the Armenians* consisted mainly of narrative accounts of the deportation and massacre of the Armenian population, arranged region by region. The accounts were accompanied by a preface by Bryce, a brief history of Armenia by Toynbee and several letters from eminent professors and a lawyer commenting on the veracity of the accounts.[23] It was a product of co-operation between government, diaspora and Armenophile societies in Britain and abroad. Toynbee relied on the contacts of Bryce and other Armenophile organisations to obtain this information. He also requested information from the American Missions Board which co-ordinated the work of the many Armenian missionaries in the Ottoman Empire and relief organisations such as the Comité de Secours aux Arméniens in Geneva, the ANDP in Paris and the American Red Cross at Cairo.[24]

A guide for readers was provided in case the 'ordinary' reader did not wish to read through all of the 149 accounts included in the volume. The provision of this guide was part of the attempt to shape public perceptions of the massacres, drawing attention to dramatic 'key' events. The reliability of the evidence was thought to be of paramount importance: Toynbee spent months cross-checking reports and obtaining details of place-names, dates and events in order to separate 'facts' from rumour, exaggeration and confusion. The emphasis on accuracy related to the possibility that the documents could play a role in bringing the Turks to account after the war. It also related to ambiguous perceptions of the Armenians, who, despite their sufferings, as 'orientals' were still considered by many to be potentially unreliable witnesses. Armenian testimony was thought inadequate and confirmation was sought through the 'reliable' and supposedly neutral accounts of Western European missionaries or diplomats. In a supporting letter printed as part of the introduction to the volume Professor Gilbert Murray made this very clear:

> I realise that in times of persecution passions run high, that oriental races tend to use hyperbolical language, and the victims of oppression cannot be expected to speak with strict fairness of their oppressors. But the evidence of these letters and reports will bear any scrutiny and overpower any scepticism . . . The statements of the Armenian refugees themselves are fully confirmed by residents of American, Scandinavian and even German nationality.[25]

The publication of *The Treatment of the Armenians* brought the Armenians back into the public eye, prompting another round of press interest. The government, Armenophiles and the Armenian diaspora were all keen to have the volume distributed as widely as possible. However their motives for supporting the publication of the volume varied. Bryce stated that it had been produced, 'in the interests of historic truth, as well as with a view to the questions which must arise when the war ends'.[26] The attitude of the government was less idealistic; they seem to have seen its value primarily as a piece of propaganda to sway public opinions in neutral countries and influence post-war settlements. In June 1916 Masterman echoed this sentiment, stating in a letter to Bryce, 'I am very anxious that it should be published as soon as possible for general reasons connected with the influencing of public opinion, especially in regard to any ultimate settlement in the Near East.'[27] Later that summer Toynbee expressed similar opinions, explaining to Bryce that adding further material to the volume would risk their missing 'an unrivalled opportunity of getting the book widely pushed and distributed in America'.[28]

At this stage in the war the aims of government propagandists and pro-Armenian ideals did not seem contradictory; the split in their agendas would occur later, as the war drew to a close and the peace conferences began.[29] At this stage all parties sought to highlight the suffering of the

Armenians and vilify the Turks. Therefore all were willing to collaborate closely with Toynbee.[30] Many of the accounts that he included were drawn from the Armenophile press or pamphlets that had previously been published in Britain or the United States. When it came to the distribution of the volume the Armenophiles saw it as a valuable tool and were keen to use it to their own advantage. Nubar Pasha, for example, expressed a wish that it should be translated into French in the hope of arousing interest in the fate of the Armenians across the Channel.[31]

Many parties thus had a stake in the representation of the Armenian genocide to the British public. On the surface they had a great deal in common and in the early stages of war their representations of the massacres were remarkably consistent in content and imagery. Under the strains of war, however, the agendas and actions of these parties and the images of the Armenians they chose to employ diverged dramatically.

Atrocity, orientalism, history

> Nearly the whole nation has been wiped out, and I do not think that there is any case in history, certainly not since the time of Tamerlane, in which any crime so hideous and upon so large a scale has been reported.[32]

Bryce's characterisation of the massacres as a unique occurrence was reiterated throughout the war. Yet it is clear that understandings of 1915 were shaped by the history of cycles of violence, oppression and intervention on behalf of Christian minorities in the Ottoman Empire which had characterised the 'eastern question'.

In 1915 public appetites for atrocity stories had not diminished. The graphic language of atrocity from the era of the 'Bulgarian Horrors' was still in usage, having since been reused in other circumstances: the outcry over the Belgian Congo atrocities, the Balkan wars and the controversy over concentration camps during the Boer War.[33] As in the 1890s, reports emphasised the extreme and ingenious methods developed by the Turks to inflict pain. Gratuitous descriptions of acts of wanton cruelty and sadism were common. A pamphlet describing the escape of an Armenian family typically provided a detailed description of the tortures they had undergone, 'There was no limit to the tortures he endured. They crushed his hands and feet in the press, and pulled out his nails with pincers; they pierced his face with needles . . .'[34] This kind of description bore a striking similarity to the descriptions provided by Dillon in 1896.[35] Pamphlets and books regarding the massacres sometimes avoided the graphic, emotive language of the press, focusing instead on the Armenian past and future. Even so, they almost always made at least veiled reference to this kind of violent imagery.

The violence perpetrated by the Turks was represented as beyond the boundaries of 'normal' conflict or warfare between civilised nations. Turks were portrayed as taking a particular delight in inflicting pain and killing, hence the attention paid to incidences of torture or mutilation. At the same time British audiences were reminded once again that the Armenians were not 'oriental' but a civilised and Christian people, part of the European world. The adoption of this language of civilisation and barbarism in the reporting of the massacres had particular resonance for British people. Orientalist stereotypes provided a vital explanatory tool, making a clear statement that the massacres were a barbaric attack on European civilisation.

Interpretations of the events of 1915 also drew upon established readings of the history and character of the region. Throughout the first decades of the twentieth century the issue of minorities in the Ottoman Empire had been kept alive by ongoing crises in the Balkans and Macedonia. The fate of these peoples and that of the Armenians was often represented as one and the same. As a speaker at a conference on Macedonia suggested, 'It is impossible, morally and politically, to separate the sacred cause of Armenia from that of Macedonia and the whole of Turkey.'[36]

For those involved in these causes and for the public, the nature of the violence in these different regions was virtually the same; oppression, massacre and atrocity were portrayed as the inevitable consequences of Ottoman rule.[37] The Armenian massacres were fitted into this framework as the culmination of almost a century of 'atrocities' committed against Christian minorities. As Bryce put it:

> In Chios, nearly a century ago, the Turks slaughtered almost the whole Greek population of the Island. In European Turkey in 1876 many thousands of Bulgarians were killed on the suspicion of an intended rising, and the outrages on women were, on a smaller scale, as bad as those here recorded. In 1895 and 1896 more than a hundred thousand Armenian Christians were put to death by Abd-ul-Hamid, many thousands of whom died as martyrs to their Christian faith . . . All that happened in 1915 is in the regular line of Turkish policy. The only differences are in the scale of the present crimes and in the fact that the lingering sufferings of deportations in which the deaths were as numerous as the massacres, and fell with special severity upon the women, have in this latest instance been added.[38]

In some cases the roots of the massacres were portrayed as even deeper and authors recounted a history of centuries of violence against Armenian Christians by the Turks or other 'eastern invaders'. These histories were shaped to a large extent by orientalist discourses portraying the Turks as part of a violent and uncivilised 'East' in perpetual conflict with the civilised 'West'. Central to this argument was the idea that the Ottoman Empire was unchanging and incapable of progress without the intervention of Western European nations.[39]

Yet although reference to such readings of history provided a powerful tool for convincing the British population that it was possible for massacres on such a scale to occur, they also presented a problem. If the British public believed this was a region locked into perpetual conflict through 'ancient hatreds', the argument for British intervention and support for the Armenian cause was somewhat weakened, for this implied that British intervention could not make a long-term difference. For this reason, it was necessary for British supporters of the Armenian cause to differentiate between these massacres and earlier instances of violence.[40]

The Armenian massacres as a war atrocity

Previous massacres of Armenians and other Christian minorities in the Ottoman Empire had usually been explained in reference to the particular characteristics of the empire or the nature of 'the Turk'. Explanations were couched in terms of racial difference, religious conflict, degeneracy and the nature of the Ottoman state or the conflict between 'East' and 'West'. These explanations, though often portrayed as 'scientific' or objective, were not used in a systematic or logical manner; they were conflated or manipulated almost at will in order to create a negative stereotype of 'the Turk' and a sympathetic image of the Armenians. Common to all sectors of British public opinion was an acceptance that the Ottoman Empire, particularly its borderlands, was prone to descend into violence at the slightest cause.

Such explanations, which focused on the unstable nature of the region or the characteristics of its inhabitants, were not deemed sufficient to explain the events of 1915. Newer explanations were therefore sought which related the Armenian massacres more specifically to wartime circumstances. The massacres and deportations were assigned to the new category of 'war atrocity'. Thus the massacre of Armenians was treated as the same 'type' of phenomenon as the invasion of Belgium, the sinking of the *Lusitania*, the use of poison gas and the shooting of the British nurse, Edith

Cavell.[41] These acts were all portrayed as having transgressed the boundaries of 'civilised' modern warfare. Such 'atrocities' would become not only powerful images in war propaganda but a central part of wartime culture.

The categories of 'atrocity', which emerged during the First World War, must be related to the development of the idea of 'lawful' war and the attempts which had been made to codify what was, and what was not, acceptable practice in wartime. Such debates over the rights and wrongs of conducting warfare were not restricted to those engaged in combat. In fact it was the position of the civilian, and the civilian's rights to immunity and indeed to self-defence, that had been of greatest concern to those involved in writing the 'rules'.[42] This attempt at codification began in the late nineteenth century with the Geneva Convention of 1864, establishing standards for humanitarian intervention in battle. Such legislation had been developed in a piecemeal manner and culminated in the Hague Convention. The effectiveness of the convention before the war seems to have been limited – however this did not prevent its invocation to vilify the enemy after war had broken out. Nicoletta Gullace has pointed out the way in which it was 'rehabilitated' as 'British publicists and international lawyers succeeded in investing the rules of war with a public meaning that they lacked at the time of the conference.'[43]

Reports of atrocities were a feature of the war from the start; they played an important role in wartime propaganda but also assumed a broader cultural significance. Atrocity stories were a means through which a variety of collective fears and beliefs about the war could be expressed and understood. Narratives of atrocities and the myths that developed around them were both shaped by and helped to shape these fears and beliefs. They were one way of giving the war meanings that often drew upon pre-existing cultural assumptions or popular beliefs.

In the decades after the war doubts were aired about the authenticity or accuracy of these atrocity stories.[44] Some suggested they were a product of exaggeration or falsification by wartime governments eager to mobilise support for the war. Recent work on German atrocities has shifted the debate away from simple questions of truth or falsehood to more complex questions of the construction and meanings of atrocity stories. Such questions are particularly relevant for the understanding of the depiction of the Armenian massacres. 'Atrocities', as Horne and Kramer point out, 'are a culturally constructed and historically determined category.'[45] Defining what exactly constituted atrocity was subject to selection and manipulation, shaped by specific concerns and contexts. This is not to suggest that atrocities are 'made up'; rather to claim that their form is shaped by ongoing processes of interpretation and re-interpretation: 'Like any inter-pretation they were also an expressive and creative act. They vented fear and trauma and helped impose some kind of narrative order, and hence meaning on what were usually chaotic experiences.'[46]

The experiences of those who endured the Armenian massacres were re-shaped and re-ordered for the British audiences in a manner which reflected contemporary concerns and fears. Their portrayal was heavily influenced by the investigation and representation of the massacres in Belgium that preceded them. News of the Armenian massacres reached Britain around the time that the report into the German atrocities in Belgium was published. This investigation had also been carried out by Bryce.[47] By this time, Trevor Wilson points out, 'atrocity mongering [had] reached its peak'.[48] This choice of words is telling, reflecting the doubts that such stories inspired, as well as their power.

Despite the fact that what occurred in Belgium and Armenia was very different, the same themes and motifs were used to define both events. As in the case of Belgium, the themes of violence against women and chil-dren preoccupied reports of the Armenian massacres. Sexual violence seems to have been treated as characteristic of the behaviour of the enemy. A British investigator of the atrocities in France stated that, 'outrages upon the honour of women by German soldiers have been so frequent that it is impossible to escape the conviction that they have been condoned and indeed encouraged by German officers'.[49] When Bryce first addressed the House of Lords on the massacres he remarked, 'it is needless to say that their present participation has been accompanied by numerous outrages upon women'.[50]

In the atrocity discourses of this period certain 'types' of events were accorded special attention, regardless of the frequency of their occurrence. Rape and violence against children were the most frequent and highly symbolic motifs in atrocity narratives of the First World War, evoking not only an attack on the innocent but also symbolising the violation of the nation.[51] Some acts of violence would also assume a mythical, emblemic status, in the case of Belgium; this was the image of children with severed hands, which, although rare in reality, recurred in images and narratives. Reports of severed hands also appeared in narratives of the Armenian genocide, 'In many places on the road from Mosul to Aleppo, he had seen children's hands lying hacked off in such numbers that he could have paved the road with them.'[52]

These similarities in the imagery used to depict acts of atrocity were reinforced by texts attempting to provide a coherent explanation of these events. For example, in his pamphlet *The Attitude of Great Britain in the Present War*, Bryce attempted to justify Britain's involvement in the conflict, describing the wrongdoings of the enemy. He included the Armenian massacres, the invasion of Belgium, and also the sinking of the *Lusitania* and Zeppelin raids. All of these acts were portrayed as being contrary to 'civilisation' and to British values.[53]

Atrocities and perpetrators

The definition of the Armenian massacres as part of a category of wartime atrocities must be related to the specific ways in which the perpetrators were constructed. Although accounts of the massacres were primarily concerned with the fate of the innocent Armenian victims, they also devoted a great deal of attention to describing and analysing the behaviour of those who carried out the massacres. Narratives of the Armenian massacres helped to re-define the Turks as the wartime enemy. Though an emphasis on supposed Turkish barbarism remained, images of the Turks as the perpetrators of organised violence shifted subtly to meet the needs of portraying them as a wartime adversary that must be defeated.

After the outbreak of war pre-existing images of the Turk as lustful, barbaric, backward and fanatically religious were recycled and enhanced. Prior to the war some British observers had expressed a hope that, with western guidance, this 'barbarism' could be reformed into something resembling western 'civilisation'. Now, faith in Turkish capacities to reform evaporated. The Turks were deemed 'incurable', incapable of just and peaceful rule.

In some cases observers tried to provide a more considered judgement on the Turks. Toynbee, for example, suggested that up until 1878 Ottoman rule in Armenia had been 'on the whole beneficial'.[54] In general these 'balanced' statements were overshadowed by the negative and emotive stereotypes of barbarism that dominated the press and propaganda materials. Even Bryce, who elsewhere had devoted careful analysis to the situation in the Ottoman Empire, felt able to assert that 'the Turkish government is of course a thoroughly barbarous government'.[55]

Barbarism was associated in the British imagination with the fact that Turkey was part of the 'East'. Representations of the massacres therefore played upon orientalist notions of opposition and difference between 'East' and 'West' in order to suggest that Turkey was devoid of the values that the western powers claimed to be fighting for. Bryce contrasted Turkey with 'civilized Europe' where 'Christian nations have during the last few centuries softened the conduct of war by agreeing to respect the lives and property of innocent non-combatants.'[56]

Wholesale condemnation of the Ottoman Empire by British observers was relatively new, brought about by wartime enmity. In the past few critics of the Ottomans had been so openly opposed to the continued existence of the empire in any form. Now, the Armenian massacres were viewed as part of a problem which could only be solved by the wholesale destruction of the empire. British commentators used the massacres to illustrate longstanding claims about the despotic nature of the Ottoman Empire, claiming that it was illegitimate, unnatural and innately oppressive. Toynbee stated that 'Turkey, the Ottoman State is not a unity, climatic, geographic, racial or economic; it is a pretension, enforced by bloodshed and violence whenever or wherever the Osmanli government has power.'[57]

Longstanding assumptions about the nature of eastern 'despotism' were applied in a very specific manner to the contemporary Ottoman Empire and the 'Young Turk' regime was interpreted as a particularly virulent strain of 'barbarism'. In Britian, Armenophiles and authorities attributed blame to the Ottoman government rather than the people of the empire, implying that the defeat of this government would definitively solve the problem. British commentators also desired not to appear to be simply prejudiced against Islam, as they feared this could aggravate the Muslim population in British-ruled India. This attitude was evident in the 'official' propaganda. Thus Bryce remarked in one pamphlet, 'No Moslem passion, not religious fanaticism, all was done by the will of the Government.'[58]

In popular representations things were not so clear cut. Discourses of race, religion and civilisation overlapped and intersected and the meanings of 'Islamic' and 'eastern' were often interchangeable. The imagery and the language associated with the massacres therefore continued to evoke religious persecution and conflict between Christianity and Islam. Popular preconceptions and misunderstandings of Islam were played upon, particularly in the press, in order to evoke images of a bloodthirsty, amoral and fanatical faith, an integral part of which was claimed to be attacking or converting Christians.

Armenia, in contrast, was once again presented as the last outpost of Christianity, playing an important role in the defence of the Christian and civilised world: 'For thirteen centuries she has preserved the integrity of her creed amongst unspeakable oppression and persecution, as the representative of the cross against the crescent.'[59] The 1915 massacres were treated as the latest manifestation of Islamic persecutions of the Christian world. Religious imagery played an importance role in defining the differences between Britain and the enemy.

In Britain, the massacres were not only utilised to condemn the Ottoman Empire. Blame for these events was also extended to Britain's other enemy, Germany. Germany was imagined to have become tainted with the 'barbaric' characteristics associated with the Ottoman Empire. In the words of Bryce, Germany had taken 'a step backward towards barbarism'.[60] In his own report into the Belgian atrocities, J. H. Morgan, author of a pamphlet on the German atrocities in Belgium, also condemned Germany by designating its behaviour in Belgium 'eastern':

> A Nation thus acquiring the destructive resources of the West, while retaining the peculiar morality of the East – Its ruthlessness, its contempt for human life, its sombre fatalism, its indifference to personal liberty . . . can discipline its mind but cannot control its appetites, which can acquire the idiom of Europe and yet retains the instincts of Asia or rather of some pre-Asiatic horde, presents the greatest problem that has ever perplexed the civilisation of man.[61]

Such statements were effective because of the powerful connotations of barbarity, lustfulness, immorality and backwardness which orientalist discourses had associated with the 'East'. Of course another effect was to make the rest of Europe – including the Armenians – appear united, part of the same civilisation. Germany, like the Ottoman Empire, was portrayed as beyond the boundaries of this moral universe, 'Germany no longer counts among the civilised nations of this world.'[62]

German influence in Turkey on the other hand was believed to have led to greater organisation and militarism which made carefully planned and systematic deportations possible. This implied that German involvement had brought about the 'modern' elements of the genocide. Such observations were commonplace in the press. The *Manchester Guardian* suggested that the system of massacres, 'in its conception has something of the thoroughness of the Germans, in its execution it is as brutal as the Turk can make it'.[63] *The Times* similarly observed that, 'this union of German Kultur and old fashioned Turkish barbarism has produced a real Frankenstein monster that now stalks through this eastern world'.[64]

Such abstract theories of cultural or political influence were not the end of the story. Though the extent of German involvement was difficult to discern, British propaganda sought to demonstrate that the Germans had either been complicit in carrying out the massacres, or at the very least had failed to intervene and to prevent them when they alone were in a position to do so.[65] The eyewitness testimonies of Armenians and missionaries were said to provide evidence of this.[66] The evidence of German eyewitnesses was also particularly sought-after in Britain since it proved that the massacres were not simply exaggerated by the British government.

Extermination and genocide

Representations of the massacres of the Armenians, I have suggested, were conditioned by longstanding orientalist stereotypes and beliefs about the nature of the Ottoman Empire. However the events of 1915 were regarded by contemporary observers as having unique features which differentiated them from other instances of Ottoman violence and from other wartime atrocities. A key difference was that of scale. *The Times*, for example, reported that, 'the nature and scale of the atrocities dwarf anything perpetrated in Belgium or under Abdul Hamid'.[67]

British commentators argued that the 1915 massacres took an unprecedented form. Previous attacks on the Ottoman Armenians had been limited to certain regions, mass deportations had not occurred, and although the results were devastating, the violence was sporadic rather than sustained. The British Armenophiles and government were keen that the 1915 massacres should not be dismissed as yet another inevitable explosion of this kind of endemic regional violence. Thus elaborating upon the distinctiveness of the 1915 massacres was essential.

Images of the 1915 massacres therefore located them within a long-term history of violence, but also highlighted unique features such as the extent of government involvement and planning. Toynbee stressed that the Ottoman authorities 'worked out a uniform method of procedure, dispatched simultaneous orders to the provincial officials and gendarmerie to carry it into effect'.[68] *The Times* also highlighted the new features and differences in the intensity of the massacres in 1915 through making comparisons with earlier massacres:

> The Red Sultan's abominations were seldom accompanied by the wholesale deportation of survivors: The violation and abduction of women and the conversion of children, though sadly frequent in some places, were by no means general in 1894–1896. Then the wild beast was allowed to run amok for twenty four hours and was then usually chained up.[69]

Although it was clear to contemporaries that the massacres of 1915 constituted something new, they sometimes struggled to define what had occurred. They relied upon older terms such as 'atrocity' and 'massacre', elaborating upon and attaching new meanings to these terms. Although the massacres of the Armenians are now recognised by many scholars and growing sections of the international community as genocide this term may only be applied retrospectively.[70] As Helen Fein has pointed out, 'no legal term or concept of genocide existed' at the time.[71] However the description of the massacre of the Armenians by contemporary commentators echoes Article 2 of the United Nations Convention on the Prevention and Punishment of Genocide (1948).[72]

Certainly, contemporary observers believed that the Ottoman government aimed to rid itself of the whole of the Armenian population. The terminology often used to describe this process was the 'extermination' of a nation.[73] This word appears frequently as an overarching description of the intended fate of the Armenians. In the preface of *The Treatment of the Armenians*, Bryce described the massacres as an 'attempt to exterminate a nation'.[74] *The Times* and the *Manchester Guardian* also employed this term in their reports.[75] The word 'extermination' had featured in descriptions of the massacres in Armenia in 1895–96, but at that point its use reflected the dramatic rhetoric associated with Gladstone and the sensationalist language of the 'new journalism' rather than a genuine fear for the 'end' of the Armenians. At this point it seems that British observers thought the Ottoman government used the massacres as warning or punishment, aiming to subdue Armenian ambitions or weaken an Armenian population perceived to be a threat rather than eliminate them completely. Leo Kuper has described these massacres as having:

> Limited objectives, being designed as a sort of ambassadorial note to the European powers to refrain from intervention in the domestic affairs of Turkey, and a most bloody warning to the Armenians themselves against seeking the intercession of these powers on their behalf or aspiring to autonomy.[76]

In 1915 on the other hand, the fear of 'extermination' was much more powerful, reflecting the belief that it was the intention of the Ottoman government to empty the Ottoman Empire of its Armenian population. The use of the term 'extermination' points to a racialised understanding of what it meant to be Armenian, suggesting that nationality lay 'in the blood'. This marked a contrast with the emphasis that had previously been placed upon the Armenian Church as the repository of Armenian identity and was linked to both fears for Armenian survival and intensified aspirations for the establishment of an Armenian nation state.

The belief that the Ottoman government intended to 'exterminate' the Armenians was related by British observers to the aims and ambitions of the 'Young Turk' regime. Some observers expressed the belief that the massacres were a product of the emergence of pan-Turkist ideologies which were intolerant of the religious and ethnic minorities living in the Ottoman Empire. Although the 1908 revolution had initially raised hopes for the improvement of the situation of the Armenians these hopes were rapidly dashed as 'between the Young Turk Revolution in 1908 and the outbreak of the First World War in 1914 extreme Turkish nationalism triumphed over multinational Ottomanism'.[77] At the start of the war the Ottomans espoused a pan-Turkist ideal of the creation of a homogenous Turkish nation stretching far across Asia. In the words of the Armenian activist A. P. Hacobian, 'They had formed a design for the extermination of the non-Mohammedan elements in the population of Asiatic Turkey in order to make what they called a homogenous nation, consisting of Mohammedans only.'[78]

British Armenophiles, including Toynbee, suggested that the Turks had massacred the Armenians as they were 'in the way' of the creation of a homogenous Turkish nation, racially, religiously, culturally and physically. In the LMF pamphlet, *The Murder of a Nation* it was suggested that 'The Armenians both by character and by religion are impossible to assimilate in Turkey. And moreover they stand as the direct obstacle in the way of the pan-Turanian ideas encouraged in Germany.'[79] The process of extermination of minorities, it was claimed, would not stop with the Armenians. In his pamphlet, *Turkey: A Past and a Future*, Toynbee suggested that 'Every non Turkish nationality in the Empire is threatened with extermination.'[80]

This argument offered a more complex explanation of the massacres as a modern political or ideological phenomenon. However, perceptions of pan-Turkism were not unified. Some identified it as a religious phenomenon whilst others focused upon the racial dimension. Pan-Turkism was often regarded as only one element within multi-layered explanations drawing heavily upon traditional negative stereotypes and cultural assumptions about the Turks. Nonetheless, the role of this ideology in prompting the massacres was accorded a great deal of importance amongst British observers, as it placed responsibility for the massacres directly in the hands of the Ottoman government.

Representing Armenia: civilisation, suffering and the nation

Alongside these shifts in the interpretation of violence and massacre there were equally significant changes in the way that Armenia and the

Armenians were portrayed. These changes related particularly to debates provoked by the massacres over the future of Armenia. To recapitulate, images of Armenian suffering were rife in both press coverage of the massacres and in the propaganda material produced by the government, Armenophiles and the diaspora. Missionaries and diplomats provided shocking accounts of events which, even to those familiar with the traumatic history of the Armenian people, seemed almost beyond belief. Photographic evidence of the massacres was scarce because deportation was arranged in such a way that it could be concealed from the rest of the world. For the few observers who witnessed the massacres, providing photographic evidence posed enormous difficulties.[81] Witnesses therefore struggled to convey in words the scale of suffering and death that they observed, describing the ubiquitous corpses in rivers and roads, huge numbers of suffering Armenians making their way across the desert in deportation conveys and horrendous conditions in camps at the end of the routes.[82]

The portrayal of the Armenians in the aftermath of 1915 was not however a straightforward matter of describing events and demonstrating their status as 'victims'. Representations of the massacres also engaged with broader questions of how to represent the Armenians. In a context where the destruction of the Ottoman Empire had become desirable, Armenian independence had become for the first time a real possibility and it was no longer adequate to define the Armenians as an oppressed Christian minority. Instead, there was an increasing tendency from all parties to represent the Armenians as a coherent 'national' body. Even before the question of national independence became pressing, the representation of Armenian suffering and the question of the defence and survival of Armenia were formulated in a national framework.

National suffering

Preoccupation with Armenia as a 'nation' in images of the 1915 massacres cannot be understood in isolation. War had engendered wide concern for the fate of small or defenceless nations on the part of the Allied powers. This was triggered specifically by the invasion of Belgium by Germany in August 1915, portrayed in Britain as the brutal violation of a small, innocent nation by a powerful barbaric enemy. For British Liberals, many of whom held strong anti-war sentiments, a war in defence of Belgium was therefore morally acceptable. As Peter Clarke explains, 'the point was that a war on behalf of Belgium was not seen as an assertion of realpolitik in the national interest, which the conservatives would have supported anyway, but a struggle of right and wrong in the Gladstonian tradition'.[83] Such a war could be understood as a war for traditional Liberal values, as over the past few decades the defence of the rights of small nations against despotic powers had become an important part of these values.[84]

Thus war was conceived of as a 'moral crusade in defence of small nations'. This viewpoint was not restricted to the self-justifications of the British Liberals but became part of the popular understanding of the war and an important dimension of war culture.[85] This formed the core of British propaganda, aimed not only at convincing the 'home' population that the war was both just and necessary but also to convince neutral countries of the need to fight. It was within this context of concern for small nations then, that the British government could frame an apparent change of heart over Armenia's status as a nation.

Professed concerns for small nations encompassed a range of peoples and places. Belgians, Poles and Serbs all found themselves characterised as 'victim nations', nations which had suffered at the hands of the enemy and which Britain and the Allies had a moral duty to protect.[86] Attacks upon the Belgians, Serbians or Poles were understood not as attacks on individuals or communities but as attacks upon the fabric of the nation. Suggested remedies or reparations were formulated around the principle of national self-determination and reconstruction. It is indicative of the belief in national claims that the organisations which offered humanitarian assistance took a national form. Networks in Britain supported Poles, Serbs and Belgians, providing humanitarian relief and protection and campaigning for the recognition of their 'national rights'.[87]

Armenia was part of this new category of 'victim nations'. Although the Armenian experience was very different to that of other regions, the Armenians were presented as the victims of the same type of crime against the nation:

> Now since the European War, their fate has been so similar that it is almost as common for those who are acquainted with its history to characterise the Armenians as the 'Belgium of Asia' as it is for the world to characterise the Germans as the 'Turks of Europe'.[88]

Comparative scales of national suffering emerged, with the supporters of various nations arguing the case that their chosen cause was the most deserving. Grace Knapp, for example, an American missionary from Van, claimed that 'no race has suffered so much as the Armenians in Asiatic Turkey'.[89] The fate of the Armenians was often utilised as an index against which the sufferings of other nations could be measured. The reports of Morgan Philips Price, correspondent of the *Manchester Guardian,* who encountered Armenian refugees in north-west Persia, expressed similar sentiments, describing a chain of suffering and displaced nations across Europe:

> Much has been said about the sad exodus from Poland before the German advance and we have been made almost to see the endless processions of carts piled with the household goods and weaker members of the homeless Poles. And our hearts have been wrung with the sufferings of Belgians driven from their land, and Servians fleeing from the ruthless Bulgars. But the deportations in Armenia contained more elements of horror, a condensation of agony that almost defies the human imagination.[90]

The idea of the Armenian nation

Although there were common themes in the portrayal of 'victim nations' there were also significant differences relating to the ways in which their pasts and futures were imagined. Representations of Armenian national suffering drew upon discourses of Armenian national identity and cultural meanings attached to Armenia since the late nineteenth century. In the case of Armenia the themes of Christianity, civilisation and culture, and the idea of the Armenians as an 'ancient' people who had survived centuries of conquest and oppression recurred frequently.

The emphasis placed on Armenian nationhood also reflected the changing geopolitical circumstances. Geopolitical changes wrought by the First World War and the prospect of the destruction of the Ottoman Empire offered the Armenians a real chance of national autonomy. This chance was seized upon by both Armenophiles and the Armenian diaspora. Even as the massacres continued they had begun to construct a vision of the future liberty of the Armenians. Prior to the war most Armenian nationalists and their supporters had been cautious. After the massacres, both diaspora and Armenophiles became bolder, pushing for the creation of an autonomous nation state.

Explicit statements of Armenian national aspirations regularly featured as an opening or a conclusion to publicity material. A pamphlet written by the British Armenophile Aneurin Williams and published in 1916 stated:

> The modern problem before the Allies with regard to this land and people is the establishment of an autonomous Armenia under conditions which open to the new Armenian state a vista of settled, ordered and progressive national existence.[91]

Such calls for the future liberty of the Armenians were echoed in the statements of the British government and played a significant role in determining the image of the Armenian massacres in Britain. Humanitarian efforts to aid the Armenians were frequently couched in terms of saving a potential nation.

Opinions on Armenian nationhood in the later nineteenth century had echoed the ambiguity with which Armenia was regarded generally during this period. It was rare for British observers to accept wholeheartedly the idea of Armenian national independence. Armenian nationalism was regarded, even by harsh critics of Ottoman rule, as deeply suspicious – the pursuit of a small, troublesome minority. The American missionary, Edward Munsell Bliss, echoed the views of many British Armenophiles in his view that it was 'conceived in conceit, in treachery and in falsehood, its fruit has been ruin and misery of the worst type'.[92] As for 'Armenia', this was 'scarcely more than a historical name'.[93]

In 1915 ambiguous British discourses of Armenian national identity and history were re-shaped in the context of war and the Allied aim to defeat the Ottoman Empire. Negative connotations that had been associated with the Armenians and the notion that Armenia was 'unready' to become a nation were swept aside. In their place renewed emphasis was placed on the 'positive' characteristics of the Armenian people. In other words the ambiguities of the image of the Armenians came to an end. The Armenians were reclaimed from their 'in-between' position, made part of the civilised European world and their suitability as a nation was proclaimed with renewed vigour.

Civilisation, church and nation

The massacres generated a renewed general interest in the Armenian people, prompting the publication of numerous pamphlets and books concerned with Armenian history, culture and society.[94] A thorough knowledge of these subjects was considered essential to a proper understanding of both the causes of the massacres and the future of the Armenians. Thus a history of the Armenians accompanied the definitive accounts of the massacres and deportations provided in *The Treatment of the Armenians*.[95] Such narratives of the Armenian past tended to continue to present the history of the Armenians as a perpetual struggle between East and West, good and evil, or Christianity and Islam. In the words of Emily Robinson, secretary of the Red Cross and Refugees Fund, Armenian history was 'one long record of murder, rapine, burning, desolation'.[96] The 1915 massacres were presented as the latest episode in this traumatic narrative.

Such statements added weight to the argument that the Ottoman Empire was 'incurable' and must be destroyed. They also helped to arouse sympathies for the long-suffering Armenians, highlighting the need for the creation of a safe national home. Yet this image of Armenian history as the continued oppression of a nation had another dimension. The Armenians may have become fixed in the British imagination as the victims of the Turks, but they were equally imagined to be 'survivors' and were admired for their strength and courage. Emily Robinson, a devoted admirer of the Armenians, expressed this point of view: 'So marvellous are the powers of endurance of the Armenian race that after each terrible visitation by Asiatic hordes who decimated the population, before many years had passed homes and towns rose from the ashes and the land flourished again.'[97] Survival of conquest and oppression was seized upon by British Armenophiles as clear evidence that the Armenians were worthy recipients of British support and protection.

Attempts to cast Armenia in a positive light also frequently referred to its status as an 'ancient nation' or ancient people and to associations through biblical myths and ancient civilisations with British origins. Others referred to historical achievements of the Armenian people or looked to Armenian history, particularly the crusades, to find examples of bonds between Armenia and the nations of Europe. Typically, the author of one pamphlet suggested that 'it was very natural that Armenian Christians should aid their fellow Christians in their attempts to recover the holy places from the hands of the infidel Turk'.[98]

Stressing historical and cultural bonds between the Armenians and the British created a sense of identification with the victims of the massacres. An attack on a 'civilised' people, a people not unlike the British, seemed more worthy of British attention than the suffering of 'uncivilised' or 'exotic' peoples elsewhere in the world. An emphasis on Armenian history and culture served not only to improve the standing of Armenians in Britain. Portraying the Armenians as part of civilised Europe allowed the massacres to be portrayed as an attack upon 'civilisation', not just upon a minority in the Ottoman Empire.

Christianity was also integral to wartime images of Armenia. Despite an emerging emphasis on 'nationhood' and the more secular articulations of Armenian identity that this entailed, traditional images of the Armenians as 'fellow Christians' persisted. Thomas C. Leonard has pointed out the importance of these associations in generating American support for the Armenians in 1915: 'The mental landscape of the Near East was crucial. Armenians died on bible lands. Mount Ararat, Tarsus and Constantinople were names that formed part of a common sacred tradition for American Catholics, Protestants and Jews.'[99] The same was true for British observers.

In reality the boundaries between Armenian national and religious identities, in the eyes of British observers, were often blurred. Many viewed the Armenian Church as the repository of Armenian national values and traditions; others imagined nationality to have been 'preserved' only by the continued existence of the Church. Either way, Christianity was presented as integral to the Armenian nation. Images of the Church and of the nation were intertwined. Indeed, the nation itself came to be regarded as sacred and the massacres as a kind of martyrdom.

Christianity acted as a marker of 'civilisation'. This was in turn related to the idea of the nation. For a people such as the Armenians to be deemed 'fit' to become a nation state, certain culturally constructed standards of 'civilisation' had to be met. Christianity helped the Armenians to ascend established hierarchies of progress, and 'qualify' as a civilised people. Any doubts about the nature of Armenian Christianity, for example that it was based on 'superstition', were swept aside in 1915. The Armenians were embraced as 'fellow Christians'.

Armenians were represented as martyrs for their nation and even for the entire Christian world. The language of martyrdom, revived from the 1890s, was especially resonant during this period as the Great War was often constructed as 'a Latin Christian campaign against barbarian incursion'.[100] Images of barbarity often had religious associations. Accounts of crucifixion of Christians emerged from Armenia, but also from Belgium, where it was reported that Allied soldiers had been crucified by German soldiers.[101] This report was widely circulated though unconfirmed. Wartime rhetoric employed Christian language and symbolism and religious language abounded in depictions of the Armenians. Even the usually sober and reasoned voice of Toynbee stated that 'the redemption of these innocent peoples from the hell into which they have been cast and where they will remain in agony as long as Ottoman and Prussian militarism holds out, is incumbent upon the Allies if they are to redeem their blighted world'.[102]

Images of the destruction or defilement of sacred places or objects played a key role in the depiction of the massacres as an attack upon Christianity. One report from Constantinople stated, 'When the people were deported, the churches were pillaged and turned into mosques, stables or what not. Besides that they have begun to sell at Constantinople the sacred objects and properties of the Armenian Church.'[103] Another account from Moush reported the defilement of sacred relics, claiming that the Turks entered the Armenian church and 'opened the tomb of St. Garabed and destroyed everything'.[104] Such images symbolised the destruction of Armenian faith, tradition and values. They also provided vivid images of the immorality and barbarity of the enemy. Attacks on sacred objects and sacred places could also be thought of as attacks on universal symbols of Christianity, an affront to the faith of the European Christian readers of the accounts as well as to the Armenians.

Attacks on sacred sites were not only a matter of religious persecution. These acts of destruction had a wider significance for perpetrators, victims and European observers. Armenian religious architecture was destroyed as part of an effort to erase any trace of Armenian presence in the lands of the Ottoman Empire. This related to the pan-Turkist agenda of the Ottoman government and the desire to create a homogenous Turkish state. Dickran Kouymijian has suggested that 'during the years 1915–23, some one thousand Armenian churches and monasteries were levelled to the ground while nearly 700 other religious structures were half destroyed'.[105] The destruction or defilement of these religious buildings came to represent the tearing away of the Armenian population from their traditional homeland and the Turkish attempt to 'exterminate' the Armenian people and destroy any material evidence of their presence.[106]

Armenian churches were particularly distinctive in form and regarded as intertwined symbols of Armenian faith and nation, representative of historic cultural achievements. During the nineteenth century British scholars and travellers had come to recognise Armenian religious architecture as an important dimension of Armenian and European cultural and religious development. They not only admired the buildings from an architectural point of view but also regarded them as powerful symbols of the Christian heritage in an otherwise Islamic landscape. As such they were regarded as part of a common heritage of European civilisation.

In October 1915 the *Manchester Guardian* published photographs of Armenian monasteries prior to the massacres, as an attempt to remind their readers just what was at stake in the massacres and to illustrate what was meant by 'Armenian civilisation'.[107] Leonard suggests that the fact that Armenia was regarded as a site of 'western heritage' was essential in spurring on the response to the massacres; other areas which did not share the same 'cultural associations' did not receive the same kind of attention.[108] Few images of the destruction or defilement of Armenian religious architecture were available to the British public but heavy reference was made in the press and in pamphlets to the extent of the material destruction. Such reports and images worked on a variety of levels. For those who were more familiar with 'Armenia' and the Armenians, these reports would provoke a multi-layered response. The medieval church or monastery could act as a national symbol, especially as the medieval kingdoms of Armenia had been regarded as a high point of Armenian national development. Their destruction thus embodied the idea of an attack on the nation. It could also embody a more general attack on civilisation, echoing the destruction of the churches of the medieval city of Ani by 'eastern hordes' centuries previously.[109] But even for those with no knowledge of Armenia, the image of an attack on a Christian site and the desecration of consecrated artefacts could generate outrage.

Reports of destruction in Armenia evoked memories of the destruction of important cultural and religious sites in Belgium and Northern France by the German army during the invasion. At Louvain, the university library was burned during the German advance and much of the historic centre of the town was destroyed, as was the historic cathedral of Rheims in France. Such acts of deliberate destruction of sites representative of cultural and historical achievements were regarded by the Allies, as Horne and Kramer point out, as 'the ultimate proof of barbarism'.[110] Like attacks on innocent women and children, they were considered to have broken the laws of civilised conduct of warfare.

Gender and the representation of national suffering

In the construction of atrocity narratives, descriptions of 'real' events may be transformed in the practice of telling and re-telling of stories. Because of the shifts in perceptions of the fate of the Armenians and the possibilities for their future, images and themes from the tradition of representing violence against the Armenians came to be employed in new ways. Information about the Armenian massacres was initially sparse, and therefore a limited number of events and images were repeatedly re-circulated and elaborated upon. Through this process certain events and images took on a special significance, having the power to relay to the public the horror of the situation, one dramatic example being the drowning of hundreds of Armenians off the coast of Trebizond.[111]

For the British public the archetypal image of the Armenian massacres was that of violent attacks on women and children. These images permeated all forms of representation. Press and propaganda pamphlets alike described in detail the fate of Armenian women; narrative accounts focused on women's experiences and visual images were overwhelmingly of suffering Armenian women and children.

Appeal posters for the LMF, for example, depicted a mother holding a child, whilst in the background houses burned (see Figure 1). *The Friend of Armenia* also used images of Armenian women and children on their cover. The September 1917 issue, for example, featured a young Armenian women, barefoot, with children clinging to her skirts, smoke billowing in the background (see Figure 2). Their appearance is marked by standard images of the orient – their heads are covered and they do not wear European dress. This 'othered' these women, seemingly contradicting the emphasis placed on British–Armenian bonds which characterised narratives of the massacres. Such images of mother and child also had religious resonance, evoking images of the Virgin and child. This had a special significance in the case of Armenia, where the massacres were considered a kind of martyrdom.

Another cover image from *The Friend of Armenia* in April 1918 depicted a woman holding a baby, with her children by her sides. All are dressed in rags and the woman and her daughter carry sticks, alluding to the distance they have been forced to travel. The caption reads 'The Aftermath of Massacre'. This image was re-used by the Friends of Armenia at least three times, having first appeared on the cover in spring 1910, to accompany the reports of the Adana massacres, and again in 1914 before the 1918 issue. This re-use highlights the way in which the image of the suffering woman and child came to be a symbolic of the fate of the Armenians. It also perhaps reflects the image of the region as a timeless site of conflict and violence, a place that would be unchanging without European intervention.

Of course, the emphasis on female victimhood in the reporting of the massacres reflected the realities of the situation in Armenia where massacre and deportation was from the very beginning a gendered process. As Eliz Sanasarian has pointed out, almost all accounts of the massacres begin with the separation of the sexes and the killing of the adult male population.[112]

The Turks had first targeted the men – the physically 'stronger' part of the Armenian nation, whilst women, thought to pose less of a threat, were kept alive longer. Women were then subject to different kinds of violence, enduring deportation to the desert and repeated rape and sexual violence. Many women were forced to convert to Islam, or converted to save themselves. Others were taken as the wives of Turks and their children brought up as Turkish Muslims.

Figure 1   Armenia – The Lord Mayor of London Appeals for Help,
Louis Raemakers, 1917

THE

FRIEND OF ARMENIA.

(FOUNDED 1897.)

Organ of the Society of the "Friends of Armenia."

PUBLISHED QUARTERLY.

Office: 47, Victoria Street, Westminster, S.W.1.

Telephone No.: "VICTORIA 1198."

ARMENIA.

London : MARSHALL BROS., Keswick House, Paternoster Row, E.C. 4, and the Society, 47, Victoria St., Westminster, S.W 1

Figure 2   The *Friend of Armenia*, cover illustration, April 1918

Emphasis on female suffering at the hands of the Turks was not unique to the 1915 massacres. In 1894–96, images of Armenian women raped, massacred or forced into Turkish 'harems' had also proliferated. The portrayal of these women reflected the interpretation of the massacres as an attack on a Christian minority.[113] They were portrayed as devout virgins preyed upon by lustful fanatical Turks. Reports of women who committed suicide rather than convert were common. They were portrayed as martyrs for the Christian faith. These images later accompanied narratives of the massacres at Adana in 1909 when *The Friend of Armenia* reported the story of a group of Armenian girls, who, rather than convert, braided their hair together so that they could not be separated and remained inside a burning church. The fate of Armenian women thus provided a potent image of the martyrdom of the nation.[114]

Images of suffering Armenian women which populated accounts of the 1915 massacres resonated with the British population, evoking long-established stereotypes of the lustfulness of the Turk, of polygamy, of persecuted Christians and of oppressed women living as virtual slaves in the harems of the 'oriental' world. Toynbee described women 'exhibited like slaves in a public place . . . and every Moslem inhabitant was allowed to view them and take his choice of them for his harem'.[115] British observers claimed that the fate of Armenian women in 1915 was 'worse' than their fate in previous massacres. However the representation of the massacres through images of female victims did not only relate to these traditions, it also bore a striking similarity to representations of other acts of atrocity, particularly German atrocities in Belgium.

The suffering of women and children was central to most atrocity narratives of this period. 'The images of violence and cruelty were images, primarily, of acts against women, so that the rape and sexual mutilation of women dominated contemporaries' imaginings and representations of the war.' Women and children were portrayed as idealised, innocent victims subjected to acts of cruelty and barbarity by the enemy. Many accounts provided graphic details of humiliation, sexual violence and bodily mutilations. Women's bodies provided 'evidence' of the nature of the enemy: their cruelty, barbarity and 'unnatural' behaviours. This evidence was readily utilised by press and propagandists and recounted in graphic detail in some parts of the press.[116]

Depictions of violence against women not only reflected fears or beliefs about the nature of the enemy. They were also shaped by contemporary discourses of gender and sexuality. Since the 1870s, the ideology of 'separate spheres' had been central to the articulation of different roles for men and women and the concepts of masculinity and femininity. The argument was as follows: 'The womanly woman was gentle, domesticated and virginal: the manly man was athletic, stoical and courageous.'[117] Though the experience of war in part re-shaped such constructions of gender it seems that in the case of atrocity narratives these traditional images and ideals of male and female remained powerful.[118]

It was important that Armenian women matched up to this ideal and therefore their piety, morality and role in the family were stressed. Fulfilling these ideals was not straightforward because Armenian women occupied such an ambivalent position in the British imagination. They were not eastern or Islamic but neither were they accepted as European women. As a result it was found necessary to emphasise that Armenian women were 'like' their British counterparts. It was as if any sense that they were not 'respectable' or moral would devalue their status as victims. *The Times* saw fit to remind their readers that:

> The belief that the Armenians 'do not mind' is a falsehood. The Armenian woman of the country's towns is nowadays often quite well educated and always strictly brought up, and her sufferings are doubtless as great as those of the average English or French farmer's daughter would be were she subjected to similar cruelty.[119]

This particular ideal of femininity also related to other aspects of the representation of Armenian women, creating an image of them as passive victims rather than agents.[120] Although the occasional account of female heroism or survival by a resourceful Armenian girl emerged – usually with the help of western observers – the vast majority of these individuals were depicted as completely powerless, with suicide their only chance to escape from their fate. In fact it seems that suicide was presented as the most virtuous course of action for an Armenian woman faced with conversion or life in a Turkish harem.

One result of this depiction of Armenian women was that individual experience and agency were 'lost' as their sufferings were displayed for the British public. As female victims had their experiences recounted by journalists, missionaries or Armenophiles they were more often than not reduced to a 'type', a vehicle for portraying the sufferings of Armenia.[121] This treatment of female victims continued to shape their fate after the war, as international governments and agencies would dictate what was in their 'best interests'.[122]

The exploitation of female suffering for western audiences is best illustrated by the experience of Aurora Mardiganian. Mardiganian was an

Armenian deportee who managed to escape to the United States where she recounted her experiences to her new American guardians who published them as a book. She was persuaded to play herself in a film version of her experiences, *Ravished Armenia* or *The Auction of Souls*. The film graphically depicted the tortures undergone by Aurora, dwelling on the theme of sexual violence, evoking stereotypical images of the oriental harem and culminating in the crucifixion of Christian girls. The makers of the film professed that their motives were altruistic; however the film was clearly sensationalist in tone with an 'obvious effort by the producer to titillate the audience – to pander to its demand for sex and violence'.[123]

The use of images of women and children in the representation of the Armenian massacres had another important dimension. This related less to discourses of femininity and more to changing perceptions of Armenia itself. Female victims of the massacres thus became symbolic of the national body, martyrs not only for their faith but also for their nation. This conflation of female suffering and national suffering is by no means unusual. National discourses are always gendered and the multiple ways in which gender and national identities intersect is well documented. Women are involved in the construction of the nation in numerous ways, as 'biological producers of members of ethnic collectivities and of the boundaries of ethnic and national groups, as transmitters of culture, as signifiers of ethnic or national differences and symbols of ideological discourses, as participants in national, economic, political and military struggles'.[124]

In the case of the 1915 massacres in Armenia and also in Belgium it is clear that images of raped and mutilated women were used to represent, in a graphic manner, the violation of the nation. Rape and sexual violence represented the transgression of boundaries and the pollution of the nation. In the case of Armenia the image of raped women was a particularly powerful symbol of an attack on the nation because religious and national identities were, in British eyes, so closely entwined. The idea of chaste and pious Armenian women had been central to the British idealisation of Armenia, and the widespread sexual violence accompanying the massacres had breached this vision of religious and national purity.

Women are not only viewed as a repository of national culture or spirit in an abstract sense; they are also viewed as the 'carriers' of the nation in a biological sense. This becomes important in racialised discourses of the nation. In this framework, then, rape poses a threat to national purity and homogeneity whilst the mass killing of women poses a direct threat to the continuity of the race or nation.

Such racialised approaches to the nation were present in representations of the Armenian massacres. The widespread concern that the Armenian people might be 'exterminated' was reflected in the emphasis placed on the fate of mothers and women of childbearing age.[125] Elderly victims of the massacres, in contrast, featured little in accounts of the massacres. There were however innumerable descriptions of women, young girls and children. Assaults on the family were also frequently depicted: 'Very many mothers had been cut to pieces and lay swimming in their blood; wounded children were screaming; little babies of eight to nine months old hung on the breasts of their mothers.'[126] Similarly images of the fate of pregnant women and the killing of unborn children added to fears about the threat to the biological continuity of the Armenians at the hands of the Turks. For example, 'Another witness saw a Turk tear a child out of its Armenian mother's womb and hurl it against the wall.'[127]

The Armenian male population was strikingly absent from the majority of representations of the massacres.[128] This was largely due to the nature of their fate. For a press seeking to provide sensational or shocking material in order to arouse public outrage, the rapid killing of the Armenian male population was of less interest than the prolonged sufferings of women, children and the elderly. If at all, their fate was alluded to relatively briefly; sometimes from the point of view of wives and children and focusing upon their loss and subsequent vulnerability.[129]

However it was deemed important that the British public knew what had happened to the Armenian men. Toynbee described the way in which men were rounded up by the local authorities and, rather than being subjected to deportation, 'halted and massacred at the first lonely place on the road'.[130] In part this sprang from a desire to demonstrate that the massacres were an attempt to 'exterminate' the whole population, not simply a case of Turks preying upon Christian women. It was linked to a desire to demonstrate that Armenian men were not 'weak' and had not failed to defend their wives, children or nation through any fault of their own. Control of their fate had been taken out of their hands.

The passive victimhood which characterised images of Armenian women was incompatible with contemporary constructions of masculinity and definitions of the male role in the nation, especially the nation at war. These constructions of masculinity focused upon the heroic role of men as defenders of the nation and protectors of women and the home.[131] To have failed in this role could be viewed as inadequacy on the part of Armenian manhood. Supporters of the Armenians therefore strove to counter these ideas by emphasising the qualities of Armenian men.

Aneurin Williams of the BAC reported his desire to publish a pamphlet on the 'fighting qualities and virtues of the Armenian race'.[132] Such a pamphlet would both demonstrate the Armenian contribution to the Allied cause and appeal to constructions of the nation in which men were understood as its active agents and defenders.

Such a pamphlet would also have appealed to popular wartime conceptions of masculinity in Britain and created an image of the Armenian man sharing in the characteristics of an 'ideal' British male: courage, physical strength, endurance and so on.[133] This represented part of a desire to 'westernise' or 'Europeanise' Armenians, making them appear fit for a future as a European nation. Concerns about the future of the nation also conditioned the portrayal of Armenian men. Defending the nation was linked to national belonging because, as Joanna Bourke has observed, 'men who were incapable of fighting were not deemed to be worthy of active membership in the wider body politic'.[134] Supporters of the Armenian cause were therefore keen to show that the Armenians had proved their fitness for nationhood through defence of their nation.

Conclusions: national suffering/national futures

The apparent demand for 'proof' of Armenian fitness for nationhood through either the capabilities of males or Armenia's historical achievements was determined at least in part by the way in which the Armenians had been perceived in Britain during previous decades. Even sympathetic British images of the Armenians had not presented them as 'equals' and had been shot through with suspicions about their 'character' or nature. The status of Armenians as victims did not change this situation. Supporters of the Armenian cause were thus keen to utilise images of the massacres to display evidence of their national virtues and potential and dispel possible negative connotations.

Representations of the massacres had drawn selectively upon preexisting images of the Armenians, emphasising 'positive' characteristics such as Christianity and highlighting their cultural proximity. This meant that the 'otherness' of the Armenians had temporarily been set aside; the 'oriental' failings assigned to them in the past were minimised in an effort to claim them as part of the civilised world of the Allies. Nonetheless, the Armenians were still not regarded as fully part of the 'self', but their otherness was expressed and negotiated in new ways.

Although great emphasis had been placed upon Armenian nationhood and the threat to 'national' existence, this did not necessarily entail an acceptance of Armenia into the world of nation states. As the next two chapters will demonstrate, wartime propaganda did not easily map onto the geopolitical realities of the post-war world. Nor did it mean the Armenians would be able to articulate their own agendas or determine their own future. The voicelessness and enforced passivity of female victims in British representations of the massacres would be paralleled by the position of Armenian leaders at the peace conferences. In turn this would also be echoed by the situation of Armenian refugees who found themselves at the mercy of diplomacy and international visions of reconstruction.

Notes

1 For example, Arslanian, 'Britain and the Transcaucasian Nationalities', p. 296, and Nassibian, *Britain and the Armenian Question.*

2 Quoted in Hovannisian, 'The Historical Dimension of the Armenian Question, 1878–1923', p. 30.

3 For oral accounts see D. E. Miller and L. Touryan Miller, eds, *Survivors: An Oral History of the Armenian Genocide* (Berkeley: University of California Press, 1999).

4 On the effects of total war on the Armenian genocide see Jay Winter, 'Under Cover of War: The Armenian Genocide in the Context of Total War', in Winter, *America and the Armenian Genocide of 1915.*

5 News arrived faster in the USA due to continuing diplomatic and missionary presence. An American commission of inquiry into the massacres reported in September 1915. Ambassador Morgenthau sent reports from Constantinople which were gathered from consuls in the interior: see Leslie A. Davis, *The Slaughterhouse Province, An American Diplomat's Report on the Armenian Genocide, 1915–17*, edited by S. K. Blair (New York: A.D. Caratzas, Orpheus Publications, 1989). In America Morgenthau continued to intervene on behalf of the Armenians, and wrote an account of the massacres: H. Morgenthau, *Ambassador Morgenthau's Story* (Detroit: Wayne State University Press, 2003), originally published in 1918 by Doubleday, Page & Co. The massacres were covered in the *New York Times* before they reached the British press: Fein, *Denying Genocide* p. 11. For long-term American support for the Armenian cause see P. Balakian, *The Burning Tigris* (London: William Heinemann, 2004). In Germany the clergyman Johannes Lepsius (who had reported the massacres in the 1890s) published what he had discovered after visiting Constantinople in 1915. He managed to distribute much of his report before it was censored by the German government – it would later reach Britain. Johannes Lepsius, *Le Rapport Secret sur les Massacres d'Arménie* (Paris: Payot, 1917).

6 Nassibian, *Britain and the Armenian Question*, pp. 70–73.
7 See *The Friend of Armenia, Quarterly Journal of the Friends of Armenia*, Vols. 1–61 (1900–1915). This organisation had a long history of corresponding with the American missions in the Ottoman Empire.
8 The Armenian Red Cross and Refugee Fund was launched in January 1915. Its purpose was to provide relief and medical supplies for Armenian volunteers in the Allied armies but it soon extended its activities to refugee relief. See *Armenian Red Cross, Annual Reports 1915–1923*. It emerged from the Armenian Society of London, of which G. W. E. Russell was president.
9 See BAC minute books for details of their work: British and Foreign Anti-Slavery Society Archive, Rhodes House Library, Oxford, G506, British Armenia Committee.
10 Nubar Pasha was the son of an Egyptian government minister. His background gave him access to European diplomatic circles. He was, in Hovannisian's words, 'a polished Levantine gentleman – fluent in French, wealthy and conservative and well known to the European diplomatic corps'. R. Hovannisian, *The Republic of Armenia*, Vol. 1 (Berkley: University of California Press, 1971), p. 257.
11 See Bryce papers, Mss. 201, Correspondence 1915. Bryce was in contact with Nubar Pasha and A. S. Safrastian (who travelled to the Caucasus early in the war) and A. P. Hacobian of the Armenian United Organisation. He was also in contact with missionary organisations. Aneurin Williams, an MP and a prominent member of the BAC was also in touch with a wide range of supporters of the Armenian cause and provided Bryce with information.
12 Bryce was called upon to authenticate information about the Armenian massacres. He is credited in the titles of the American film 'Ravished Armenia' which told the story of a young girl, Aurora Mardiganian who escaped the massacres and fled to America. See Anthony Slide, *Ravished Armenia and the Story of Aurora Mardiganian* (London: The Scarecrow Press, 1997), p. 207.
13 *Hansard*, Parliamentary debates, Lords, 1915, vol. XIX, 3 June–20 October, p. 1002.
14 'Destroying a Nation', *Manchester Guardian* 25 September 1915. The *Manchester Guardian* was particularly supportive of the Armenian cause. The editor, C. P. Scott, sat on the BAC for some time and was a longstanding friend of Bryce.
15 *The Times*, 30 September 1915.
16 See chapter 2.
17 *The Times*, 10 November 1916, quoted in Nassibian, *Britain and the 'Armenian Question'*, p. 107. See also R. Hovannisian, 'The Allies and Armenia, 1915–18', *Journal of Contemporary History*, Vol. 3, No. 1 (January 1968) pp. 147–150.
18 Arslanian, 'Britain and the Transcaucasian Nationalities', p. 296.

19 M. Kent, 'Great Britain and the End of the Ottoman Empire 1900–1923', in M. Kent, ed., *The Great Powers and the End of the Ottoman Empire* (London: Frank Cass, 1996), second edition, p. 185.

20 The Propaganda Bureau was created in September 1914 in an attempt to counter German propaganda. It was headed by the Liberal MP Charles Masterman. Masterman was in close contact with Archbishop Charles Gore, another supporter of the Armenian cause. See G. Messinger, *British Propaganda and the State in the First World War* (Manchester: Manchester University Press, 1992) and Cate Haste, *Keep the Home Fires Burning* (London: Allen Lane, 1977).

21 Toynbee was a young historian from Oxford employed by the Government Propaganda Bureau. In October 1915 he was asked to work on *The Treatment of the Armenians* with Viscount Bryce. See A. Toynbee, *Acquaintances* (London: Oxford University Press, 1967) for further information. Toynbee became a strong supporter of the Armenian cause but would later on reassess his condemnations of the Turks.

22 NA FO 96/205, Toynbee: Armenian Correspondence Nov 1915–March 1916, letter from Toynbee to Barton, 1 February 1916.

23 These letters were provided by Professor Gilbert Murray (Toynbee's father-in-law, Oxford professor and supporter of the League of Nations), the historian and later biographer of Bryce, H. A. L. Fisher and Mr Moorfield Storey, ex-president of the American Bar Association.

24 NA FO 96/205, Toynbee: Armenian Correspondence, November 1915–March 1916.

25 Bryce and Toynbee, *The Treatment of the Armenians*, p. xxxi.

26 Ibid., Preface.

27 MSS Bryce 202, Files Relating to Armenia, Correspondence January–June 1916, letter from Masterman to Bryce, 14 June 1906, p. 152.

28 NA FO 96/206 Toynbee: Armenian Correspondence 12 August 1916–14 December 1916, copy of letter, Toynbee to Bryce. Toynbee later distanced himself from the 'propaganda' dimension, stating that neither he nor Bryce would have been as keen to work on the volume had they been aware of this at the time. See *Acquaintances*.

29 These issues are discussed in chapters 4 and 5.

30 Co-operation of this nature was not unusual, Messinger points out: 'The most conspicuous feature of British propaganda at the start of the Great War appears to be the extreme care taken by the British, even more than was the case in other nations, to let non-governmental sources do the work of opinion manipulation that the Government wanted done.' Messinger, *British Propaganda*, p. 23. Nassibian describes the way the Government shared its information regarding the massacres: Nassibian, *Britain and the Armenian Question*, pp. 83–85.

31 NA FO 96/206, Toynbee: Armenian Correspondence 12 August 1916–14 December 1916.

32 *Hansard*, Parliamentary debates, Lords, 1915, vol. XIX, 3 June–20 October, p. 1003.
33 Individuals who had campaigned about the events in Armenia were also involved in humanitarian causes elsewhere – transferring the concepts, categories and language which they used between 'causes'.
34 Esther Mugerditchian, *From Turkish Toils: The Narrative of One Family's Escape* (London: C. Arthur Pearson, 1918), p. 15.
35 See chapter 2.
36 Mgr F. de Pons at the International Conference on Macedonia at Caxton Hall. Quoted in *The Friend of Armenia*, No. 17 (Spring 1904), p. 3.
37 See Todorova, *Imagining the Balkans*, Introduction.
38 Bryce and Toynbee, *The Treatment of the Armenians*, p. xxvi.
39 Mazower has pointed out that the former Ottoman Empire is still regarded as a place locked into ancient hatreds, that the Balkan wars of the 1990s were 'the latest in a series of massacres and counter massacres which according to them constituted the stuff of Balkan history'. 'The conflict in Bosnia', British premier John Major stated in 1993, 'was a product of impersonal and inevitable forces beyond anyone's control.' A century earlier the French foreign Minister Hantaux had similarly termed anti-Armenian massacres in Anatolia as 'one of those thousand incidents of struggle between Christians and Muslims'. Mazower, *The Balkans*, p. 43.
40 Winter suggests that a lack of understanding of the region was one reason for inaction: 'Besides, western European attitudes were marked by massive ignorance deep enough to lump together Armenian Christians and Turkish Muslims in one undifferentiated mass of people who – supposedly wise heads nodded – share eternal and uncompromising hatreds.' I would suggest that a lack of knowledge amongst the general population encouraged the Armenophiles to try to inform them about the Armenians. This task was made easier because of the history of British interventions in Armenia and pre-existing images of the Armenians as persecuted Christians. Winter, *America and the Armenian Genocide of 1915*, p. 2.
41 Cavell was a British nurse working in Belgium who was executed by the Germans on 12 October 1915. Her execution was widely exploited for propaganda. The image of Cavell as an innocent young woman dying at the hands of a barbaric enemy echoes the representation of female victims of the Armenian massacres.
42 G. Best, *War and Law since 1945* (Oxford: Clarendon Press, 1994), pp. 44–48.
43 N. Gullace, 'Sexual Violence and Family Honor: British Propaganda and International Law during the First World War', *American Historical Review*, Vol. 102, No. 3 (June 1997), p. 734. See also Gullace, *The Blood of Our Sons: Men, Women and the Renegotiation of Citizenship during the Great War* (Baingstoke: Palgrave, 2002).
44 For example, A. Ponsonby, *Falsehood in Wartime: Containing an Assortment*

of Lies Circulated throughout the Nations during the Great War (Sudbury: Bloomfield, 1991), reprinted from 1928 edition.

45 J. Horne and A. Kramer, *German Atrocities: A History of Denial* (London and New Haven: Yale University Press, 2001), p. 430.

46 Ibid., p. 201.

47 Bryce's report was based on the testimony of British and Belgian soldiers and refugees. It concluded that Germany was guilty of breaking the Hague conventions; committing widespread atrocities against non-combatants, including rape, mutilation, murder of civilians, robbery and destruction of property. The Bryce Commission was subsequently castigated for failing to investigate and verify the evidence properly.

48 T. Wilson, 'Lord Bryce's Investigation into the German Atrocities in Belgium 1914–15', *Journal of Contemporary History*, Vol. 14, No. 3 (July 1979), p. 369. See also K. Robbins, ed., *Political Diplomacy and War in Modern British History* (London: Hambledon Press, 1994).

49 J. H. Morgan, *German Atrocities: An Official Investigation* (London: T. Fisher Unwin, 1916), p. 57.

50 *Hansard*, Parliamentary debates, Lords, 1915, vol. XIX, 3 June–20 October 1915, p. 774.

51 Gullace shows these images were a powerful way of illustrating what was at stake in the war: 'Images of mutilated children and violated women were much more effective than the idea of broken treaties in rousing public sympathies. Regardless of the actual flexibility of the written rules of war, the humanitarian public was rigid in its ideas of right and wrong. British propagandists exploited this knowledge when they crafted an evocative image of international law suitable for arousing public feeling during a war increasingly understood in terms of violence against women and children.' She also points out that such imagery portrayed the enemy as a threat to the idea of the family, the 'civilised' social order and British values. Gullace, 'Sexual Violence and Family Honor', p. 734.

52 Dr M. Niepage, *The Horrors of Aleppo . . . Seen by a German Eye-Witness* (London: T. Fisher Unwin Ltd., 1917). The image of children with severed hands first appeared in reports of the Belgian Congo atrocities.

53 J. Bryce, *The Attitude of Great Britain in the Present War* (London: Macmillan and Co., 1916).

54 Bryce and Toynbee, *The Treatment of the Armenians*, p. 606.

55 Bryce, *Attitude of Great Britain*, p. 15.

56 Ibid., p. 15.

57 A. J. Toynbee, *Turkey: A Past and a Future* (London: Hodder & Stoughton, 1917), p. 9. The need to bring to an end the Ottoman Empire was a recurring theme in the propaganda pamphlets produced by Toynbee for the government; see Toynbee, *The Murderous Tyranny of the Turks* (London: Hodder & Stoughton, 1917).

58 Bryce, Preface to A. J. Toynbee, *Armenian Atrocities: The Murder of a Nation* (London: Hodder & Stoughton, 1915), p. 7.

59 *Manchester Guardian*, 18 October 1915 (report on service commemorating the massacres in Manchester Cathedral).

60 Bryce, *Attitude of Great Britain*, p. 15.

61 Morgan, *German Atrocities*, p. 31.

62 W. L. Williams, *Armenia: Past and Present: A Study and Forecast*, With an Introduction by T. P. O'Connor MP (London: P. S. King and Son, Ltd., 1916), p.vi.

63 *Manchester Guardian*, 11 September 1915.

64 *The Times*, 24 August 1916, p. 6.

65 E. F. Benson suggested 'Germany – official Germany – knew all about them and she permitted them to go on.' Benson, *Crescent and Iron Cross* (London: Hodder and Stoughton, London, 1918), p. 195. The extent to which the German authorities were complicit in carrying out or planning the massacres is still highly contested. For one viewpoint see V. N. Dadrian, *German Responsibility in the Armenian Genocide: A Review of the Historical Evidence of German Complicity* (Watertown, MA: Blue Crane Books, 1996).

66 See, for example, see 'Foreword' in Mugerditchian, *From Turkish Toils*.

67 *The Times*, 30 September 1915.

68 Toynbee, *Turkey: A Past and a Future*, p. 22. For modern perspectives on the planning and development of the genocidal policy see Bloxham, 'The Armenian Genocide of 1915–16'.

69 *The Times*, 8 October 1915.

70 On recognition of the massacres as genocide see the introduction. In this chapter I use 'massacres' to avoid confusion as it was the word used in the contemporary reports I am discussing. It is not intended to imply that they should not be considered genocide.

71 Fein, *Denying Genocide*, p. 11.

72 'Any part of the following acts committed with intent to destroy, in whole or in part, a national, ethnical, racial or religious group, as such: A. Killing members of the Group, B. Causing serious bodily or mental harm to members of the group, C. Deliberately inflicting upon the group conditions of life calculated to bring about its physical destruction in whole or in part, D. Imposing measures intended to prevent births within the group, E. Forcibly transferring the children of the group to another group.' Quoted in Samantha Power, *A Problem From Hell*, chapter 1, Race Murder.

73 On contemporary terminology in America, M. Housepian-Dobkin, 'What Genocide, What Holocaust? News From Turkey, 1915–1923: A Case Study', in Hovannisian, *Armenian Genocide in Perspective*.

74 Bryce and Toynbee, *The Treatment of the Armenians*, Preface, p.xxi.

75 *The Times*, 8 October 1915.

76 L. Kuper, 'The Turkish Genocide of the Armenians 1915–17', in Hovannisian, *Armenian Genocide in Perspective*, p. 55.

77 Hovannisian, *The Armenian Genocide: History, Politics, Ethics*, p. xvii.

78 A. P. Hacobian, *Armenia and the War* (London: Hodder & Stoughton, 1917), p.xxi. Pan-Turkism was an ideology espoused by the Young Turks. It differed from the more tolerant ideology of pan-Ottomanism which allowed for religious or racial diversity in that it focused upon the creation of a homogenous Turkish nation stretching across Asia. Great importance was attached to ethnic and religious homogeneity (unlike pan-Islamism which focused solely on religious identities). The Armenians therefore did not 'fit in' to this agenda. See R. Melson, 'Provocation or Nationalism, A Critical Enquiry into the Armenian Genocide of 1915', in Hovannisian, *Armenian Genocide in Perspective*, pp. 74–79, Bernard Lewis, *The Emergence of Modern Turkey* (Oxford: Oxford University Press, 1961) and Somakian, *Empires in Conflict*, chapter 2.

79 LMF, *The Martyrdom of a Nation*, included in Mss. Bryce 209, Fol. 123.

80 Toynbee, *Turkey: A Past and a Future*, p. 30.

81 On photographs of the genocide see T. Hofmann and G. Koutcharian, 'Images that Horrify and Indict: Pictorial Documents on the Persecution and Extermination of Armenians from 1877–1922', *Armenian Review*, 45, 1–2 (1992). Particularly important are the photographs taken by the German soldier Armin T. Wegner at the Armenian camps in the Middle East in the summer of 1915. Wegner was able to send some of his work to Germany and the USA, but he was arrested and returned to Germany in 1916.

82 See eye-witness evidence in Bryce and Toynbee, *The Treatment of the Armenians*.

83 P. Clarke, *Hope and Glory: Britain 1900–1990* (London: Penguin, 1996), p. 72.

84 Bentley suggests that Belgium was used by Liberal Anti-war politicians 'as a convenient opportunity to change their stance, once it became clear that Asquith was not going to fall.' Michael Bentley, *The Liberal Mind 1914–1929* (Cambridge: Cambridge University Press, 1977), p. 17.

85 Horne and Kramer, *German Atrocities*, p. 235.

86 Mazower highlights British support for Balkan nationalism, '"The Allied powers"', stated the British Foreign Secretary in June 1915, "hope that as a result of the war, the political balance in the Balkans will be established on a broader and more national basis." Mazower, *The Balkans*, p. 113.

87 A fund for Serbian relief was created by the scholar R. W. Seton-Watson. Organisations to assist the Belgian refugees who had fled to Britain were also established. See P. Calahan, *Belgian Refugee Relief in England during the First World War* (New York: Garland, 1982).

88 *The Friend of Armenia*, No. 61 (June 1915), p. 10.

89 Bryce and Toynbee, *The Treatment of the Armenians*, p. 75. An LMF pamphlet, *The Martyrdom of a Nation*, also claimed that 'no nation has suffered from the War as Armenia has suffered'.

90 *The Friend of Armenia*, No. 63 (April 1916), p. 15. Morgan Philips-Price's report was widely reprinted.
91 Williams, *Armenia: Past and Present*, p. 159.
92 Bliss, *Turkey and the Armenian Atrocities*, p. 344.
93 Ibid., p. 558.
94 A number of books which dealt with Armenian history, culture or religion were produced, during the peace conferences, with the aim of swaying public and political opinion in favour of an Armenian nation state.
95 Bryce and Toynbee were historians; this may in part explain the emphasis placed on the Armenian past in British publications regarding the Armenian massacres. Often the prefaces Bryce provided for books or pamphlets made reference to Armenian history even if the main body of the work did not.
96 E. J. Robinson, *Armenia and the Armenians* (1917).
97 Robinson, *Armenia*, and see also her earlier pamphlet, *The Truth about Armenia* (1913).
98 Williams, *Armenia Past and Present*, p. 117.
99 T. C. Leonard, 'When News Media is Not Enough: American Media and Armenian Deaths', in Winter, *America and the Armenian Genocide of 1915*, p. 304.
100 R. Harris, 'The "Child of the Barbarian": Rape, Race and Nationalism in France during the First World War', *Past and Present*, No. 141 (November 1993), p. 175.
101 This report was widely circulated though unconfirmed.
102 Toynbee, *Murderous Tyranny*, p. 14.
103 Bryce and Toynbee, *The Treatment of the Armenians*, p. 15.
104 Ibid, p. 95.
105 D. Kouymjian, 'Confiscation and Destruction: A Manifestation of the Genocidal Process', *Armenian Forum*, 1, Vol. 3 (Autumn 1998). See also D. Kouymjian, 'Destruction des Monuments Historiques Arméniens, Poursuite de la Politique Turque Du Génocide', in Tribunal Permanent des Peuples, *Le Crime de Silence. Le Génocide des Arméniens* (Paris: Flammarion, 1984).
106 For the protection the medieval manuscripts of Etchmiadzin from the Turkish advance see A. Simcowantz, 'The Etchmiadzin Manuscripts during the First World War', *Armenian Review*, Vol. 36, No. 4, (1983).
107 *Manchester Guardian*, 7 October 1915, p. 5.
108 Leonard, 'When News Media is not Enough', p. 31.
109 On Ani, see chapter 2.
110 Horne and Kramer, *German Atrocities*, p. 218. The issue of cultural heritage and its destruction as a policy in wartime remains significant in the modern Armenian Republic, particularly as a result of the war with Azerbaijan over Nagorno-Karabagh: see Kohl and Tsetskhladze, 'Nationalism, Politics and the Practice of Archaeology' and Dolukhanov, 'Archaeology and Nationalism'.

111 This incident was detailed in Bryce and Toynbee, *The Treatment of the Armenians*, p. 292. The Italian consul-general described Armenians 'placed by hundreds on board ship in nothing but their shirts and then capsized and drowned in the Black Sea and the river Deyirmen Dere'.

112 Eliz Sanasarian, 'Gender Distinction in the Genocidal Process, A Preliminary Study of the Armenian Case', *Holocaust and Genocide Studies*, Vol. 4, No. 4 (1989).

113 Emphasis on religion may also have been a product of the attitudes of those who reported the massacres. Many reports came from missionaries who supported the Armenian cause as a Christian duty.

114 *The Friend of Armenia*, No. 38 (Summer 1909), p. 13.

115 Bryce and Toynbee, *The Treatment of the Armenians*, p. 643.

116 S. Kingsley-Kent, *Making Peace: The Reconstruction of Gender in Inter-War Britain* (Princeton: Princeton University Press, 1993) p. 25. Kent highlights the way in which the depiction of atrocities reinforced traditional constructs of gender identity: 'The reassertion of traditional norms of masculinity and femininity and of separate spheres for men and women found expression in the efforts to legitimise and justify the war itself' (p. 22).

117 J. Bourke, *Dismembering the Male. Men's Bodies, Britain and the Great War* (London: Reaktion Books, 1996), p. 13.

118 The experience or war could transform or reinforce constructions of gender: 'war must be understood as a gendering activity, one that ritually marks the gender of all members of a society, whether or not they were combatants'. 'Introduction', in M. Higonnet, J. Jenson, S. Michel and M. Collins-Weitz, eds, *Behind the Lines, Gender and the Two World Wars* (London: Yale University Press, 1987), p. 4.

119 *The Times*, 8 October 1915. Other accounts stressed that Armenian women were educated or prosperous, living in comfortable homes. The pamphlet which recounts the story of the escape of Esther Mugerditchian stresses that before the massacres she and her family lived a 'normal' family life, more similar to the domestic arrangements of Britain that the stereotypical image of the Turkish harem. Mugerditchian, *From Turkish Toils*.

120 Ronit Lentin highlights the problems in defining women as a homogenous group of 'victims': 'Viewing women as homogenously powerless and as implicit victims does not allow us to theorize women as the benefactors of oppression or the perpetrators of catastrophes, which in turn makes it impossible to understand/challenge domination.' Lentin, *Gender and Catastrophe* (London: Zed Books, 1997), pp. 11–12.

121 Harris suggests that it is men's fantasies and anxieties rather than the experience of women that shapes discussions over sexual violation and the war. Harris, 'Child of the Barbarian', p. 175.

122 On refugee women see chapter 4.

123 Slide, *Ravished Armenia*, p. 13. Afterwards Mardiganian was unable to cope

with the demands placed upon her. The film was screened in 1919 in the USA and later that year in Britain where the League of Nations arranged for twice-daily screenings at the Albert Hall for three weeks. In Britain there were problems with censorship and the crucifixion scene was cut.

124 Lentin, *Gender and Catastrophe*, p. 9.

125 Pat Thane states 'Fears about race and empire created a rhetoric than more explicitly than before identified women with the role of preserving, perpetuating and enhancing the physical quality, and the numbers of the race in their role as mothers and, more mystical, embodying the essence of each race as its physical conduit to the next generation.' Thane, 'The British Imperial State and the Construction of National Identities' in B. Melman, ed., *Borderlines, Genders and Identities in War and Peace* (London: Routledge, 1998), p. 31.

126 Mugerditchian, *From Turkish Toils*, p. 31.

127 Niepage, *Horrors of Aleppo*, p. 13. This kind of incident represented the enemy's willingness to attack the most defenceless.

128 The men who do appear in accounts of the massacres are the Armenian clergy. Attacks on the clergy had a dual significance, representing not only an attack on the individual but also an attack on the Church and nation. The depiction of the sufferings of the male clergy seems to have been regarded as acceptable as these men were not expected to share in the same masculine characteristics as the male population in general.

129 This is the theme of Mugerditchian's *From Turkish Toils*, which describes a family's fate after the father is taken away.

130 For a more comprehensive description see Bryce and Toynbee, *The Treatment of the Armenians*, pp. 638–641.

131 See J. Horne, 'Masculinity and Politics in the Age of Nation-States and World Wars', in S. Dudink, K. Hagemann and J. Tosh, eds, *Masculinities in Politics and War: Gendering Modern History* (Manchester: Manchester University Press, 2004). Horne refers to 'a powerful myth that portrayed the army as a direct expression of the nation' (p. 28). See also Michael Roper, 'Between Manliness and Masculinity: The War Generation and the Psychology of Fear in Britain 1914–1915', *Journal of British Studies*, Vol. 44, No. 2 (April 2005), p. 343.

132 BAC Minute Books, 1915–1935.

133 Melman observes the importance of certain conceptions of masculinity for wartime culture more generally, 'Male purity, identified with heterosexuality, masculinity and valour in Battle – was central to the propaganda, and popular iconography of all belligerent powers.' B. Melman, 'Introduction', in Melman, *Borderlines*, p. 10.

134 Bourke, *Dismembering the Male*, p. 77.

4

Armenian refugees:
representation, relief and repatriation

Introduction

By October 1918, when the Mudros armistice brought about a fragile peace between the Ottoman Empire and Britain, the Armenian population of Anatolia had already been decimated. Hundreds of thousands of Armenians had been executed or died as a result of the terrible conditions on mass deportations through the desert. Armenian refugees who managed to escape the deportations and massacres were dispersed across the Middle East, Transcaucasia and Eastern Europe. From May 1918, a small independent Armenian Republic led a precarious existence in Transcaucasia, struggling to cope with the continuing influx of refugees and to defend itself against Turkish aggression. Though the very existence of the republic was a powerful symbol of Armenian national survival, its future was by no means guaranteed.[1]

The 'Armenian question' remained unresolved. In particular the future of the thousands of displaced Armenians became a matter for international debate.[2] Meanwhile, Armenians in the Transcaucasian Republic and the diaspora tried desperately to salvage something from the tragedy, attempting to convince the rest of the world of the need for the creation of an independent Armenian state. British Armenophiles continued to support the Armenian cause, turning their attention to both the fate of the displaced and the broader question of the future of the nation.

This chapter examines humanitarian responses to the post-war predicament of the Armenians and to population displacement on an unprecedented scale. The first section concerns the image of the Armenian refugee, focusing upon the gendering of representations of the displaced and its implications, and the representation of Armenian refugees as a 'problem' population in need of moral as well as material intervention.

The second part of the chapter concerns the practice of refugee relief, and the attempts of humanitarian and Armenophile organisations to provide emergency relief and safeguard the future of the refugees. Their response to the Armenian refugee crisis sheds light on the development of new international approaches to population displacement in the post-war period. The case of Armenia thus offers the opportunity to examine the perceptions and motivations underpinning humanitarian intervention.

As will become clear, solving the Armenian refugee crisis was framed as a process of preserving and protecting an 'endangered' nation, a process thought to encompass both concern over the biological continuity of the Armenian 'race' and the desire to return Armenians to their 'homeland'. The refugee crisis and subsequent attempts to manage displacement had long-term consequences, playing a significant role in shaping the future development of both Soviet Armenia and the Armenian diaspora.

Post-war settlements and the Armenian refugees

By the end of the war, eastern Anatolia had been systematically 'emptied' of its Armenian population. Only a few pockets of survivors remained in regions which had been spared the massacres and deportations, for example Constantinople. The cessation of systematic programmes of massacre and deportation however did not herald an immediate improvement in the situation of the Armenians. For survivors of the deportation marches, the situation at their destinations, makeshift camps in the Middle East, was dire. There was little food, shelter or sanitation. Disease and starvation were rife and Armenians continued to perish.[3] Even for those who had reached refugee camps conditions were often dire as the authorities were completely overwhelmed by the crisis. For example, the British High Commission at Constantinople reported in November 1919 that at the nearby Haider Pasha refugee camp 'men women and children were huddled into tents until there was hardly room to move, the decencies could not be preserved and in wet weather the whole place was deep in mud'.[4]

For the refugees from eastern Anatolia who had reached Transcaucasia the situation was often little better.[5] Armenian refugees had begun to arrive here soon after the deportations began in 1915, hoping to find safety from Turkish attacks in this Russian-controlled region. Hopes for the swift repatriation of these refugees to their former homes in Anatolia had been raised as the Russians had advanced into Turkey in 1915–16, but this had soon given way to the realities of a prolonged refugee crisis, with the attendant problems of starvation and disease. The Russian revolutions of 1917, though initially offering hope to the Armenian nationalist aspirations, ultimately compounded their plight.[6] As the Caucasian front collapsed and the Bolsheviks made peace with the Ottoman Empire, the Armenians in Transcaucasia once again became vulnerable to Turkish attack. In early 1918 the Turks broke the armistice and advanced towards Transcaucasia and by April the Armenian city of Kars had been captured.

In the face of a renewed Turkish advance, coupled with Russian collapse, the embryonic states of Georgia, Armenia and Azerbaijan saw little other choice than to form a Transcaucasian Federation.[7] This short-lived alliance was fraught with difficulties. After Georgia and Azerbaijan quickly abandoned the federation the Armenians, struggling to hold back the Turkish advance, were left with no choice other than to declare their own independence.[8] On 28 May 1918 the Armenian Republic was created, with its capital in Yerevan and under the control of the Dashnak party.[9] The existence of this independent Armenian Republic provided hope, a 'basis for a vision of survival' for the Armenian people, yet it faced enormous difficulties.[10] In October 1918 the defeat of the Ottoman Empire and the Mudros armistice finally gave some respite to this small, beleaguered state.

The Armenian Republic had been forged in the crisis that engulfed Transcaucasia at the end of the war and represented a desperate attempt to salvage and protect what remained of Armenia and the Armenians. It occupied only a small part of the land regarded as 'historic Armenia' and was home to only a fraction of the population. Its capital, Yerevan, did not live up to the standards of the traditional home of Armenian intellectuals and elites, Tbilisi. As such the republic could not live up to the grand aspirations of many the Armenian nationalists who dreamed of a reconstructed 'greater Armenian' nation. The conflicts that this situation would cause and its long-term consequences are examined further in the following chapter.

Besides providing a focus for national hopes, the Armenian Republic was also the site of a serious refugee crisis. The surrender of the Ottoman Empire in October 1918 and the armistice did nothing to ease this crisis which became acute over the winter of 1918 as famine and typhus hit.[11] In these difficult circumstances the under-resourced and ill-prepared republic struggled to survive. As diplomatic wrangling over the future of the region began, around 300,000 refugees remained stranded in

Transcaucasia, unable to return to their homes. Around 285,000 more Armenians found themselves in the Middle East.[12] These refugees were dependent for their survival upon the goodwill of the surrounding populations and international aid. In Transcaucasia the native Armenian population had organised relief since the start of the war, but they struggled to cope with the scale of the crisis, and also came to depend upon international help.

The image of the Armenian refugee: victimhood and voicelessness

The figure of the Armenian refugee fleeing Turkish violence had become familiar to the British public over the course of the war. Representations of the Armenian refugee, most often a mother with children, dressed in rags and carrying a few miserable possessions, were frequently exploited to tug at the heartstrings of the British public, evoking a sympathetic and hopefully charitable response. In this respect the Armenians were not alone. The entire war had been characterised by mass population displacement. As populations fled violence and national boundaries were drawn and re-drawn, Serbs, Poles and Belgians all entered the British imagination as refugees, populating the innumerable publications of charitable appeals and propaganda campaigns.

Images of the displaced, stressing their status as the victims of enemy violence, were a key feature of British war propaganda. These propaganda images stressed the status of the refugee as victim, emphasising helplessness and innocence. In the case of the Armenians, the refugees were incorporated into a narrative of national and religious martyrdom at the hands of a barbaric Turkish enemy. Yet these propaganda images reveal only one dimension of the British image of the Armenian refugee, an image which was in reality complex and multilayered, shaped by fear and hostility as well as empathy and compassion.

Such images of Armenian suffering often masked or homogenised the experiences of Armenian refugees. Peter Loizos has pointed that out approaches to refugees have been and are still often underpinned by assumptions of universal victimhood and 'helplessness'.[13] These kinds of assumptions have the effect of rendering refugees voiceless and failing to take account of individual experience or agency. This means that the displaced 'cease in the narratives of both contemporaries and historians, to play the role of active historical agents'.[14]

It is important to recognise then, that the images of Armenian refugees which appeared in the press and the propaganda of governments and humanitarian organisations were based on external perceptions which drew upon emerging assumptions and stereotypes of the displaced. They were deployed to evoke particular types of response from the British public rather than to acknowledge or to accurately reflect the experiences of the Armenian refugees or the realities of refugeedom.

Gender and the Armenian refugee

Representations of the refugee, like those of atrocity and massacre, were gendered. In the Armenian case this gendering of refugee images drew upon the stereotypes of Christian female virtue and the assumptions about Turkish tendencies to sexual violence that have been discussed in previous chapters. Being forced from the family home and having to survive deportations with little food, shelter or clothing was seen as particularly dangerous and difficult for women, especially mothers. Being outside the safety of the home and deprived of the protection of husbands or fathers Armenian women were thought to be extremely vulnerable to violence, particularly of a sexual nature. The feminisation of Armenian suffering and victimhood also continued to be a dominant theme in the representation of displacement long after the deportations and massacres had ended.

For humanitarian agencies the image of the female refugee and particularly of the mother and child represented a timeless and universal figure of victimhood and powerlessness.[15] Even though after the initial waves of violence and deportation had ended representations of Armenian women changed, the image of female refugees would still be permeated by the theme of vulnerability. Although the imminent danger of enemy attack had passed, the condition of refugeedom was still thought to pose an innate physical, mental and moral threat to women.

Such views conditioned the types of relief undertaken with refugee women and helped shape the belief that it was the relief agencies rather than the women themselves who were best equipped to decide their future. This was important as a central part of the programme of refugee relief was the reclamation of women who had been abducted or bought into Muslim homes and forced to convert to Islam, and children in Turkish homes and orphanages who had been given Turkish identities. This had been a concern since early in the war. In summer 1916 for example, the BAC had expressed concerns about the 'sale' of Armenian girls. However, until the war had ended and the Allies could gain access to the areas where such 'sales' were alleged to have taken place, little action could be taken.[16]

In 1920 a co-ordinated attempt to resolve the problem of 'stolen' Armenian women and children was made when the League of Nations established a Commission of Inquiry for the Protection of Women and Children in the Near East. In Aleppo, Karen Jeppe, a Danish missionary, led the work of the commission. In Constantinople its work was initially carried out by an NER officer, Emma Cushman, and Dr W. A. Kennedy, a British doctor.[17] Their work consisted of the 'rescue' of women and children taken into Turkish homes who would then be brought to a 'neutral house'. From there, it was hoped, their original identities would be determined and they would be returned to their families, adopted, encouraged to emigrate or given hospital treatment.[18] In Constantinople, Cushman and Kennedy worked with women and children of all nationalities, whilst in Aleppo, Jeppe focused solely on the Armenians.

The League continued to support the work of the Commissions until 1927; thereafter the work of Jeppe in Aleppo was supported by voluntary organisations including the Friends of Armenia and LMF. The length of time this work continued testified to the scale of the problem. In 1930 the British journal *Slave Market News* (associated with the Anti-Slavery and Aborigines Protection Society) was still featuring images and stories of 'Armenian girls saved from foul captivity', though by this stage British concern for the Armenians had declined and their fate was only of interest to a small sector of the British population.[19]

The importance attached to the rescue of Armenian women and children stemmed at least in part from the gendered manner in which the massacres had been carried out.[20] It was also a product of public perceptions of the massacres and deportations and the depiction in press and propaganda of these events as the martyrdom of Armenian women. In representations of the experience of deportation, Armenian women had been portrayed as particularly vulnerable, not only to violence, but also to mental breakdown. Esther Mugerditchian was amongst those who reported witnessing 'maddened mothers and women'.[21] The idea of rescue and reclamation was therefore imagined as a kind of antidote, administering care to those women who could no longer look after themselves.

The fate of these women was represented in terms of orientalist images which were already embedded in the public imagination: slavery, polygamy and the harem. The harem was re-imagined only as a site of cruelty, oppression and corruption. The idea of a Christian woman having to endure life in a harem where she would be 'brutalised by degrees – blows and caresses, opium and persuasion are used in turn', was thought by many western observers to be intolerable.[22] Toynbee described the 'living death of marriage to a Turk and inclusion in his harem'.[23] Their rescue provided a dramatic and heroic narrative, which not only demonstrated Armenian survival but also highlighted the continued barbarity of the enemy, underlining the argument that the Turks should not rule over the Armenians.

The kind of attention accorded Armenian women and children was not at all unusual. As Peter Gatrell has pointed out, 'when publicity was given to gender, it tended to emphasize the need to protect feminine virtue, to sustain women's duties relating to motherhood and domesticity, or to draw attention to the vulnerable female psyche'. Male refugees, in contrast, were notably absent, as Gatrell goes on to point out: 'To maintain silence on this score may have been a deliberate device to draw a veil over the de-masculinisation of the male refugee.'[24] Just as male victims were absent from British representations of violence and suffering, so they were absent from narratives of refugee relief. In the context of post-war Armenia, the supporters of the Armenian cause highlighted the contributions of Armenian men to the war effort, their 'fighting qualities' and their potential capacities as nation-builders rather than their place as the recipients of charity.

The rescue of women and children became an attempt to restore the norms of family life and gender roles in the aftermath of violent dislocation. It reflected a desire to restore and rebuild the nation. Although the commissions saw themselves in apolitical and purely 'humanitarian' terms, framing rescue in national terms inevitably gave their work a political dimension.[25] Besides, the deportations and massacres were widely thought of as an attempt at 'extermination', which drew attention to the importance of women as the 'root and stem of the race'.[26] The project of reclaiming women underscored their role in the biological reproduction of the nation.[27]

The desire to prevent the Armenian population from diminishing further also encouraged efforts to rescue Armenian children from Turkish homes and orphanages. Children were brought to the 'neutral house' in order to establish their original ethnic identity. Once this had been determined the commissioners believed the children could relearn how to be Armenian: 'In these American houses, rescued children once again learned the Armenian language and sang Armenian hymns.'[28] This was by no means a straightforward task because the children had not only been wrenched from their homes but had also begun to form new emotional attachments. However, Armenian patriots and their sympathisers made it a priority to 'restore' their identity.[29]

The problems of rescue were very real. In addition to the difficulties of locating Armenians the reluctance of some to be rescued posed another challenge. Jeppe hoped the difficulties of rescuing children who had been taken into nomadic families would be resolved through the ineradicable 'Armenianness' of the refugees: 'After all, they could not forget their people and their faith and the whole spiritual atmosphere that was their birthright.'[30] When working with women this problem was intensified. Some were reluctant to leave their new surroundings, because of fear or because of bonds they had established in their new surroundings, especially if they had borne children in their new setting. Jeppe stressed that these women had to decide for themselves whether they would leave the houses where they were detained or not.[31]

The choice to remain in Muslim households was evidently not uncommon. Mary Caroline Holmes, a relief worker at the Urfa Orphanage in the south-east of the empire, reported that 'quite as often as not, they do not wish to leave their Moslem men, are happy and contented and to my mind quite as well off as with men of their own race'. This was not however the statement of support for the Armenian women that it may seem. The choice made by Armenian women was for Mary Holmes just yet another thing which contributed to her 'disappointment' with the Armenians and her views that in their bad habits, 'lying, deceit, thieving, blackmail . . .' they were no different from the other races they lived among. Others were less fiercely critical, and presented choosing to stay as a tragedy: 'There are cases, but thank God they are rare, where these unhappy women return voluntarily to their bondage. All Turks are not wicked and often they treat their victims with cruel gentleness.'[32]

This statement reinforces the difficulty of overcoming the image of Armenian women as passive victims. Within these narratives of victimhood and rescue, epitomised by the story of Aurora Mardiganian, individual experience was subsumed. This left little space for the refugee women to articulate their own experiences or desires as exemplified in Donald Miller and Lorna Touryan Miller's collection of oral histories of the genocide: 'A survivor told us, "I had girlfriends who had married Turks. They used to say 'I want my effendi.' They wanted their husbands. They had a comfortable life."'[33] However, personal choices do not seem to have been a priority. Women were thought to be in need of protection and it was assumed that the experience of deportation and violence had rendered them less able than ever to determine what was in their own interests. Many relief workers, it seems, therefore felt able to make their own judgements.[34]

Refugees as a 'problem' population

Although an emphasis on female suffering remained, during the post-war period the image of the Armenian refugee presented to the British public changed. The image of the Armenian fleeing Turkish violence became less prevalent and focus shifted to the long-term effects of population displacement. There was clearly a need for relief agencies to demonstrate to the public that the end of the war had not lessened the plight of the Armenians. Public appeals warned of the problems of starvation and disease facing the Armenians. At the same time those working on behalf of the Armenians sought to counter negative images and suspicion of the refugees, emphasising that they were 'deserving' of British support. However, whilst charitable appeals strove to create sympathetic images of the Armenians, official reports, personal observations and press coverage revealed the ambiguity of responses to the refugees.

That the experience of displacement for the Armenians was deeply traumatic was not doubted.[35] However, as the refugee crisis persisted the refugees were increasingly seen as a 'problem' rather than simply as victims. In this respect the Armenian 'refugee question' anticipated many of the debates over the 'problem' of displacement which would recur throughout the twentieth century. This problem was not only envisioned in terms of the practical and material difficulties involved in feeding, clothing and returning the refugees to their homes. The condition of being a refugee was itself regarded as inherently damaging. James Barton, director of the American agency Near East Relief (NER), for example, stated that being in exile 'is paralysing on character . . .'.[36]

Such fears conditioned the image of the Armenian refugee. Descriptions of refugees recalled the descriptions of Armenian peasants by nineteenth-century travellers examined in chapter 2, highlighting the extent to which displacement was thought damaging and threatening. Use of animal imagery was not uncommon. Harold Buxton, arriving in Batum in 1921, described 'ravenous wolves, that once were human beings, prowling about the wharves and warehouses of the port'. Such language highlights the 'otherness' of the refugees, even in the eyes of relief agents who encountered them at first hand. Displacement was thought to have dehumanised them; they no longer belonged to modern, civilised society, but to the untamed, natural world.

British perceptions of the 'otherness' of the refugees was clearly evident in the writings of these authors. This was not however the same kind of 'otherness' that had been thought to distinguish 'eastern' populations from the British in their past. This otherness stemmed from the refugees, perceived detachment from social and moral norms and transgression of social and political boundaries. It also related to the supposed unpredictability and uncontrollability of the refugee population.

A language of otherness, which had in the past been commonly used to describe the Turkish enemy, was now imbued with new meanings and utilised in the depiction of the Armenian refugees. Relief workers, journalists and other observers spoke of 'refugee hordes', conjuring up images of threatening, undifferentiated and uncontrolled masses.[37] The term 'savage' was in frequent usage, implying a descent of the refugees into a 'lower' stage of civilisation, or a passing into the past. The NER publication, *New Near East* described shocking scenes of refugee behaviour for its readers: 'Hundreds of children, diseased, starving, uncared for, were roaming around the streets like little animals, in fact they were savages. To our horror we came upon one group who were tearing to pieces a dead horse and with ghoulish cries were devouring it like vultures.'[38] Such descriptions highlighted the need for international intervention, not only to provide material relief but also in order to restore the norms of civilisation and human behaviour.

The idea of dehumanisation or loss of civilisation was a common theme in reports from the British administrated Ba'quba refugee camp in Mesopotamia (Iraq). In 1919 this camp had become home to 14,612 Armenians from the regions of Van, Mosul and Urmia and also to 24,579 Assyrian Christian refugees.[39] On arrival, refugees were described as 'only partially civilised', 'retaining many primitive characteristics'.[40] It is important to note that such comments were not a new feature of British responses to the Armenians. For at least the previous fifty years the question of Armenian 'civilisation' had vexed British scholars and travellers, politicians and humanitarians. Thus it is sometimes unclear whether the negative features attributed to the Armenian refugees were thought to be a result of the experience of displacement or understood to be the consequence of a perceived innate 'otherness'.

Images of Armenians remained highly unstable; shifting between categories of civilisation and barbarism. In the case of the refugees, the balance had been tipped towards barbarism and it was the 'otherness' of the Armenian refugees that was most striking to British observers. Of course this was a marked contrast to the image of the Armenians as a civilised and Christian people circulated by the pro-Armenian lobby. The two images coexisted uneasily.

Generalised notions about the 'savagery' of displaced people were accompanied by a more specific set of characteristics associated with the refugees. These centred upon the untrustworthiness of the Armenian refugee and related to doubts as to whether they were worthy recipients of British aid. At Ba'quba, for instance, the Armenians were never simply regarded as passive victims; but as an unknown quantity, a source of potential trouble. Camp administration reports create the impression that the purpose of the camp was not simply provision of material relief; but also supervision and control of a 'problem' population.

Anxieties about the nature of the refugees were expressed in a number of ways. There was an expectation that crime rates amongst refugees would be high and a belief that they would not readily comply with rules and regulations. Indeed surprise was expressed at the way the refugees rapidly adapted to the camp. Idleness was a recurring complaint: refugee men were reported to be 'very poor workers, [who] need much supervision and resent being separated from their families'.[41] Perceptions of idleness must however be placed in the context of limited opportunities and choices.

In other areas fears were expressed regarding the moral impact of displacement on the refugees, a fear associated especially with females. The morality of Armenian women was also a longstanding concern; however this time the threat was not perceived to be from external agents such as the Turkish perpetrators of sexual violence but from the condition of displacement itself. These concerns were voiced by Harold Buxton. On a visit to Transcaucasia to investigate famine conditions he claimed to have witnessed 'women of the old aristocracy selling themselves to any ship's officer who will take them out of the country'.[42] Similarly the British relief worker Dudley Stafford Northcote feared that if the refugee camp at Ba'quba was closed, there would be no 'respectable' work for women.[43]

Anxieties about refugee behaviour were coupled with concern for the threat that they posed to their surroundings. This operated at a number of levels. One concern was health and sanitation. Authorities were aware of the threat of the spread of disease both inside and outside refugee camps or settlements. At Ba'quba refugees had to pass through a 'disinfecting area' before they could enter the camp; hospitals were quickly established in order to contain the spread of disease. Another threat was thought to be the disruption that the refugees could cause to the social and economic order, thus leaving the Ba'quba camp to find work in Baghdad was seen as a serious problem: 'Numbers of Armenian refugees secretly ran away from the camp to Baghdad and other places to seek work, thus increasing the unemployed and poor in Baghdad. The situation became rather grave, but prompt measures were taken and many of them returned to the camp.'[44]

The view of the refugees as unreliable or untrustworthy related to the tendency to deny the Armenians the chance to tell their own stories. One camp administrator, attempting to construct a history of the refugees' experiences, complained, 'I have had to write on knowledge derived from intercourse with the refugees themselves, much of which on close examination having proved to be quite unreliable.'[45] Terence Ranger's more recent response to doubts about the usefulness or reliability of refugee oral testimony form an interesting counterpoint to this point of view. Ranger suggests that these doubts may have a positive side as they help us to form a more complex and sophisticated view of refugees, that is:

> reinsert refugees and returnees into the general stream of history and society rather than remove·them into some special problematic category. The more we insist that refugees are agents rather than helpless victims, the more we restore them to a history in which they must necessarily reveal, like everyone else, their capacity for deceit and fraud and force as well as for endurance and courage.[46]

In the case of the Armenians, perceptions that they were unreliable witnesses to their own experiences primarily related to the idea that as 'traumatised' refugees they were unfit or unable to determine what was in their own interests. Secondly, it related to the desire to impose order on the refugee population and to determine that their future would unfold in an organised manner. Underlying all of this was the desire to improve, to 'civilise' the refugee population, a theme running through refugee relief work with many different displaced populations.

Managing relief/managing refugees

In Britain a number of voluntary organisations were involved in the provision of refugee relief. Longstanding Armenophile associations such as the Friends of Armenia, which had provided support for American missionaries working in Armenia, intensified their efforts.[47] Local Armenian diaspora communities also contributed to the relief effort. The Armenian community of Manchester, for example, ran a refugee clothing fund.[48] It became clear at a very early stage that the scale of the crisis required a large-scale, more co-ordinated effort. To this end the Lord Mayor's Fund for Armenian refugees was created. Operated by many of the same individuals who were involved in the BAC, including the Buxtons and Aneurin Williams, the LMF soon became 'the best organized, most active and influential of agencies'.[49]

These organisations not only co-ordinated appeals to the British public for aid, but their work began to take a new direction as they became involved in the administration of relief in the Middle East and Transcaucasia. The fate of these thousands of refugees now became the focus of both their campaigns and their relief work. In 1916 a team was sent to assess how their funds could be used most effectively. It included Revd Harold Buxton, a longstanding supporter of the Armenian cause who eventually became the LMF's Director of Relief.[50] They became involved in caring for orphaned children and finding employment, usually spinning and weaving, for women. However their activities were virtually ended by the 1918 Ottoman invasion of the Caucasus.[51]

In the long term the task of providing relief and 'solving' the refugee crisis was not straightforward. By 1918 there were still approximately 500,000 refugees in Transcaucasia, with 350,000 of them in the Yerevan region.[52] The relief effort which began in Transcaucasia continued to operate even after the establishment of Soviet rule. In Soviet Armenia W. H. Harcourt led a team of thirteen field directors who organised several schemes including orphanages for refugee children, feeding stations and work programmes.[53] The LMF continued to work with the Armenians until the 1930s when the British government ceased to play a role in refugee relief and handed on to it responsibility for the resettlement of the Armenian refugees.

In the Middle East the work of these British agencies, although significant, was dwarfed by the relief effort led by the American organisation Near East Relief. NER had emerged from missionary organisations which had previously worked in the Ottoman Empire. During the First World War it operated throughout the Ottoman Empire, from Lebanon to Transcaucasia, caring for Assyrian Christians and other war victims as well as the Armenians.[54] During the post-war period NER ran an extensive network of hospitals, orphanages and feeding stations for the refugees. British organisations thus worked alongside NER, often in collaborative relief schemes.

The American missionaries who worked with NER had adopted a 'hands on' approach to spreading 'civilisation' amongst the Armenians. Missionary work did not simply mean conversion; it entailed education, employment and the cultivation of moral and behavioural standards. Whilst few British missionaries followed the Americans to Armenia,

British Armenophile organisations, including the Friends of Armenia supported their work and reported their progress to the British public.[55] The notion of 'improving' the Armenians was thus established before the First World War and transposed onto the ideology of NER post-war relief.

The image of the refugees that NER presented also recalled missionary rhetoric. It depicted the Armenians as having the potential to be bastions of Christianity and civilisation in the Near East. The fact that the Armenians were Christians was repeatedly referred to in NER material. For example, it was remarked in the NER journal *New Near East* that: 'As the introduction of Christianity was a decisive process by which Armenians obtained a distinct national character, so it has been the link that has bound their interest and culture with the western world'.[56]

Even without their connection to NER many British Armenophiles, often drawn from Nonconformist or Anglican backgrounds, shared much of the missionary ethic. There were those however who were not wholly comfortable with the missionary aspect of relief. In July 1919 Admiral Calthorpe, the British Commissioner at Constantinople, warned Balfour of his fears of missionary involvement with the American relief efforts, 'Missionary zealots in Turkey differ in no way from those elsewhere and I am somewhat apprehensive that in their new capacity as administrators in Armenia under American auspices they will be found applying discriminatory measures against Muslims which little accord to HMG's policy of religious non-interference'.[57] Calthorpe was clearly amongst those who had a specific vision of British relief divorced from religious or other prejudices.

The work of the various international agencies engaged in refugee relief in the former Ottoman Empire and the Caucasus was carried out in conjunction with the American Relief Administration (ARA). This body was formed in February 1919 with the aim of easing the post-war crises and was led by Herbert Hoover. The creation of the ARA meant that there would be a US government-funded supply of provisions for the Armenian refugees in Transcaucasia who had previously been reliant upon charitable donations made to NER.

Food supplies from the ARA began to arrive at Batum for the Armenians in April 1919. British troops assisted with its delivery via the railways and the 20,000 tons of flour, grain, condensed milk and other foodstuffs delivered between then and August helped to keep alive the thousands of refugees threatened with starvation.[58] In July 1919, in the absence of any peace settlement in the Near East, Colonel William Haskell was appointed High Commissioner for Armenia on behalf of the Allies. Due to the scale of population displacement in the region a large part of his work would focus on refugee relief, co-ordinating the various agencies already at work in the region.

The practice of relief: the camp at Ba'quba

The example of the Ba'quba refugee camp provides an example of the nature of post-war refugee relief and the motivations, practices and ethos which shaped it. The Ba'quba camp represented an attempt to provide systematic and comprehensive relief, unlike the piecemeal and voluntary work that had occurred during the war and previous times of crisis. This form of relief provision was not however an ideal, but came about because of the impossibility of quickly repatriating a large number of refugees. Reports from the camp indicate the attempts made to make relief efficient and disciplined on every level, from spatial organisation through to daily routine:

> The whole camp which covers roughly an area of one square mile has been divided into three areas, 'A', 'B', and 'C' respectively. Each of these areas are subdivided into sections, varying from 11 to 13 in number in each area. Over each area there was a British officer, and each section had a British officer looking after it assisted by 3 or 4 British soldiers.[59]

In part this ordered approach was due to the need to find ways to manage this scale of crisis. The need to feed, clothe, accommodate and prevent the spread of disease amongst so many refugees in a relatively small area meant that they were subject to a strict routine. The camp also had to be run in a cost-effective manner, as the refugees could not be supported indefinitely. It relied on government funds and therefore its administrators had to prove that it was being run in an efficient and rational manner. A report provided for the British government compared the camp's efficiency – in terms of improving the health of the refugees – with the South African concentration camps of the Boer War in order to prove that 'the heavy expenditure in the camp has been justified by results'.[60]

Considering the attitudes and experiences which shaped Armenian refugee relief also offers important insights into the way in which humanitarian relief in a broader sense was imagined in the immediate post-war period. For the type of relief that was administered did not solely concern meeting basic material needs but was intended to act on the refugees themselves, 'improving them' and directing their development in the desired direction. This approach was not exclusive to Armenian refugees. As Lisa Malkki has pointed out, refugee relief is often conceived of as a remedy to problems thought inherent in refugees:

> They are not ordinary people but represent rather, an anomaly requiring specialised correctives and therapeutic interventions. It is striking how often the abundant literature claiming refugees as its objects of study locates 'the problem' not in the political conditions or processes that produce massive territorial displacements of people, but, rather, within the bodies and minds (and even souls) of people categorized as refugees.[61]

In the Armenian case the provision of relief was framed in terms of the discourses of 'civilisation' and national development which had helped shape British perceptions of Armenia over the last five decades. Thus the approach to refugee relief was conditioned not only by the circumstances of displacement but also by historical relations between Britain and Armenia. As a result, programmes of refugee relief had two interrelated themes, that of reconstructing the nation and that of 'civilising' the refugees.

Before considering the way this related to the refugees themselves it is important to reiterate the background which led to this specific understanding of relief. The Armenians had long been the objects of British and American attention. The relative levels of civilisation of the Armenians had been a matter of interest to western audiences since the nineteenth century. Armenophiles had long lamented the detrimental effect of Ottoman rule upon the development of the Armenians, suggesting that with the help of European intervention the Armenians could eventually be a civilising force in the region.[62]

But even those who saw relief as a non-religious project placed great importance on 'improvement' and 'civilisation'. British interest in the Armenians had emerged in the context of a particular Liberal vision of the British Empire which stressed its role as a civilising force and expressed a particular concern for 'minorities' such as the Armenians. Armenophiles had frequently contrasted the evils of despotic Ottoman rule with an image of the British Empire as a tool for spreading civilisation and justice.[63] In the post-war period, although imperial politics and beliefs about the nature and role of empire had changed somewhat, attitudes to refugee relief still drew upon the imperial idea of Britain's civilising mission and the idea of Britain as a benevolent force in the world.[64]

For the Armenophiles, Britain had an important role to play in preparing the Armenians for their national future. They felt that even if Britain had failed Armenia in the forum of international politics, British duty towards the Armenians could be fulfilled and cultural and social influence maintained through refugee relief.

If relief was thought of in terms of 'civilising' or improving the Armenians, it follows that the Armenians first had to be imagined as different to their European providers. This difference or 'otherness' was articulated in a number of ways. As I have described, a range of negative characteristics were attributed to the refugees; many were associated with a lack of civilised habits, including illiteracy and lack of cleanliness. Reports from Ba'quba stressed the problems in 'teaching the people sanitation, and how to keep clean and free from disease'.[65] These doubts as to standards of hygiene and cleanliness amongst the refugees echoed the observations of the British travellers who witnessed the realities of the domestic arrangements of Armenian peasants during the nineteenth century.[66]

Difference was also expressed through the ethnographic approach to the refugees taken by some of the relief workers. Dudley Northcote, a British army officer who would later become a relief worker, used his time working at the Ba'quba camp in order to 'study' the way of life of the refugees. In letters home he described the Armenian traditions he witnessed in the camp, including the Armenian wedding, with the priest dressed in a 'gorgeous blue vestment' and the couple standing against one another for an hour while a Bible is held over their head.[67] In his eyes the ceremony was 'pathetic and ludicrous' but nonetheless had a 'quaint prettiness'. At Easter he observed another Armenian service and decided to keep the Eucharist as a 'souvenir'.

Northcote was obviously deeply interested in the refugees and had a great deal of sympathy for their plight – he went on to write an unpublished book on their history and culture. Nonetheless his approach served to underline their 'otherness' and exoticism, marking out the refugees as the passive objects of study. The refugee camp was thus viewed as a place to witness a dying way of life, a more primitive culture or even 'living history'. In Ba'quba camp administrators attempted to describe the 'national customs' of the Armenian people, listing beliefs and practices unfamiliar to themselves:

> On a certain day called Asdvazasin, grapes are forbidden to be eaten until consecrated in Church. It takes place in the beginning of autumn and is also the Mother of Christ's day. With the grapes, all other fruit and seeds that are to be sown during the coming year are consecrated. It is considered that this consecration destroys any disease that might be in the fruit.[68]

The summary of national customs, like Northcote's anecdotes, constructed an image of the Armenians as primitive, exotic and strange. Of course this contrasted somewhat with accounts of the deportations which emphasised the high standards of civilisation in Armenia. It implied that the Armenians belonged to a different age: 'Though influenced and modified by ruling powers, the majority of the ancient customs have remained.'[69] It also reinforced pre-existing beliefs that Armenian religious practice was based on superstition. The response to this 'primitiveness' was however ambiguous. Whilst the implication that the Armenians were inferior was clear, there was also a romantic admiration for their way of life and a desire to preserve it. This ambiguity was expressed in the summary from Ba'quba, which included the rather cryptic observation that all of the refugees 'are tainted by the influence of western civilisation'.[70]

Finding out about the Armenians in this manner was not simply a matter of curiosity or scholarly interests. The process of information gathering was regarded as important in determining what to 'do' with the Armenians in terms of both day-to-day organisation of the refugees and their long-term future. In terms of relief provision any attachment to the 'primitive' way of life was overridden by the demands of organising large-scale relief and the desire to 'improve' the refugees and equip them for the future.

At Ba'quba the process of civilising began at the basic level of imposing order and discipline on a population thought of as inherently unruly and difficult. The refugees were subject to strict military organisation and planning. They were divided up into sections, each of which had section administrators responsible for 'cleanliness, welfare and discipline'.[71] Photographic images of life in the camp, for example children organised into neat rows for exercise, and even its immaculate layout, highlight the ways that this ethos was put into practice. Refugees were encouraged to take some responsibility for organising themselves through 'national committees'. However these bodies were thought in need of improvement as, 'their natural methods of administration are in direct variance with ours, thus their teaching and training to our methods being necessitated'.[72]

The idea of relief as 'improving' had its clearest expression in the schemes for self-help, employment and education. The aim was to allow the refugees to become self-supporting. Self-help was at the core of refugee relief programmes. In *New Near East* it was declared that, 'No opportunity is lost to develop the largest measure of self-support in connection with all relief work. The people naturally are frugal, thrifty and eager for their industrial independence. Given a single year of peace and the adult population would regain complete self-support.'[73] Dependence upon international aid was thought damaging to the refugees' moral and physical well-being; instead relief workers strove to instil a work ethic and make the refugees responsible for themselves.

The relief effort of the immediate post-war period could not be sustained indefinitely. Public interest waned and so it was essential that the refugees became self-supporting. British Armenophiles believed that self-help would also equip Armenians for the long-term future of their nation. In the first phase of the relief effort refugees were expected to return to life in an independent state. It was imperative to provide them with the skills and education which would allow Armenia to become a 'civilised' and prosperous modern nation. Armenophiles regarded this as essential for the future of the region because, in Bryce's words, 'the Armenian element is the only one numerous enough to be capable of civilising it and of hereafter administering it as a civilised state'.[74] As the chance for independence passed, Armenians needed to be equipped to survive as a 'useful' population in their host countries.

Self-help was also thought to be important in order to demonstrate to the rest of the world that the Armenians were worthy recipients of aid. The format of self-help was gender-specific and based on pre-war ideals of masculine and feminine roles and abilities. Lace-making and sewing were deemed 'respectable' tasks for women and children. For example the American Persian Mission provided sewing rooms at the Ba'quba camp. Some forms of self-help related to concerns that Armenian identities must be kept alive. Teaching traditional lace-making to Armenian girls both allowed them to support themselves and ensured that an Armenian traditional craft did not die out.[75] The provision of an orphanage for the camp by the Baghdad Armenian community, led by Bishop Moushegh Seropian, was also envisioned as a means to prevent the dispersal of children and ensure they did not lose their Armenian identity.[76]

For men, manual labour was more usual. Work opportunities were limited after the war; at Ba'quba the Armenian men were given various jobs, inside and outside the camp, 'for transportation and distribution of supplies throughout the camp, for the construction of roads, drains and bridges and in many other useful directions'.[77]

Self-help for adults was accompanied by education for children. This included the teaching of Armenian language and the provision of a broader education, once again designed to allow the Armenians to support themselves in the future. Education was not limited to academic instruction of children and this wish to educate the refugees into a

European or 'civilised' way of life shaped educational programmes. This involved creating order and discipline, and setting norms and standards of behaviour.

This is clearly demonstrated by the dress and appearance of the refugees in the camp at Ba'quba. Images of the refugees escaping the Turks revealed dishevelled, shabby figures, stick-thin, unwashed and dressed in rags that in no way resembled Western European dress. In other words, the refugees appeared far removed from the modern world. In contrast, photographs from the Ba'quba camp present a very different image of refugees, who are clean, neat and uniformly dressed in a European style. Female dress was often viewed as an indicator of levels of progress and development.[78] Therefore for refugee women to appear in this way not only demonstrated improved material conditions, it also implied improved standards of morality and behaviour, inculcation with 'western' ideals. In *New Near East*, it was explained that such a change was exactly the intention: '400 more little kinless wanderers settled down to absorb American ideals of wholesome living and to grow into useful manhood and womanhood according to American standards and by American methods.'[79]

Although British agencies do not seem to have made such explicit statements of their purpose, it is evident that they intended to export a way of life and set of values. The implications of British cultural superiority were clear but it seems that the Armenians were regarded as having made good progress: 'It is perhaps one of the most wonderful feats on record, the way in which these refugees, comparatively only partly civilised, adapted themselves to strict British discipline and organisation in an amazingly short space of time.'[80]

The pattern of disciplined, camp-based relief at Ba'quba was not repeated everywhere. The nature of refugee relief varied from region to region, according to need and available resources. In many regions the British government and voluntary relief organisations worked hand in hand with organisations based in other nations or funded by the Armenian diaspora. Armenian refugee relief was very much an international undertaking and the organisation of relief agencies evolved as new international bodies were created and the support of governments and the public ebbed and flowed.

After Versailles the work of humanitarian and Armenophile agencies was augmented by that of the League of Nations. In the post-war period the problem of displaced persons stretched far beyond Armenia and the League attempted to grapple with this problem. Claudena Skran emphasises its scale: 'In terms of size and scope, refugee movements in inter-war

Europe dwarfed all previous ones. They were mass migrations that significantly affected the refugee-producing countries and the refugee-receiving ones.[81]

The scale of the refugee problem meant that new international bodies, primarily the League, became engaged in the attempt to resolve the problem of displaced peoples. In 1921 a League of Nations High Commission for Refugees was created, initially to look after Russian refugees.[82] The High Commissioner for Refugees, Fridtjof Nansen, took responsibility for the Armenian refugees reluctantly, but was left with little other option as the Allies tightened their borders and would not take long-term responsibility for them.[83] The League became involved in the future of the Armenians in a number of ways.[84] In 1924 'Nansen passports' were created for Armenian refugees who lacked documentation which allowed them to travel in the heightened international security of the post-war period.[85] The problem was not easily solved; even with the support of the League and throughout the twenties Nansen continued to advocate schemes for irrigation of the land in order to facilitate resettlement of the remaining refugees in the Soviet Armenian Republic, most of which foundered due to lack of international support.[86]

Resolving the crisis: repatriation, resettlement, abandonment?

The provision of refugee relief, although focused initially on the provision of material aid, was in the end inseparable from the question of the future of the Armenian nation and the creation of a 'homeland'. This was in part because the vast majority of western Armenians saw the ideal solution of the refugee question in terms of the repatriation of Armenians to their homes in the former Ottoman Empire.[87] Outside the Armenian diaspora the need for repatriation was also recognised. Richard Hovannisian has pointed out that 'even the most outspoken advocates of purely philanthropic aid could at best merely sustain the homeless people on a day-to-day basis until a political settlement cleared the way for reconstruction.'[88] The realities of the situation in the region however made such a repatriation scheme a distant prospect. The region had been decimated by the war and even after the armistice it had not been fully occupied by Allied troops. This would leave any returning Armenians vulnerable to Turkish attacks.

Nonetheless, the ideal of repatriation continued to colour visions of the Armenian future. As attempts to provide refugee relief and to reach an international political settlement progressed, Armenophiles, the diaspora and relief workers called for some kind of 'national' home for the

Armenian people. The fate of the refugees was seen as key to the preservation of the nation, thus attempts to initiate the complex process of repatriation and resettlement of displaced Armenians began.

In 1918 James Bryce indicated his own belief that the post-war period would witness the return of Armenian refugees to Asia Minor:

> The Armenian population has been terribly reduced by the massacres of 1915 but a large body of refugees who escaped are likely to return, some from the territory which was Russian and some from Egypt, while a great many of those who emigrated to Europe, and still more to the United States in previous years, may also be expected to return to their native land as soon as they can do so with safety.[89]

This view was shared by most of the British Armenophiles and was based on the assumption that after the war an Armenian nation state would emerge which would incorporate all of the Armenian inhabited territories which had previously belonged to the Ottoman Empire. For Armenian nationalists repatriation was integral to the attempt to create an Armenian nation state, an attempt which will be discussed in depth in the following chapter. For without an Armenian population in the region, Armenian territorial claims to the lands of the former Ottoman Empire, despite historical Armenian connections to these territories, seemed tenuous. An Armenian nation state without Armenians would not, in the eyes of the international community, be a viable option. Without an Armenian population there was little hope of its development and regeneration.[90]

Repatriation was viewed as essential because, as Lisa Malkki has explained, in the modern world being outside the nation state is often perceived as damaging, whilst 'rootedness' in the soil of the homeland is viewed as a natural or healthy state of being. This is a way of thinking arising from a world thought to be clearly divided into national territories:

> It is when the native becomes a national native that the metaphysical and moral valuation of roots in the soil becomes especially apparent. In the national order of things, the rooting of people is not only normal; it is also perceived as a moral and spiritual need.[91]

This point is particularly relevant to the case of the Armenians after the First World War, as the diaspora, the leaders of the republic and international organisations and governments sought to tie Armenian nationality to a particular territory, even though the boundaries of such a territory were by no means clear-cut. The existence of historical roots in the homeland had long been a feature of Armenian national claims.[92] The identification and elaboration of these Armenian roots in the homeland made the position of the refugees seem even more anomalous. The condition of being in exile, regardless of the material and physical hardships, was identified as damaging not only to the individual but also to the nation.

Throughout 1919 as the future of Armenia was debated by the victorious powers, Armenian representatives pressed for the speedy repatriation of the Armenians. The ANDP warned the British government of the consequences of delay and pressed for the occupation of Eastern Anatolia by British forces in order that repatriation could take place safely. Part of the desire for repatriation was driven by practical concerns. Conditions for the refugees in Transcaucasia were dire, there were food shortages and it was feared that if the refugees could not return home to plant their crops the harvest would fail once again and thousands would starve. The British High Commissioner in Constantinople agreed with the view that occupation was essential if the refugees were to return to their homes. He stated that, 'The situation is very precarious, [the] presence of allied troops will be indispensable before repatriation of Armenians can commence . . . delay in announcing peace terms is having the worst possible effect.'[93] Colonel William Haskell, the allied High Commissioner in the Caucasus, agreed that occupation was a matter of urgency, for the Armenians 'may be exterminated at any time otherwise'.[94]

The British General Staff were well aware of the problems posed by repatriation. In their eyes repatriation had to be well managed and organised. They were particularly concerned about the consequences of repatriation at an inappropriate time.

> The Armenians as a race possess a great homing instinct and if, as is feasible, a small number were repatriated now to this area, it is more than probable that large numbers of Turkish Armenians, of whom there are 300,000 now in the Caucasus would consider repatriation on a general scale had begun and wander over the border on their own account, the movement would get out of control and thousands would perish in the coming winter.[95]

The perspectives of the General Staff reflected contemporary perceptions of the refugees as a 'problem' population, a potential threat to themselves and others. The mass of Armenian refugees were thus regarded as an unpredictable and irrational body driven by primitive urges, often characterised as a 'homing instinct'. For this reason their movements had to be carefully planned and controlled.

Despite these concerns about controlling the movement of refugees the British government proved unwilling to provide the troops necessary for the occupation of Anatolia.[96] When the war had ended British troops had arrived in Transcaucasia and occupied the Transcaucasian railway. British troops had also landed at Baku in an occupation that would eventually end in disaster as they unceremoniously evacuated the city. For the time being though their presence allowed them to assist with the implementation of relief and also offered a degree of security and reassurance to the population. Despite these actions, Sir Henry Wilson, chief of the Imperial General Staff, resolved to rid the overstretched British troops of their responsibilities in Transcaucasia and the Near East.[97]

In summer 1919 British troops were withdrawn from the region. This action reflected the now diverging aims and priorities of the British authorities and the Armenians and their Armenophile supporters. Over the following years deciding the fate of the Armenian refugees would become even more conflict-laden and fraught with difficulties. The ill-judged Greek landing in Smyrna in June 1919, for example, fuelled Turkish nationalist sentiments and therefore made return to the eastern provinces even more dangerous for the Armenian refugees. The subsequent growth of Turkish nationalism and the ultimate outcome of the peace conferences would mean that repatriation to Eastern Turkey remained impossible.

Repatriation from Ba'quba

The problem of repatriation did not only apply to the Armenian refugees from Eastern Anatolia stranded in Transcaucasia. There were of course thousands of refugees also stranded in the Near East. Whilst decisions regarding the future of this region also remained unmade their future was equally uncertain. The story of one such group of refugees, the Armenians of the Ba'quba refugee camp, demonstrates both changing attitudes towards the Armenian refugees and the complexities of resolving the refugee crisis.

The fate of the refugees at Ba'quba camp was quite different from that of the refugees stranded in Transcaucasia; however it was equally problematic. The camp had been established in a time of dire need; when it opened in 1919 Northcote reported terrible conditions, with Armenians arriving on the brink of starvation and up to 80 deaths every day.[98] He soon came to recognise that the problem was long term, that the Armenians would have to be 'looked after and rationed for some considerable time by us'.[99] Northcote made the common assumption that a return to the Armenian homeland was simply a matter of time, accepting that the Armenian refugees would remain together and be retuned to 'their own country'.[100] His view reflected the aims of the ANDP, who pressed the British authorities to repatriate the refugees. In June 1919 Nubar Pasha wrote to the British government on behalf of the refugees requesting that they be repatriated, if not to Van then at least elsewhere: Aleppo, Adana or Constantinople. The climate at Ba'quba, he argued, was causing disease amongst the Armenians.[101] These demands were not met but were reiterated again, also unsuccessfully, in 1920:

> Arsen Kittur, another western Armenian deputy, was sent to Baghdad to assist 20,000 refugees, mostly natives of the Van Vilayet, and to urge the British authorities to repatriate them or at least transport them to Yerevan to get them away from the alien, disease-ridden plains of Mesopotamia.[102]

The setup of the Ba'quba camp seems to have reflected the view that the fate of its inhabitants would be settled on a national basis. As soon as possible the camp administration recognised these divisions as it went about 'unmixing':

> For the first month or so the people were all mixed up, Armenians and Assyrians together. But as they became more settled, a census was held, and the people arranged throughout the sections according to their tribal divisions and affiliations.[103]

Armenians and Assyrian Christians were organised separately, and treated as distinct problems requiring different actions. It was also decided that 'all matters connected with their customs and national life' would not be 'interfered with' and therefore that refugee committees would be formed to deal with 'questions of national customs and religious duties'.[104] A report from the camp administration which included a section entitled 'Notes on the National Customs of the Armenian Refugees' also suggests that the Armenians were accepted as a national community. The recording of national religious practices, traditions and beliefs was regarded as an important dimension of camp administration.

In the eyes of the camp administration the refugees coped well with the delays to their repatriation:

> Although the longing for their fatherland is so strongly implanted in them that it has led many of them into trouble, they have realised up to the present the difficulties standing in the way of their repatriation, and accepted the decisions and orders of the British administration, philosophically and willingly.[105]

Nonetheless, the problem of 'longing for fatherland' loomed in the background and over the following years reconciling this longing with British agendas and the international political situation would prove problematic. Aside from the practical considerations of the post-war period, the nature of the 'longed-for' fatherland in itself posed a problem. Though there was clearly an assumption that an Armenian 'homeland' existed, what it meant in the aftermath of war, when borders were contested and unstable and whole populations had been forced from their homes, was a matter of debate. In the years to come reconciling constructions of the historic Armenian homeland with the realities of the post-war world would prove problematic.[106]

The repatriation of Armenians from Ba'quba highlights some of these problems. Though repatriation was viewed from the outset as the eventual fate of the refugees, its organisation was hindered by the lack of security in the former Ottoman territories that had been the homes of the refugees. Those involved were painfully aware that the areas to which the refugees wished to return were unsafe and that any programme of repatriation would require not only military protection but economic aid in order to rebuild livelihoods and homes. Local factors played an important role: *New Near East* reported in 1920 that repatriation had been abandoned for the present due to 'strained diplomatic relations with Persia'.[107] In October 1919 it was still impossible to repatriate refugees to Van, Bitlis or the Caucasus. Some had returned to Adana via Aleppo, but many of these repatriates were forced to leave once again as the French evacuated Cilicia.

In August 1920 the Ba'quba camp was closed as a result of Arab uprisings.[108] The refugees were moved north to Nahr Umar where Northcote became the administrator for the Armenian part of the camp. The move coincided with the Treaty of Sèvres. Sèvres raised hopes of repatriation by promising the creation of an independent Armenia. In the months that followed these hopes were dashed by the Sovietisation of Armenia and the rise of Turkish nationalism. Armenian nationalists, relief workers and the refugees themselves were forced to re-imagine their notions of homeland and nationality. Of course this affected the desire for repatriation and meant that new solutions were needed: 'Thus the close of 1920 found one still with the repatriation problem to a great extent unsettled and with fresh measures to be devised which should get rid of these people somehow or other before the coming spring.'[109]

In 1920, even before the imposition of Soviet rule in the Armenian Republic had finally brought home the impossibility of repatriation to Eastern Anatolia for the refugees at Ba'quba and elsewhere, an alternative scheme to repatriation had been proposed. This involved the settlement of Armenian refugees on an agricultural colony in Kirkuk, Mesopotamia. A similar scheme was launched in Syria at Ali Begdjili, supported by the Friends of Armenia, and met with some success. Various other schemes advocated by Nansen at the League of Nations and other philanthropic bodies to resettle the Armenians 'on the land' in Syria were also undertaken.[110] Settlement 'on the land' appealed to international agencies as it seemed to offer a way for Armenian communities to continue to live together as a community, preserving their national identities whilst allowing them to become self-supporting. On the other hand it also avoided refugees' presence in towns, which was regarded as disruptive to the social and economic order and dangerous to the refugees.

The matter of colonies was a rare instance of the refugees having a say in the determination of their own future. Despite the difficulties of their situation on this subject they were neither voiceless nor powerless. The Kirkuk scheme was rejected outright by the Armenian Committee in the Ba'quba camp and the Armenian Relief Committee in Baghdad. The Armenians, it was reported, 'categorically declined to colonize that country on any condition. They desire to join their compatriots in Armenia.'[111] The refugees, unlike the camp administrators, did not accept that repatriation to Armenian soil was no longer a possibility, 'still clinging to the hope that there would be, sooner or later, a possibility of repatriating overseas and of uniting all their refugees in a new Armenian republic with its government at Yerevan'.[112] A colony was no replacement for the return to the homeland that the Armenians pinned their hopes upon.

The matter of repatriation eventually led to a clash between the British government, relief workers and refugees. In summer 1921 the British government, which had never anticipated caring for the refugees for such a long period, announced plans to close the Ba'quba camp: 'It is quite impossible, with financial constraints as they are at present, to find any more money from public funds for these refugees.'[113] This measure was indicative of the change in the attitude of the British government towards the Armenians. Support for an independent Armenia had given way in the face of a changing international situation and the more urgent pressures of post-war reconstruction. This reflected a more general decline in interest in the fate of the Armenians amongst the British public.

In a striking change from the wartime rhetoric of responsibility to the Armenians, the government declared that responsibility for the welfare of Armenian refugees lay in the hands of private charity, calling upon 'all those who are interested in the fate of the Armenians' to assist the philanthropic bodies.[114] This change of policy met with hostility from both the Armenians and the civil administration of the camp. Dudley Northcote resigned in protest, along with his superior. With his resignation in July 1919 he submitted a memorandum critiquing the government's decision.[115]

In his memorandum, Northcote reiterated the words of other Armenophiles, maintaining that British wartime promises, coupled with Armenian support for the Allies during the War, imposed upon the British government an obligation to care for the Armenian refugees. He was also deeply concerned about the effect of the closure on Armenian culture and identity. He echoed common fears about the dispersal of Armenian refugees in his protests that the abandonment of the Armenians in Mesopotamia would lead to 'the end of them as a community'.[116]

Northcote sought to recreate an image of the Armenian refugees which appealed to the charitable instincts of the British people. He maintained that they were only in the camp because they had fought with the Allies, claiming they 'have already had more than their fair share of suffering as a direct result of their having taken the Allied side during the Great War'.[117] Clearly aware of the concerns of the public, he also wanted to dispel any ideas that the Armenians were taking advantage of British generosity. If Armenian refugees were unemployed, no blame should be attached to them; they were simply unable to find work:

> The Government have only succeeded in finding work for a few hundred and as the men themselves have been discouraged from looking for it on their own, it cannot possibly be considered the fault of the refugees that they have remained a burden on the shoulders of the British taxpayers for so long.[118]

He emphasised that the refugees suffered real hardship. He proceeded to describe in detail what fate would befall them, should the refugee camp at Ba'quba be closed. According to Northcote it was proposed that as the camp was closed, the refugees would be 'evacuated' and given fourteen days' rations and a small amount of money, but they would have to find their own transport. However, as the camp was '24 miles from anywhere', it was the hottest part of the year and most of the refugees were penniless, Northcote believed deaths from heatstroke and starvation, especially amongst women and children, would inevitably follow. Even if the refugees survived a journey from the camp, he thought that their successful settlement in the region was highly unlikely. The Arab population was hostile and few of the Armenians could speak Arabic. There was no demand for unskilled labour, and as the Armenians came mainly from agricultural backgrounds there was no other work they could do.[119]

The proposal to close the camp renewed waning public interest in the fate of the Armenians for a brief period. The government's announcement met with a great deal of hostility in the press. One writer, styling himself 'Armenus', argued that it was mistaken to believe that there were numerous wealthy Armenians living in Europe who could afford to assist the refugees. Most of the 3,000 Armenians living in Britain, he argued, lived in very humble circumstances. Private charity, in his view, was not a realistic option, contrary to the opinion of the British government.[120]

Archbishop Charles Gore, another public figure who had become involved in the Armenian cause, also protested publicly about the government's plans. Gore was in no doubt as to the 'national' status of the Armenians. In his letter he evoked a range of positive images of the Armenians which had been a staple of Armenophile discourse since the late nineteenth century. He spoke of their ancient past, their 'tenacity in holding on to their faith' and their artistic, industrial and commercial gifts, concluding that the British government had a duty to assist another civilised Christian country.[121]

Such arguments may have been familiar from wartime propaganda but by this time seemed outdated and even irrelevant to a public struggling to recover themselves from the strains of four years of war. So although dedicated Armenophiles and those involved in humanitarian work championed the cause of the Armenians at Ba'quba, they did not capture the full sympathies of the general public. The 'Armenian question' had once again become the interest of a minority and would remain so during the following decades.

In autumn 1921, despite the renewed public protests, the Ba'quba camp was closed and the process of transporting the refugees to Transcaucasia began. This region was not the homeland that the Armenian patriots envisaged but under the circumstances it seemed to be the best or only substitute. In the aftermath of genocide and the dispersal of the Armenian population, homeland had taken on new meanings and importance. Given the determination of the Ba'quba refugees to go there it appears that this was now conceived of as a place of refuge to which exiled Armenians could safely return. To those who had suffered the hardships of long-term displacement, the precise borders of this territory now seemed to matter less.

Conclusions: refugees and the changing image of Armenia

The post-war Armenian refugee crisis meant that British Armenophiles and the British government and public engaged with Armenia and the Armenian population in new ways. The protracted crisis brought about another shift in representations of the Armenians, bringing to the fore once more the ambivalent British attitudes to the Armenians which had been masked by the pro-Armenian tone of wartime propaganda. Although the British public initially demonstrated their sympathy for the Armenian refugees through charitable works and donations, as time passed concern for the condition of the Armenian refugees was eclipsed by other concerns, primarily British post-war reconstruction. Sympathy gave way to wariness and fears regarding the refugees' reliability, honesty and morality. In response to this dedicated humanitarians and the Armenophile lobby sought to reassure the public and the government that the Armenian refugees were 'deserving'.

However, even the relief workers who encountered Armenian refugees at first hand responded to those in their care in a highly ambivalent manner. To be sure, the refugees were the objects of sympathy but they were simultaneously regarded as exotic specimens to be studied and a problem to be 'solved'. An examination of the practices of relief at the Ba'quba camp reveals highly unequal power relations and the nature of the camp as a site where the belief in the superiority of British civilisation could be exercised and the Armenian refugees trained to conform to British norms and values.

As the experience of the Ba'quba refugees demonstrates, shifting attitudes to Armenian refugees and the practice of relief were entangled with the complex question of repatriation. Repatriating the refugees was in the eyes of many British humanitarians and politicians the ideal way to 'solve' the refugee problem; that is to both relieve the British of their responsibilities for caring for refugee populations and to resolve the anxiety caused by a population 'out of place' in a world where clearly defined nation states containing homogenous populations was increasingly accepted as the ideal.

The various attempts to finally 'solve' the Armenian question and fit the Armenians into this new order of nation states through the peace settlements are addressed in the following chapter. This project was fraught with difficulty as idealised schemes for the future of the Armenian nation state were rudely disrupted by developments 'on the ground'. Ultimately the Armenian question was resolved in a manner which neither the Armenophiles nor international governments had anticipated.

Notes

1 For a comprehensive history of the Armenian Republic see the four-volume study by Richard Hovannisian, *The Republic of Armenia* (Berkeley: University of California Press, 1971–1996).

2 For in-depth discussion see Somakian, *Empires in Conflict*, chapter 5, Bloxham, *Great Game of Genocide* and Hovannisian, 'The Historical Dimension of the Armenian Question'.

3 Raymond Kevorkian, *Revue d'Histoire Arménienne Contemporain (Numéro Spécial):L'Extermination des Déportés Arméniens Ottomans dans les Camps de Concentration de Syrie-Mesopotamie (1915–1916): La Deuxième Phase du Génocide* (Paris: Bibliothèque Nubar, 1998).

4 NA FO 608/79, 368 Telegram from British High Commission, Constantinople, 11 November 1919.

5 Walker estimates that by the time the republic was established there were 300,000 Armenian refugees in Transcaucasia. C. J. Walker, *Armenia: The Survival of a Nation.* (London: Croom Helm, 1980), p. 349.

6 On the impact of revolution in Transcaucasia see R. Hovannisian, *Armenia on the Road to Independence* (Berkeley and Los Angeles: University of California Press, 1967), chapters 5 and 6.

7 On Transcaucasian politics and the military and political pressures in the region see Hovannisian, *Armenia on the Road to Independence*, chapters 7 and 8, Somakian, *Empires in Conflict*, chapters 4 and 5 and Richard Pipes, *The Formation of the Soviet Union* (Cambridge, MA: Harvard University Press, 1964), revised edition, pp. 193–195.

8 The breakdown of the Transcaucasian Federation is described in Hovannisian, *Armenia on the Road to Independence*, pp. 183–194.

9 The republic was to be initially led by the Armenian National Council which had been created in Tiflis (home to a large part of the educated Armenian middle class and elite). After the Russian revolution it transferred to Yerevan in summer 1918.

10 Somakian, *Empires in Conflict*, p. 177.

11 P. Gatrell and J. Laycock, 'Armenia: The "Nationalisation", Internationalisation and Representation of the Refugee Crisis', in N. Baron and P. Gatrell, eds, *Homelands: War, Population and Statehood in Eastern Europe and Russia 1918–24* (London: Anthem Press, 2004), p. 183.

12 Figures from Hewsen, *Armenia: A Historical Atlas*, p. 268.

13 Peter Loizos, 'Misconceiving Refugees', in Renos K. Papadopoulos, ed., *Therapeutic Care for Refugees: No Place Like Home* (Karnac: London and New York, 2001) pp. 45–49.

14 N. Baron and P. Gatrell, 'Population Displacement, State Building and Social Identity in the Lands of the Former Russian Empire, 1917–1923', *Kritika: Explorations in Russian and Eurasian History*, Vol. 4, No. 1 (Winter 2003),

p. 53. See also L. Malkki, 'Speechless Emissaries: Refugees, Humanitarianism and De-Historicization', *Cultural Anthropology*, Vol. 11, No. 3 (1996).

15 Ronit Lentin highlights the problems in defining women as a homogenous group of 'victims': 'Viewing women as homogeneously powerless and as implicit victims does not allow us to theorize women as the benefactors of oppression or the perpetrators of catastrophes' which in turn makes it impossible to understand/challenge domination. *Gender and Catastrophe*, pp. 11–12.

16 BAC minute book, August 1916.

17 H. Spaull, 'Mothering Children for the League of Nations: Froken Jeppe', in Hebe Spaull, *Women Peacemakers* (London: Harrap, 1924).

18 V. L. Shemmassian, 'The League of Nations and the Reclamation of Armenian Genocide Survivors', in Hovannisian, *Looking Backward, Moving Forward*, p. 95. Shemmassian provides an account of the work of Karen Jeppe at Aleppo, where conditions made the rescue more complex than at Constantinople.

19 *Slave Market News*, January 1930, p. 4. See also the pamphlet, *The Rescue of Christian Slaves*, included in *Slave Market News*, January 1929 and J. H. Harris, *Salving the Outcasts of War* (1929, reprinted from the *Contemporary Review*). Harris had previously played a key role in bringing the Belgian Congo atrocities to the attention of the British public. By this time the Armenian cause seems to have been incorporated into the agenda of the anti-slavery movement. The Buxtons also played an important role in the creation of the Save the Children Fund, which was also involved in relief work with the Armenians.

20 Eliz Sanasarian, 'Gender Distinction in the Genocidal Process, A Preliminary Study of the Armenian Case', *Holocaust and Genocide Studies*, Vol. 4, No. 4 (1989).

21 Mugerditchian, *From Turkish Toils*, p. 22. See also Martin Niepage, *Horrors of Aleppo*.

22 'Statement with Regard to the Deportation of Women and Children in Turkey and the Neighbouring Countries', submitted by Mme Vacaresco, Roumanian Delegate to Fifth Committee, League of Nations Assembly, 1921 (British Library, London, Northcote Papers).

23 Toynbee, *The Murderous Tyranny of the Turks*, p. 8.

24 P. Gatrell, *A Whole Empire Walking: Refugees in Russia during World War I* (Bloomington: Indiana University Press, 1999), p. 117.

25 Shemmassian, 'The League of Nations and the Reclamation of Armenian Genocide Survivors', p. 85.

26 'Statement with Regard to the Deportation of Women and Children in Turkey and the Neighbouring Countries', Mme Vacaresco.

27 On the role of women as reproducers of the nation Pat Thane states, 'Fears about race and Empire created a rhetoric that more explicitly than before identified women with the role of preserving, perpetuating and enhancing

the physical quality, and the numbers of the race in their role as mothers and, more mystical, embodying the essence of each race as its physical conduit to the next generation': 'The British Imperial State and the Construction of National Identities' in Melman, *Borderlines*, p. 31.

28 Gatrell and Laycock, 'Armenia: the Refugee Crisis'.
29 On orphanage experiences see Miller and Touryan Miller, *Survivors*, pp. 125–136. They state that some survivors reported Armenian nationalists giving speeches at the orphanages, p. 127.
30 Report of Jeppe on behalf of the 'Commission for the protection of women and children in the Near East', 28 July 1927. Quoted in Gatrell and Laycock, 'Armenia: the Refugee Crisis', p. 198.
31 Ibid., p. 198.
32 'Statement with Regard to the Deportation of Women and Children in Turkey and the Neighbouring Countries'. Mme Vacaresco.
33 Miller and Touryan Miller, *Survivors*, p. 123.
34 One option of some of the women who survived was to marry Armenians in the diaspora. For an account of the difficult choices and problems they faced, see Isabel Kaprelian-Churchill 'Armenian Refugee Women: The Picture Brides, 1920–1930', *Journal of American Ethnic History*, Vol. 12, Part 3 (1993). Kaprelian-Churchill highlights the very limited options available to Armenian women in the aftermath of genocide: 'some remained confined to refugee camps or orphanages for many years; some managed to set down roots in the country of first asylum, usually in the Middle East or the Caucasus; others migrated to Soviet Armenia . . . and still others resettled in a third country – any country that would give them refuge' (p. 4).
35 However, on the dangers of representing all refugees as permanently 'traumatised' see Peter Loizos, 'Misconceiving Refugees', p. 44–55.
36 NA FO 608/78, Letter from James Barton, 1919.
37 *Memoranda on the Armenian and Assyrian Refugees at present in Camp at Ba'quba Mesopotamia* (Baghdad: Government Press, 1919), p. 4.
38 *New Near East*, Vol. 7, No. 6 (April 1922), p. 16.
39 *Memoranda*, p. 34. On the Assyrian Christians at the camp, see Herbert H. Austin, *The Baqubah Refugee Camp: An Account of Work on Behalf of the Persecuted Armenian Christians* (London: Faith Press, 1920).
40 *Memoranda*, p. 6.
41 Ibid., pp. 6–7.
42 H. Buxton, 'Transcaucasia', *Contemporary Review*, Vol. 121 (January/June 1922) p. 560.
43 British Library, London, The Northcote Papers, *Memorandum Concerning the Proposed Dispersal of Refugees in Mesopotamia*, D. S. Northcote, 19 July 1921.
44 *Memoranda*, p. 7.
45 Ibid., Prefatory Note.
46 T. Ranger, 'Studying Repatriation as Part of African Social History', in T. Allen

and H. Morsink, eds, *When Refugees go Home* (London: UNRISD in association with James Currey, 1994).

47 This is evident from wartime editions of *The Friend of Armenia.*

48 B. Jerazian, *The Armenian Merchants and the Armenian Community in Manchester* (Local Studies Collection, Central Library, Manchester).

49 Nassibian, *Britain and the Armenian Question*, p. 63.

50 Harold Buxton was the brother of Noel Buxton, MP, a member of the Balkan Committee and BAC, and co-author of *Travels and Politics in Armenia.*

51 Hovannisian, *The Republic of Armenia*, Vol. 1, p. 134.

52 Ibid., p. 126.

53 The work of the LMF in Transcaucasia is described in the report of Dr Armstrong Smith of the Save the Children Fund. Dr Armstrong Smith, *Famine in Transcaucasia* (1922), extracts reprinted in Walker, *Visions of Ararat*, pp. 129–135.

54 On the work of NER, see the account of the director, James Barton, *The Story of Near East Relief, 1915–30: An Interpretation* (New York: Macmillan, 1930). For experiences with NER see M. E. Elliott, *Beginning Again at Ararat* (London and Edinburgh: Fleming H. Revell Company, 1924) and S. Kerr, *The Lions of Marash* (Albany: State University of New York Press, 1973). For background, see Moranian, 'The Armenian Genocide and American Missionary Relief Efforts'. Moranian states that donations to NER rose through 1916, 1917 and 1918. In 1919 $19.5 million was raised. Public campaigning ended in 1929.

55 See *The Friend of Armenia*, which suggests that the American missionaries were already familiar and much-admired figures even before their work with the survivors of the genocide.

56 NER journal, *New Near East*, Vol. 6, No. 2 (November 1920).

57 NA FO 608/80, 89, British Peace Conference Delegation, Telegram from Admiral Calthorpe, 15 July 1919.

58 R. Hovannisian, 'The Republic of Armenia', in R. Hovannisian, ed., *The Armenian People from Ancient to Modern Times* Vol. 2 (New York: St. Martin's Press, 1997), p. 312.

59 *Memoranda*, p. 5. The precise organisation also reflects the fact that the camp was run by the military.

60 Letter from Lieutenant-Colonel A. T. Wilson, Acting Civil Commissioner in Mesopotamia included in, *Memoranda on the Armenian and Assyrian Refugees*, also see Appendix D, 'A Statistical Comparison between the Refugee Camps, South Africa (1901) and the Refugee Camp, Ba'quba (1919)'.

61 L. Malkki, 'National Geographic: The Rooting of Peoples and the Territorialisation of National Identity Among Scholars and Refugees', *Cultural Anthropology*, No. 7 (1992), p. 33.

62 This argument was expressed most clearly by James Bryce. See Bryce, *Transcaucasia and Ararat.*

63 For example see the pamphlet *Mr. Gladstone on the Armenian Question* (reprint of his speech at Chester Town Hall, 6 August 1896).

64 This approach to Armenian relief which was predicated on ideas of British superiority and put into practice at Ba'quba echoes Jennifer Hyndman's comments about power relations in contemporary refugee camps. Hyndman expresses her concern that 'the means by which refugees are managed by humanitarian agencies reinscribes neocolonial and counterproductive relations of power predicated on a hierarchy of cultures in the camp and on major asymmetries of power linked to gender and political status'. J. Hyndman, *Managing Displacement: Refugees and the Politics of Humanitarianism* (Minnesota: University of Minnesota Press, 2000), p. 90.

65 *Memoranda*, p. 6.

66 See Ramsay, *Everyday Life in Turkey*.

67 Northcote Papers, Letter, 27 January 1919

68 *Memoranda*, p. 24.

69 Ibid., p. 23.

70 Ibid., Preface to Summary of Customs.

71 Ibid., p. 5.

72 Ibid., p. 7.

73 *New Near East*, Vol. 7, No. 7 (May 1922), p. 14.

74 J. Bryce, 'The Future of Armenia', *Contemporary Review*, Vol. 114 (December 1918), p. 609.

75 See A. O. Kasparian, *Armenian Needlelace and Embroidery* (Virginia: EPM Publications, 1983). D. S. Northcote reported that lace-making was organised by 'Miss Robinson's Fund' in Soviet Armenia. Nothcote Papers, Report from Erivan, January 1922. In Britain Armenian lace was sold by the Friends of Armenia.

76 On the Armenian community in Baghdad, see Vartan Melkonian, *A Historical Glimpse of the Armenians in Mesopotamia from the Earliest Times to the Present Day* (Basra: Times Press, 1957).

77 *Memoranda*, p. 6.

78 Such ideas are addressed in Lewis and Mills, *Feminist Postcolonial Theory*. See Ba'quba Camp Album, Photographic Collections of Bibliothèque Nubar, Paris.

79 *New Near East*, Vol. 7, No. 8 (June 1922), p. 8.

80 *Memoranda*, p. 6.

81 C. Skran, *Refugees in Inter-War Europe: The Emergence of a Regime* (Oxford: Clarendon Press, 1995), p. 14. Michael Marrus states that in 1926 there were 'no less than 9.5 million European refugees including 1.5 million forcibly exchanged between Greece and Bulgaria, 2 million poles to be repatriated, over 2 million Russian and Ukrainian refugees, 250,000 Hungarians and one million Germans expelled from various parts of Europe': Marrus, *The Unwanted: European Refugees from the First World War through the Cold War* (Philadelphia: Temple University Press, 2002), p. 52.

82 On the UNHCR and the problems of its role see G. Loescher, *The UNHCR and World Politics: A Perilous Path* (Oxford: Oxford University Press, 2001).

83 For example, Kushner and Knox point out the absence of Armenian refugees in Britain after the First World War. Only 200 Armenians came to Britain in the inter-war period. T. Kushner and K. Knox, *Refugees in the Age of Genocide: Global, National and Local Perspectives during the Twentieth Century* (London: Frank Cass, 1999), p. 71.

84 Detailed analysis of the work of the League with the Armenians is provided in Dzovinar Kévonian-Dyrek, 'Les Tribulations de la Diplomatie Humanitaire: La Société des Nations et les Réfugies Arméniens', in Kieser, *Die Armenische Frage und die Schweiz*.

85 On 'Nansen passports', see Marrus, *The Unwanted*, p. 95.

86 For details of Nansen's Armenian projects see F. Nansen, *Armenia and the Near East* (New York: Da Capo Press, 1976), reprint of 1928 publication.

87 Gatrell and Laycock, 'Armenia: The Refugee Cris', p. 186.

88 Hovannisian, *The Republic of Armenia*, Vol. 2, p. 40.

89 Bryce, 'The Future of Armenia', p. 606.

90 The connection between repatriation and regaining the lost lands in Anatolia was made once again in 1945 when Stalin made a formal claim to the Turkish government for the return of Kars and Ardahan, regions that had been ceded to Armenia by the treaty of Sèvres and soon afterwards invited diasporan Armenians to repatriate. See G. Mamoulia, 'Les Premières Fissures de L'URSS d'Apres Guerre: Le Cas de la Georgie et du Caucase du Sud: 1946–7', *Cahiers du Monde Russe* Vol. 46, No. 3 (2005) and 'Les Crises Turque et Iranienne 1945–7: L'Apport des Archives Caucasiennes', *Cahiers Du Monde Russe*, Vol. 45, No. 1–2 (2004).

91 Malkki, 'National Geographic', pp. 30–31.

92 Kaplan explains that the Armenians made their claims to territories in Cilicia based on forms of knowledge valid to the French officials. Thus their claims shifted from 'intangible memories' to material evidence from disciplines including anthropology and philology. S. Kaplan, 'Territorializing Armenians: Geo-Texts and Political Imaginaries in French Occupied Cilicia, 1919–1922', *History and Anthropology*, Vol. 15, No. 4 (December 2004).

93 NA FO 608/79, Telegram from High Commissioner, 25 September 1919.

94 NA FO 608/78, 411, Report of Haskell to the Peace Conference, 29 August 1919.

95 NA FO 608/79, General Staff comments on repatriation plan, 9 July 1919.

96 See for example, NA FO 608/77, Memorandum 'Situation in Armenia' to British peace delegation by Ahronian, representative of the Armenian Republic and Nubar Pasha, 28 March 1919.

97 His point of view was supported by Balfour, the Foreign Minister and even Lloyd George. Hovannisian, *The Republic of Armenia*, Vol. 1, p. 301.

98 Northcote Papers, Letter to mother, 13 December 1919.

99 Northcote Papers, Letter to father, 2 February 1919.
100 Northcote Papers, Letter to mother, 17 February 1919.
101 NA FO 608/79, 181, Letter from the Armenian delegation, 26 June 1919.
102 Hovannisian, *Republic of Armenia*, Vol. 2, p. 43.
103 *Memoranda*, p. 6. Kaplan recognises that a process of categorising and fixing the identities of Armenians was undertaken in Cilicia by the French administration in order to try and determine the future of the region. Kaplan, 'Documenting History, Historicising Documents: French Military Officials' Ethnological Reports on Cilicia', *Comparative Studies in Society and History*, Vol. 44, No. 2 (2002).
104 *Memoranda*, p. 7.
105 *Memoranda*, p. 7.
106 On how the historic landscape plays a role in defining the boundaries of Armenia, see Kohl and Tsetskhladze, 'Nationalism, Politics and the Practice of Archaeology in the Caucasus'.
107 *New Near East*, Vol. 6, No. 3 (December 1920), p. 9.
108 Events reported in *New Near East*, Vol. 6, No. 3 (December 1920).
109 *Further Memoranda on the Armenian and Assyrian Refugees in Mesopotamia* (in continuation of publication no. 36170) (Baghdad: Government Press, 1921), p. 6.
110 Syria and Lebanon had become French mandates after the war. The authorities tried to disperse the refugees but they tended to cluster in urban areas. They resisted dispersal, Greenshields suggests, out of a desire for security in numbers as well as the wish to preserve Armenian culture and identity. Only in 1929 did they accept a scheme to settle in Palmyra. T. H. Greenshields, 'The Settlement of Armenian Refugees in Syria and Lebanon 1915–1939', in John I. Clarke and Howard Bowen-Jones, *Change and Development in the Middle East: Essays in Honour of W.B. Fisher* (London: Meuthen, 1981). See also T. H. Greenshields, *The Settlement of Armenian Refugees in Syria and Lebanon, 1915–1939*, unpublished PhD Thesis (University of Durham, 1978), and Dzovinar Kevonian, *Réfugies et Diplomatie Humanitaire: Les Acteurs Européens et la Scène Proche Orientale Pendant l'Entre Deux Guerres*, unpublished Thesis (Pantheon-Sorbonne, 1998).
111 Northcote Papers, Letter from the LMF, 15 October 1921.
112 *Further Memoranda*, p. 2.
113 Northcote papers, 'Armenian Refugees in Mesopotamia', Statement received from the colonial office, 24 September 1921.
114 Ibid.
115 The BAC asked Northcote to make a statement to the press about his experiences in the refugee camps and talk to the British press in anticipation of the government's statement regarding the closure of the camps.
116 Northcote Papers, D. Northcote, *Memorandum*.
117 Ibid.

118 Ibid.
119 Ibid.
120 Northcote Papers, Clipping of letter to *The Times* from 'Armenus', 6 October 1921.
121 Northcote Papers, Clipping of letter to *The Times* from Archbishop Gore, 6 September 1921.

5

Post-war Armenia:
visions, realities and responses

Introduction

The genocidal massacres and deportations of the Armenians in the Ottoman Empire had two seemingly contradictory effects on the Armenians as a 'nation'. In one sense, the Armenian nation could be considered to be in a weaker and more threatened position than ever before. Massacre and deportation had decimated the population and left the regions they regarded as 'homeland' devoid of Armenian inhabitants. The repatriation of Armenians to their former homes in Eastern Anatolia, which many Armenians and their supporters had pinned their hopes upon, was a complex and protracted problem. With the creation of the Turkish Republic it ultimately proved to be impossible.

Nonetheless, the wartime experiences of the Armenians meant that the formation of an independent Armenian nation state now occupied a more prominent place in both Armenian nationalist discourse and in international politics and diplomacy. It was recognised that realising the ideal of an autonomous Armenia would be a difficult task, given that an autonomous Armenia had not existed for centuries and the population and territory had been devastated by war and genocide. Even so the victorious powers expressed the opinion that nationhood was the right and proper future for the Armenians. Amongst the Armenians themselves, the experience or witnessing of displacement also ignited nationalist aspirations and brought to the fore the idea of national identity and the importance of national survival, providing an opportunity for nationalists to make their claims more forcefully.[1]

In the aftermath of the war, alongside their involvement in the provision of relief for Armenian refugees, British Armenophiles also continued their campaign of support for the Armenian 'national cause', promoting Armenian claims to self-determination and the formation of an independent Armenian state. The ways in which they articulated their visions of the Armenian future and responded to the challenges of peacemaking, the rise of Turkish nationalism and the Soviet occupation of the Armenian Republic are all examined in this chapter.

A number of differing and often conflicting visions of the future of Armenia were expounded during this period by various representatives of the Armenians, Armenophile organisations, humanitarians and politicians. This made the issue of defining the borders of Armenia in the post-war period and the process of deciding how a new Armenian state should be governed highly contentious. These issues draw attention to the particular understandings of the nation state which emerged after the First World War. They also provide an example of changing perceptions of the role of the international community in the definition, establishment and protection of new states, through, for example, the mandate system.

The chapter charts the changing attitudes of international governments and the general public to the Armenian cause, examining the way that perceptions of Armenia shifted from that of a 'victim nation' which had secured the sympathies of Europe and America, to a troublesome problem for politicians, diplomats and the military which would eventually be 'abandoned' and slip from the gaze of the international community.

Finally I consider the British response to the unexpected settlement of the 'Armenian question', that is the sudden Soviet occupation of the Armenian Republic and the resurgence of a Turkish state which absorbed vast areas of the territory which Armenians considered to be their 'homeland'. I examine the perspectives of British Armenophiles on the Soviet state and their hopes and fears for the Soviet Armenian future, considering the way that this impacted on the way they understood Armenia's place in the wider world and the new national order of Europe.

Demands for nationhood

The surrender of the Ottoman Empire in 1918 initially offered renewed hope for Armenian nationalist aspirations, raising Armenian hopes of gaining control of the provinces of Eastern Anatolia as part of a 'greater' Armenian state. It also encouraged the belief that the Transcaucasian refugee crisis would ease as the Armenians could be repatriated to their homes in Eastern Anatolia, thus reducing the pressure on the struggling

Armenian Republic. Indeed some of the refugees in Transcaucasia began to make their way back to their homes in Anatolia and Cilicia, under the impression that they would now be safe from Turkish attack and that the territory would soon be under Armenian control.

In these apparently promising circumstances Armenian elites began to set out their claims to national autonomy and elaborate upon their plans for the formation of an Armenian nation state. Despite their initially idealistic tones this would prove to be a difficult and drawn-out process. The opinions of the Armenian parties (the Dashnaks who ruled the Armenian Republic, the socialist Hnchaks and the Liberal Ramkavars) which were all active in the diaspora were rarely harmonious. The unwillingness of the other powers to offer concrete support for their plans made their projects even more difficult to realise.

Armenian ideals

The call for the creation of an autonomous Armenian state was led in Europe by the Liberal Armenian leader Boghos Nubar Pasha of the ANDP. Nubar Pasha had advocated the Armenian cause throughout the war and was convinced of the need to create a large, unified Armenian state including the Anatolian provinces and Cilicia. In common with a substantial part of the diaspora and Turkish Armenians, he had little faith in the new republic, being suspicious of the revolutionary socialist politics of the Dashnak-dominated government and believing that the heartland of Armenia lay in Eastern Anatolia and Cilicia, not Transcaucasia.[2] Over the next months, therefore, the question of what constituted 'homeland' for the Armenians became fiercely contested.

As Susan Pattie has suggested, for Armenians 'homeland' is not a static or unproblematic concept, but rather a 'contested and evolving notion'.[3] This was never more so than during the post-First World War period. Pattie's work draws attention to the implications of political upheavals and reconfigurations such as those experienced during the First World War for Armenian constructions of 'homeland'. She explains that, 'The confusion increases as political parties emphasise ideological notions of homeland, detached perhaps from personal experience but rooted in the past and in contemporary political events.'[4]

In the aftermath of the First World War such 'confusion' was certainly evident. Diaspora organisations, the Dashnak government of the Republic of Armenia, international relief agencies and later the Soviet government of Armenia all articulated their own particular view of 'homeland'. Their polemics eventually influenced the perceptions of the 'ordinary' Armenians who were seeking to determine their own futures. Thus the refugees housed in the Ba'quba camp, though originally from Van or other regions of Eastern Anatolia, adopted Transcaucasia as a homeland and expressed their wish to be repatriated there, despite having no personal or familial links to the region and despite the existence of significant linguistic and cultural differences between them and the Armenians of Transcaucasia.

The notion of 'Greater Armenia' as homeland espoused by Armenian national elites such as the ANDP and their supporters during the immediate post-war period depended upon a particular reading of the Armenian past. This held that the Armenians were the remnants of an ancient nation which had survived through centuries of conquest and oppression. These understandings of history drew upon the constructions of the national past which had been undertaken by Armenian scholars and nationalists over the past two or three centuries. Within this framework, 'Armenia' meant the lands which (it was believed) the Armenians had inhabited for thousands of years before their conquest by invaders from 'the East'. This was a view espoused by many of the British Armenophiles. Their definition of the Armenian homeland relied on these theories of historical roots but also incorporated a belief in the Armenians as having the most potential to develop the land in the future.

After 1919 the future of the refugees was incorporated into arguments in favour of a large independent Armenia. A 1920 pro-Armenian memorandum presented the creation of such an Armenia as the logical way in which to improve the situation in both Eastern Turkey and the refugee crisis in Transcaucasia:

> In fact the present economic distress in the Erivan Republic is well known to be very largely due to the large numbers of refugees from the adjoining Ottoman provinces who are at present encamped there. The inclusion of these territories in the Armenian state would ease the whole situation by enabling these refugees to return home and recultivate their lands.[5]

The fact that the Armenian Republic was referred to in this text as the 'Erivan republic' underscored the fact that the majority of Armenians did not regard it as the true Armenia, but only a small part of the whole.

In the aftermath of the war the ANDP worked tirelessly to convince international governments and the general public to endorse their vision of an Armenian nation state occupying the entire 'homeland'. They focused upon the need to incorporate the eastern provinces of the Ottoman Empire and the territory of the medieval Armenian Kingdom of

Cilicia on the Mediterranean coast into a new Armenian nation state. In order to do so they embarked afresh upon campaigns of pamphlet publication and letter writing.

Nubar Pasha, leader of the ANDP, was well connected in the European diplomatic world. As a westernised moderate who saw the future Armenia as part of the European world, he gained acceptance with many influential figures and used these connections to ensure that the message of the ANDP reached those best placed to help the Armenians. He was in frequent contact, for example, with the British Foreign Office and delegations to the peace conferences, providing them with endless updates on the Armenian situation and evidence to support Armenian claims.

The ANDP and other Armenophile organisations persisted in the use of the language of a clash of civilisation and barbarism in order to describe the fate of the Armenians during the war. This was all too familiar to British audiences from the decades of Armenophile discourse and more recently from the wartime atrocity propaganda described in previous chapters. It utilised the image of the Armenians as 'an ancient people who have been the standard bearers of progress and civilisation in the Near East'. Their propaganda material also gained some new dimensions in the light of the post-war situation. It drew attention to the relevance of Armenia to the Western European powers, highlighting, for example, the potential of the Armenians as a bridge between East and West, 'by their industry and natural gifts the best intermediaries between the culture of the West and the peoples of the East'.[6]

The ANDP's *Memorandum on the Armenian Question*, meanwhile, drew upon the longstanding claim that Europe had a special duty towards the Armenians, appealing to the 'will and conscience of the civilised world' for justice. Their justification for their claims was also based upon well-known stereotypes, contrasting the 'virile and prolific' Armenians with the 'unspeakable ferocity of the Turk'.[7] The same pamphlet also illustrated the fact that the war had inadvertently given the diaspora and the Armenophiles a new weapon in promoting their cause. Not only could they call upon idealised historical images of the Armenians, they could also point to the contribution that the Armenians had made to the Allied cause during the war:

It is perhaps not generally realised that but for Armenian resistance the Turks would have overrun Persia and turned the flank of the British Army in Mesopotamia soon after the Bolsheviks came to power; and that as de facto Allies the Armenians have done their duty with unsurpassed loyalty and sacrifice.[8]

The implication was that through fighting a barbaric enemy and defending the civilised world the Armenians had come to rank alongside the other European powers. It was suggested, therefore, that recognition of Armenian nationhood would be a fit reward for their sacrifices during the war.

The Armenian lobby did not simply rely on the virtues of the Armenian nation in order to make their case to the powers. They were also well aware that the changing geopolitical agendas of the great powers would have a determining effect on the future of Armenia. For this reason the ANDP and also the BAC chose to highlight the strategic importance of Armenia for post-war British imperial policy. In one memorandum, for example, the BAC suggested that the 'territorial changes likely to be produced in the Middle East as a result of the war make the well being of Armenia an important interest of the British Empire' and compared the strategic importance of Armenia with that of the North West Frontier during the previous century.[9]

Armenia, Britain and the Versailles Peace Conference

Armenian representatives arrived at the Versailles Peace Conference in February 1919. They were not officially recognised as belligerents and as such did not have an official place at the conference. Initially the Armenians were represented by two separate delegations, one from the Armenian Republic, led by Avetis Aharonian, and the other representing the western Armenian diaspora, led by Boghos Nubar Pasha. This split reflected broader divisions between the homeland and the diaspora which would develop over the course of the twentieth century. Eventually the two bodies, who initially had different priorities regarding the future of Armenia, reached a compromise and agreed to work together to advance their claims.[10] On this basis they attempted to make their case to the conference for the existence of a large Armenian state 'extending from Transcaucasia and the Black Sea to Cilicia and the Mediterranean Sea'.[11] Later, these claims would be dismissed as extravagant and unrealistic.

Having attempted to convince the European powers that the Armenians were deserving of national recognition and that the existence of an Armenian nation would be beneficial to all concerned, the Armenians were forced to wait for the outcome of the peace conferences.[12] The Armenians were not alone in their attempts to use the peace conferences to promote their national aspirations in the aftermath of crisis. However, just as in the case of other aspiring national groups, the Armenian path towards nationhood would be by no means smooth. Reconstruction and the reconfiguration of populations and territory that peacemaking would bring would provoke further social and political upheaval and conflict. As Baron and Gatrell point out:

> The peace treaties and territorial arrangements of 1918–1920 marked the birth of a new era of nationalist and revolutionary conflict, extensive social dislocation and intense ethnic discord, grand visions of reconstruction and regeneration, and renewed population movement on a massive scale.[13]

Despite this difficult backdrop, post-war circumstances seemed initially to offer some advantages to the Armenian nationalist cause. The rhetoric of self-determination and the protection of small nations and minorities from aggressive imperialism had been central to the way in which war had been conceptualised and justified.[14] The idea of self-determination, associated particularly with President Wilson's vision of peacemaking and post-war reconstruction, would be central to peacemaking, as empires were dismantled and borders were to be redrawn to recognise the rights of small or oppressed nations.[15]

War had brought about the downfall of the empires of Central and Eastern Europe, and the rights of the minorities which they had previously encompassed were recognised, in principle at least, by the powers.[16] Like those of the Armenians, the claims of these nations were often based on historic boundaries. As Aviel Roshwald points out, 'It was precisely the immutability of territorial configurations based on frozen moments in history that lent them appeal as symbols of nationhood.'[17] In the propaganda of the Armenians the achievements and extent of past Armenian kingdoms would become a frequent reference point. Nubar Pasha himself claimed in a letter to the British government that Armenia 'has the right to invoke the glory of its own history'.[18]

In the lead up to the Versailles Conference the rhetoric of the British government had raised Armenian hopes. Since early 1918 the British government had renewed their expressions of support for the Armenians. In January 1918 in a speech on war aims to trade unionists at Caxton Hall, Lloyd George had stated that, 'Arabia, Armenia, Mesopotamia, Syria and Palestine are in our judgement entitled to recognition of their separate national condition.'[19] This intention was reaffirmed in October 1918, when Robert Cecil claimed that 'the policy of the allies towards Armenia remains unaltered . . . I am quite ready to reaffirm our determination that wrongs such as Armenia suffered shall be brought to an end and their reoccurrence made impossible'.[20]

This renewed enthusiasm for Armenian 'liberation' was linked to the desire to defend the region from Ottoman expansion following their advances towards Transcaucasia in early 1918. At this time Mark Sykes propounded a 'belt of Jewish, Arab and Armenian states' blocking any Ottoman advance.[21] This brief coincidence of aims did not, however, entail a full-scale British commitment to the Armenian cause. As Nassibian points out, British statements about the future of Armenia were always 'deliberately equivocal, vague and ambiguous'.[22]

The apparent enthusiasm for an autonomous Armenia encouraged the British Armenophiles and diaspora organisations. In May 1918 the Armenian Information Bureau, the creation of Aram Raffi, the Armenian novelist, published numerous pamphlets on the future of Armenia. Like the diaspora activists, British Armenophiles also based their claims for an independent Armenia on established images of Armenia as a site of Christianity and civilisation. In November the BAC set out their own hopes in a list of requests to be presented to the Foreign Office by Bryce. Like the ANDP they hoped for the creation of an Armenian state encompassing all of 'historic' Armenia as a mandatory of the League of Nations.[23]

British Armenophile organisations also drew upon long-established discourses of Armenian 'civilisation' in order to justify their support for the creation of an Armenian nation state.[24] Narratives and images of the deportations portrayed the Armenians as an integral part of the European world. In the aftermath of war the Armenophiles continued to try to draw the Armenians in from their ambiguous position on the fringes of Europe and banish any 'taint' of the East.[25] The events of the First World War added a new urgency to their calls for support for the Armenians and strength to their argument that they 'belonged' to the European world.

Whereas in the past even the most vocal of the Armenophiles expressed the belief that the Armenians were as yet unready for nationhood, now such reservations were cast aside. British Armenophiles portrayed the massacres as a kind of baptism of fire for the Armenian nation whose survival and endurance in the face of war, deportation and massacre indicated Armenian national qualities and potential. This was coupled with the demand that the Turks should never again rule over the Armenians: 'Turkish rule over populations of a different faith must cease forever to exist. Turkish government has been the very worst which has afflicted humanity during the last fifteen centuries.'[26]

The events of 1915–18 were built into the conception of Armenian history as a narrative of national survival in the face of conquest, oppression and suffering. This was not a new theme, but it was now expounded with greater force. The post-war period was therefore treated as a crucial stage in the history of the Armenian people, when they must finally escape centuries of oppression or be completely destroyed. This sense of urgency was vividly illustrated by the diasporan activist A. P. Hacobian:

> It is a question of 'to be or not to be' in a real and fateful sense: The rebirth of Armenian nationality from the profusion of its lost blood and heaps of smouldering ashes, or the end of that long cherished and bled-for aspiration.[27]

Armenia and the future of the Ottoman Empire

During the initial stages of the peacemaking the British government maintained their support for the creation of an independent Armenian state. Figures such as Lloyd George, who had strong anti-Turkish sentiments and had set out his commitment to the Armenians in speeches the previous year, and also Earl Curzon were particularly supportive of these plans. As Richard Hovannisian has explained, during the last weeks of 1918 the Foreign Office created draft suggestions for the Turkish settlement. According to this, the borders of an Armenia 'extended from the Cilician shores northward along the Anti-Taurus mountains to the Black Sea at a point just west of Ordy and from the Gulf of Alexandretta eastward along the Taurus Mountains, thus encompassing the six Armenian vilayets'.[28] This was of course the type of 'Greater Armenia', encompassing all of the 'historic homelands' that the Armenian lobby was hoping for. In February 1919 Toynbee noted that it was satisfying 'to note how closely the Armenian and the British proposals correspond'.[29]

Despite such sympathy for the Armenians and enthusiasm for an independent Armenia, those involved in peacemaking and reconstruction soon became aware that the process of creating such an Armenian state was fraught with difficulty. That the future of Armenia could not be decided in isolation posed the central problem. Armenia's future was entangled with the seemingly intractable task of deciding the future of the territories of the Ottoman Empire. For although the powers had been outspoken in their demands that the Ottoman government could not continue to rule over the empire, there were a multitude of differing opinions as to what should take its place and where exactly the Armenians fitted into this picture.

The Armenians were not alone in their attempt to carve out a nation state from the territories of the former Ottoman Empire. Arabs, Kurds, Jews and Greeks were amongst the other groups also demanding territory, restitution or retribution or seeking the establishment of 'homelands'. The forcefulness with which they pursued their claims was not surprising given that, as Artin Arslanian explains, 'their expectations had been raised by contradictory promises from one or more of the great powers, seeking a temporary advantage at times of pressing urgency during the war'.[30] Keeping these promises soon came into conflict with the powers' own agendas in the region.

Each of the powers had their own interests in the former Ottoman territories, for example the British in Mesopotamia and the French in Syria. In 1916 the spoils of the Ottoman Empire had originally been carved up between the Allies with little respect to the aspirations of its subject populations through the British, French and Russian Sykes-Picot agreement. Following the revolutions in Russia this agreement became defunct, which meant that a great deal of time and energy was devoted to reconciling the competing and shifting interests of the Allies. The longer the peace conferences delayed coming to a decision regarding the Turkish settlement, the more complex this task became.

The British diplomats, humanitarians and military leaders who were involved in this process soon became aware that creating a large Armenian nation state in former Ottoman territory would not be a straightforward process. The overlapping claims of these different minorities, along with the growth of Turkish nationalism, meant that dividing the territory would be a contentious process. Following the principles of 'self determination' and creating clearly defined nation states with homogenous populations proved near-impossible in the former Ottoman Empire.

Even British Armenophiles accepted that the Armenian population did not form a majority in the regions they called their 'homeland'. The Armenian population had been dispersed amongst Turks, Kurds, Greeks and other minorities, and these groups often had very different opinions regarding what the future of these regions should be. Some British observers feared that giving the Armenians priority in the region would only aggravate the Turks and Kurds, and therefore destabilise the region further, leading to a resurgence of the bloody violence that had been witnessed in these territories during the war.

The question of the future of the Ottoman Empire provoked strong feelings amongst the numerous British personnel who had been involved in the region in humanitarian, diplomatic, military or other capacities. As the Versailles Conference got under way British officials found themselves bombarded with information, evidence and demands not only from the Armenophile lobby but also from those who had experience of life in the Ottoman Empire and who were keen to offer their expertise and opinions as to its future development. The viewpoints of these individuals were welcomed as a way of improving the British authorities' somewhat sketchy picture of the complex and rapidly evolving situation in the former Ottoman Empire.

This process of information gathering and analysis which continued throughout the drawn-out process of the peace settlement echoed the work of the scholars and travellers who collected information about the Ottoman Empire in the latter stages of the nineteenth century. As explained in chapter 2, the work of these scholars and travellers also often had a political dimension: they amassed knowledge about the region and its population with the hope of improving their future development. This latter information-gathering project shared other features with its nineteenth-century counterpart. Like the work of well-meaning scholars and travellers, such as James Bryce, the reports presented to the British authorities in the post-war period also objectified the Armenians, underscoring their 'otherness'. This meant that even reports which were ostensibly positive about the Armenian future were underpinned by ambivalence and inequality.

Because Eastern Anatolia was characterised by ethnic and religious diversity, a central feature of this knowledge-gathering was the attempt to gain an accurate picture of the population distribution in the area. This was essential if the principles of self-determination were to be followed and national groups were to be able to form their own nation states in their own national territories. Available population statistics were therefore collected and analysed so as to ascertain which areas should 'belong' to whom.

Because of the upheavals of war and the inaccuracy of pre-war figures, reliable statistics were difficult to find. This was particularly true of the Armenian case. Available statistics were generally based on pre-war figures, which did not take into account the terrible loss of life amongst the Armenians that had occurred as a result of the massacres and deportations. The dispersal of the surviving population across Transcaucasia and the Middle East as a result of the war and genocide further complicated the picture and made estimating the future population of an independent Armenian state nearly impossible.

Armenian population statistics were therefore highly contested. The Armenian delegation to the peace conferences argued that the Armenians 'had formed an absolute majority in the Ottoman Eastern vilayets fifty years earlier', before Ottoman attacks on the Armenians had begun.[31] Most others, however, concluded that even taking into account the dramatic decline in the Armenian population during the war, the Armenians had never been a clear majority in the region they regarded as their homeland. For some representatives of the Armenians, such as Avetis Aharonian, representative of the Armenian Republic to the peace conferences this was not problematic, as they assumed that the pull of an independent Armenia would be irresistible to the diaspora: 'to the united country there would come back great numbers of Armenians from all over the world'.[32]

Other 'experts' viewed the future of the Armenians in a somewhat different light. In the essay on the future of Armenia received by the British delegation from Mr Louis Heck, the former American Commissioner in Constantinople, Heck concluded that, 'We admit that upon a strict interpretation of the principle of self-determination, the Armenian race can scarcely lay claim to a predominating position on the Ottoman territories where the greater portion of the race formally lived.' In the absence of clear statistical evidence Heck resorted to assessments of racial qualities and characteristics to determine the best options for the future of the region. His ambivalent attitudes to the Armenians echoed the words of nineteenth-century travellers and scholars; this is perhaps unsurprising giving his reliance on the work of the nineteenth-century traveller and archaeologist Professor William Ramsay.[33]

Heck was critical of the Armenians, whom he claimed, 'as a race do not possess characteristics of an attractive nature'. He criticised their 'love for intrigue' and the fact that they were 'greedy of gain', criticisms which had been levelled at the Armenians for at least the past half a century. Yet Heck had to weigh the problems of the Armenians against the 'flaws' of the other inhabitants of the region, for example the Kurds, whom he deemed 'ignorant and perhaps but half civilised'. He concluded that the Armenians were after all the 'race which offers the greatest possibilities of development of all the region, and which can best adapt itself to modern conditions'.[34] As previous chapters have described, the theme of Armenians as key to the development of the region had been present in British writings on Armenia since the nineteenth century and was a key idea in the work of Armenophiles such as James Bryce. It was recycled by a number of commentators during the post-war period.

Reliance on longstanding racial stereotypes in assessments of the future of the region emerged as a common theme in post-war debates. Admiral

Calthorpe at the British High Commission in Constantinople also felt able to generalise about Armenian 'characteristics', asserting that the Armenian is 'acquisitive to the point of avarice', whilst the Turk is 'lazy and indifferent to wealth'.

The British Foreign Office Peace Conference Handbook for Armenia and Kurdistan was also concerned with 'race', not only in terms of character stereotypes (the Armenians were said to be 'vigorous and virile') but also in terms of racial origins, discussing in some depth the Semitic and Aryan origins of the Armenians in the seventh century BC.[35] Armenian involvement in trade and commerce, which was viewed with ambivalence by the British, was also explained in terms of race: 'The virtues and vices of successful traders and artisans are to be expected in a race of superior capacities cut off from attachment to land.'[36] This statement also implied that these 'superior capacities' made the Armenians deserving of territory.

This set of guidelines for the delegates to the conference also took factors other than race into consideration. Once again Armenian history was used as an explanation of present characteristics and a guide for the future. For example the city of Ani figured as evidence of Armenian potential, the 'military and financial strength of the dynasty and the artistic skill of the builders'.[37] National sentiment or national identity was also discussed as distinct from race and as a determining factor in deciding the Armenian future. The authors of the handbook seemed uncertain on this subject: 'The popular opinion of so widely diffused a people as the Armenians is not easily gauged, nor can we confidently speak of national sentiment among a race which has never constituted a single and comprehensive state.'[38] It suggests however that by the time this handbook was published in May 1919 reservations about the Armenian national future were beginning to surface.

Numerous other schemes for the future of the Ottoman Empire, and particularly of its Armenian population, were sent to or sought out by British officials. Many of them were highly sympathetic to the sufferings of the Armenians yet still advised against the creation of an Armenian nation state. Newcombe, a British soldier who had been a POW in Turkey and was later based at Adana, a former Armenian capital city in Cilicia, was amongst those who suggested that a multi-national state with equal rights, rather than separate states for the various elements, would be the best way of ensuring security and stability in the future.[39]

The Newcombe scheme was amongst those presented to the British peace delegation. Arnold Toynbee, Deputy Chief Near Eastern Advisor at the British delegation, agreed with Newcombe's point of view regarding the problems of the 'mixed' population of Eastern Anatolia and its implications for Armenian nationhood. Despite his sympathies for the Armenians he still observed that 'The Armenian nationality is hardly more representative of the total population of Armenia than the Zionists are of the population of Palestine.'[40] For Toynbee equality was the best solution, but he also realised that this brought its own problems, in that it would meet with much hostility from the Armenians. 'The principle of equality for all local nationalities ought to be the basis of reconstruction here,' he observed. Hoewever he was also painfully aware that this would not easily be accepted, 'even by so moderate an Armenian as Nubar Pasha.'[41]

Dr Gates, the well-respected Principal of Robert College in Constantinople, although sympathetic to the Armenians, also believed that an independent Armenia was not a viable option. It would result, he claimed, 'in a massacre of the remnant of the Armenian nation.'[42] Instead he believed that a single mandate for the whole of Turkey was the ideal solution, but once again this raised the problem of which of the powers would take on such an enormous responsibility.

Gates' objections to an independent Armenia also provide a reminder of the gendered understanding of nations that prevailed during this period. The Armenians who remained after the massacres were, he claimed, 'for the most part widows and orphans incapable of caring for themselves and much less of contributing to the building up of the state.'[43] The women of Armenia had played their part as emblems of the suffering of Armenia but the task of constructing and defending the nation state was conceived of as a purely male role. Without strong men, he implied, the Armenian state was not viable.

Admiral Calthorpe, on the other hand, proposed a more drastic scheme for creating the desired ethnically homogenous regions in Anatolia and thus avoiding the problems of ethnic conflict otherwise thought to be inevitable. He suggested that, 'A system of exchange might be devised by which Armenians living in the Moslem state should give up their property to Moslems coming from the Armenian state and receive in exchange the property of those Moslems.' He added that, 'Every such movement of population is difficult because it is artificial.'[44] His views echoed the fact that populations had come to be seen in a new way, as entities which could be moulded, manipulated or moved in order to fit neat borderlines and avoid conflict. The effects of the later population exchanges between Greece and Turkey highlight the problems implicit in such an approach.[45]

The collection of this kind of information was important in shaping British opinions as to the best path for the future development of Armenia and of course the former Ottoman Empire in general. It was however only one stage in a complex process of decision-making. The ideal schemes developed by Armenian representatives, Armenophiles and the (often self-styled) experts were at best templates. The rapidly evolving situation in the Ottoman Empire and in particular the growth of Turkish nationalism meant none of these schemes could be implemented in a wholesale manner. They would also be tempered by the shifting aims and agendas of the powers, whose priorities changed somewhat over the course of the peace settlements, often to the disadvantage of the Armenians.

Deciding the future

Although the conference, as Suny has observed, had initially had an 'Armenophile' atmosphere, resolving the future of the Armenians had proved to be a difficult and drawn-out process.[46] Despite the apparent international support for the Armenians, none of the powers were in practice willing to translate this into a direct commitment to an Armenian nation state. This was demonstrated by the withdrawal of British troops from the Caucasus in August 1919. British priorities were clearly elsewhere, on domestic demands and reconstruction, and in international terms, on the protection of British interests in the oil-rich regions of Mesopotamia.[47]

During the peace conferences the British government endorsed the idea that the fragile Republic of Armenia should become an American mandate, a proposal also supported by Nubar Pasha and the ANDP. The concept of a mandate was a new development: it recognised, in principle, the right to self-determination, yet allowed for a degree of outside control. The belief that a mandate was the best hope for Armenian autonomy reflected lingering suspicions that the Armenians were 'unready' and were still in need of European or American guidance. As Artin Arslanian has pointed out, 'Many British politicians and an overwhelming majority of military leaders believed that the subject peoples of the former Russian and Ottoman Empires were unfit to govern themselves.'[48]

Louis Mallet, Assistant Undersecretary of State for Foreign Affairs and Chief Near Eastern Advisor at the peace delegation viewed the need for a mandatory power in Armenia as a result of the 'mixed' population in the region. In effect he was suggesting that conflict between the different ethnic groups was natural or inevitable and that such a diverse population had to be protected from itself through the presence of mandatory government. His conclusions were not particularly optimistic: 'You may call the country Armenian and make it independent, but the moral is that the tutelary power will have to govern it for a long time to come.'[49]

James Barton, Director of NER, also believed that the mandate was a long-term measure; in his opinion it would have to last for 30 years. His concerns centered on the effects of the events of the war on the Armenian population: 'The constructive thinkers have all been sacrificed and Armenia's great hope centres on the hundreds of thousands of orphans who are being gathered everywhere and are being instructed and taught trades.'[50] His viewpoint of course echoed the ethos of NER, that the Armenians had 'potential' to develop with external help, and that refugee relief should be a forum for education, development and also nation-building.

Some diasporan Armenians clearly agreed with the perspective of Barton. One diasporan pointed out in a memorandum to the British peace conference delegation that because of their history the Armenians were 'dispossessed of all practical capacities of the true art of state organ-isation and for its good government, in the English sense of the word'. For this Armenian England provided an ideal model for the future develop-ment of Armenia and the Armenians must learn from the English.[51] Such faith in the capacity of Europeans or Americans to 'improve' the Armenians was also expressed very clearly in a BAC propaganda pamphlet suggesting that 'only by the wise guidance of a powerful and impartial external authority can the peoples themselves hope to establish a stable political community'.[52]

Wilson himself was initially keen for America to take on Armenia as a mandate, an action which would fit with his ideals of self-determination and democracy. However he delayed in accepting this role on behalf of America in principle until May 1919, then became ill and unable to cam-paign to ensure that it became a reality. The mandate was eventually rejected by the American Senate in June 1920.[53] The American decision meant that official British hopes for the future of Armenia had been destroyed. Without the security of America as a mandatory power the future of Armenia seemed increasingly uncertain, especially in the face of the resurgence of Turkish nationalism under the leadership of Mustapha Kemal.

During this period of uncertainty the Armenophiles had worked to keep the Armenian cause in the public eye, their hopes still pinned on the creation of a nation state. In September 1919, the BAC had considered the possibility of sending a delegation to America to try to encourage the gov-ernment to accept the Armenian mandate.[54] In June 1920, as the chances of the establishment of an Armenian nation seemed to be slipping away, they established a 'propaganda sub-committee' in order to push the subject into the public eye once again. Though they had some success in attracting the attention of the press, they did not achieve their aims. Public interest in the Armenians was, at this point, directed towards the more urgent need for humanitarian relief for refugees rather than the politics of nation-building.[55]

The ANDP also continued to petition the powers, using a range of arguments touching on history, geography and population statistics in order to articulate the rights of the Armenians to a nation state. In January 1920 they issued the British government with three memoranda, one of which, *Transcaucasian Armenia*, 'explained claims from the ethnological point of view, according to incontestable facts and figures and official documents'.[56] In the last of the memoranda, *Armenia and the Turkish Settlement*, the delegation expressed their enthusiasm for a mandate yet acknowledged the difficulties inherent in making this a reality. However, they stressed that even a 'partial mandate' for the Armenian territories was preferable to Turkish rule. Any connection between Armenia and Turkey, they argued, must be 'severed completely'.[57] Nevertheless, later that year exactly the opposite would happen.

In August 1920 the Treaty of Sèvres theoretically settled the future of the Ottoman Empire. It divided Anatolia into zones of Italian and French influence, gave Thrace to the Greeks and placed Smyrna under Greek rule until a plebiscite was held five years later, placed the straits under an international commission and also made provision for the creation of an independent Armenia. In an attempt to appear not to have failed completely in their commitments to Armenia the conference asked President Wilson to draw up the boundaries of Armenia. The borders he drew, which included much of the territory of the ideal 'Greater Armenia', although they never became a reality, would remain a touchstone for Armenian nationalists throughout the century.

Without international enforcement Sèvres was a dead letter. Despite the provisions of the treaty the Turkish nationalist advance continued and with it the loss of territories considered integral to the Armenian homeland. Despite repeated requests the Allies had failed to protect the Armenians. Promises made during the war regarding autonomy and security remained unfulfilled, but as Artin Arslanian has explained these promises had always been 'made for achieving victory, not from sincere conviction or serious concern for the post-war world order'.[58] British postwar priorities simply could not be reconciled with those of the Armenians.

By the time Armenia's new borders were announced in November the republic was already falling victim to Bolshevik and Turkish advances. In December 1920 through 'a combination of political subversion and military operations' the Armenian Republic was forced to accept Soviet dominance as the lesser of two evils and Soviet forces occupied the small republic.[59] The Armenian provinces of Eastern Anatolia were subsequently absorbed into the new Turkey.[60] When the Treaty of Moscow finally settled the Turkish and Soviet borders a large part of the territory considered to be the Armenian 'homeland', including the provinces of Kars and Ardahan, were left under Turkish rule, devoid of Armenian inhabitants.

Hopes of an Armenian 'homeland' in Anatolia and in Transcaucasia had been destroyed. Over the course of the next year the prospect of Armenian autonomy in Cilicia, site of a medieval Armenian kingdom and regarded as an integral part of the historic homeland, also foundered. Armenians who had returned to Cilicia under French protection found themselves once again under attack. In 1922 France agreed to evacuate Cilicia and a new refugee crisis was created as around 50,000 Armenians left for Syria and Lebanon.[61]

In 1922 the attack on Smyrna created a new wave of Armenian refugees, highlighting the impossibility of an Armenian national future in the former Ottoman Empire.[62] Then in July 1923 after the Treaty of Lausanne, the provinces of Eastern Anatolia were absorbed into the new Turkish Republic. In the words of Richard Hovannisian, 'It was as if an "Armenian question" or the Armenian people themselves had never existed.'[63]

Soviet Armenia: changing perspectives

Whilst efforts to secure an Armenian nation state in Eastern Anatolia had been under way at the peace conferences, the refugee crisis and struggle for survival in the Republic of Armenia had continued. During the struggle to determine the future of the Ottoman Empire, the long-term fate of Transcaucasia had also remained unresolved. What had become clear though, through the rapid withdrawal of British troops, was that Britain was unwilling to take on political or military responsibility for the region. On the other hand the British relief workers who had become involved in the international effort to ease the Armenian refugee crisis had continued their attempts to improve the dire situation in the Armenian Republic. Many of these relief workers would continue with these efforts even after the Sovietisation of the region in December 1920.

Soviet Armenia: crisis and relief

The first impression of British relief workers and military personnel of Transcaucasian Armenia was of a region ravaged by war and near collapse due to the strain of the refugee crisis.[64] Many of those who encountered the region in the immediate post-war period struggled to describe the scenes that they witnessed. Haskell, the Allied High Commissioner in the Caucasus, reported to the peace conference in August 1919 that the situation in the Armenian Republic was 'beyond description'.[65]

During the peace conferences the leaders of the Armenian Republic attempted to inform the world of the continued plight of their tiny state. Avetis Aharonian, an Armenian Republic representative to the Versailles Peace Conference, reported the terrible situation in Armenia to the British government in March 1919. There was no bread, he said, and the orphans were in a terrible state. Alongside the physical hardships endured by the Armenian people he emphasised the dehumanising effect of the refugee crisis, famine and disease, reporting that he had seen refugee women so desperate that they were tearing the flesh from a dead horse with their hands. Because of the terrible conditions death rates were high: there were 30 deaths a day in the Ashtarak region and 25 a day in Etchmiadzin.[66] These reports were intended to stress to the Allies the urgent need for the provision of aid in Armenia. However their circulation amongst the peace conference delegations was also intended to hasten the resolution of the future of the republic and thus alleviate the crisis.

British military and diplomatic personnel in the Caucasus shared the horror of the Armenians when they encountered the situation in Armenia. Oliver Wardrop, the British Commissioner at Tbilisi, visited Yerevan in 1919 and was appalled by the conditions which he discovered. In a report to Lord Curzon he described Yerevan as 'more depressing than any place I have ever seen'. Whilst he was in Yerevan the President of the Armenian Republic spoke to him about the needs of the people and pleaded with him for further help with supplies of clothes, shoes and medicines, which despite the efforts of the relief agencies, were still in short supply. Although Wardrop had no official authority in Armenia he emphasised the urgency of the situation there to the British Foreign Office and peace conference delegation.[67]

Wardrop reported the threat to the Armenian population from disease and starvation to the authorities in Britain. He also echoed Aharonian's fears of the dehumanising effects of war, famine and a prolonged refugee crisis on the Armenian nation and society. He argued that these hardships had distorted the moral order of society at the most basic level, damaging the institution of the family, reporting from Yerevan that:

> people are selling their children for prostitution, robbery with violence has become frequent . . . Not only have the people reached the limit of physical suffering, but their moral character has been put under a strain which has in many cases passed the breaking point and in all has produced lamentable results which must last for a long time.[68]

Wardrop's description of Armenian life contrasted sharply with the image of Armenian 'civilisation' that had been idealised by diaspora activists and the British Armenophiles. For this reason it was all the more shocking. He admitted that he could not offer any easy solution to the problems in Yerevan, but he echoed the travellers and scholars of the nineteenth century in his views that the Armenians, with their 'national qualities', could overcome the situation if given the chance to work hard and 'develop'. Providing the Armenians with this chance was the problem to be faced by relief agencies over the next few years.

Harold Buxton, an LMF relief agent in Transcaucasia, was one of the best informed of the British relief workers about the nature of the situation in Yerevan and the surrounding coutryside. Following on from visits made earlier in the war, he travelled to Transcaucasia in 1921 on behalf of the LMF in order to carry out an inquiry into famine conditions for the office of Fridtjof Nansen, the League of Nations' High Commissioner for Refugees. Buxton's reports gave the impression that, despite the increasing provision of relief, the situation had hardly improved. Between 200,000 and 300,000 Turkish Armenian refugees remained in the Caucasus, unable to return to their homes.[69] Although he realised that international aid was essential for the survival of the refugees, he was well aware of the shortcomings of relief programmes which simply allowed the refugees to survive a little longer and did not 'solve' the crisis. The implication was that without a proper resolution of the future of Armenia and the surrounding regions and a long-term plan to resolve the refugee situation, the problem could not be adequately resolved.

Outside of the capital city, rural areas of Armenia, he reported, remained 'primitive' in terms of both social conditions and agricultural methods.[70] Buxton reported the plight of the Armenians for the British public in the *Contemporary Review*, a liberal publication which had long been supportive of the Armenian cause, in order to try and convince the British population of the continuing urgency of the situation. Here the balanced 'facts and figures' approach he employed in official reports was supplemented by a horrific and dramatic picture: 'Everywhere, in town and country alike, one sees crowds of human scarecrows faced with a lingering death during the coming months from cold, hunger and disease. Hundreds of thousands are destitute, and large numbers are actually starving as we ourselves have witnessed.'[71]

Buxton's reports highlighted the fact that the Sovietisation of Armenia, although it had neutralised the threat of Turkish invasion, had not yet solved the crises of famine, disease and homelessness which had gripped the republic since the war. In addition the creation of Soviet Armenia and the Turkish Republic had compounded the problems of the Armenian Republic as it had sealed the fate of the refugees in Transcaucasia. It was now impossible for them to return to their original homes which were now in Turkish territories. This meant that they would have to somehow be resettled in Soviet Armenia, a country with overstretched resources and a lack of infrastructure.

Even as the crisis progressed more refugees arrived in Armenia. The refugees from the camp at Ba'quba, for example, were repatriated to Soviet Armenia via Batumi, in Georgia, over the winter of 1920. The Ba'quba relief worker Dudley Stafford Northcote also relocated to Transcaucasia. Northcote had now left the British army and continued to work for the LMF in Transcaucasia, spending the next four years engaged in projects of relief and reconstruction in Soviet Armenia.[72]

The repatriation of the refugees from Ba'quba occurred at a less than ideal time. In January 1921, soon after their arrival, Northcote noted that because of the levels of fighting between the Armenian Republic and the Turks, the situation in Armenia was worse than the rest of Transcaucasia.[73] The following month, in a letter home he observed, 'I don't think the position of Armenia has ever been blacker than it is now, both as regards the internal famine and as regards her complete abandonment by the allies.'[74]

The Soviet Republic struggled to cope with the existing population let alone cater for thousands more homeless refugees. One Armenian resident of the republic complained about the problems of the management of repatriation of refugees in a letter to relatives in Constantinople: 'The local powers had promised much but they have until now done very little to settle them and we have had to make do as best we can. There is no work to be had in the villages and if this situation continues then we will starve.'[75]

Despite such complaints the situation was not easily resolved and would remain critical throughout the early 1920s, with the Armenians remaining in need of international aid and support. On the British side

W. H. Harcourt led a team of thirteen field directors for the LMF who organised several schemes including orphanages for refugee children, feeding stations and work programmes.[76] The LMF did not work alone. In 1921 Harold Buxton described a number of British agencies operating in Transcaucasia. The British Relief Mission, as he termed it, also included the Friends of Armenia, the Armenian Red Cross and Refugee Fund and Save the Children.

Besides working in difficult conditions with very limited resources the British relief workers faced additional problems in Soviet Armenia. Harold Buxton explained that the 'socialists' (the Soviet government of Armenia) had aroused suspicion about the 'western' relief workers amongst the Armenian population. Communist propaganda, he reported, claimed that the West was 'predatory' and created 'an entirely new mental outlook in Transcaucasia'.[77] On the other hand he conceded that Russia was providing generous aid for Armenia, 'generous, that is to say, in view of the appallingly difficult situation of Russia herself'.[78]

Hopes for the future: building an Armenian nation

Throughout the peace settlements and their attempts to relieve the Armenian refugee crisis, Armenophiles, the diaspora and relief workers had continued to hope for some kind of 'national' future for the Armenian people. Although hopes of recreating a state occupying the whole of 'historic Armenia' had slipped away, pro-Armenian endeavours continued to be framed in terms of preserving a nation. Reconciling this approach with the existence of the Soviet Armenian state was not easy. For the British Armenophiles who came from predominantly Liberal, democratic and often religious backgrounds, the presence of a Soviet government in Armenia aroused grave doubts. The Soviet Republic did not match up to the expectations of the Armenophiles who had hoped for the creation of an Armenian nation state along British lines. The fact that the Soviet Republic occupied only a small portion of 'Greater Armenia' only added to their disappointment.

Despite initial doubts the situation in Soviet Armenia gradually began to stabilise. In 1922 Harcourt reported the improvements that had occurred over the past two years: 'Erivan . . . is quite different from the town I knew in 1920. Buildings have been repaired, streets remade and trees planted. The refugee population is gradually being absorbed and there are fewer beggars about the streets than ever before.'[79] Although further problems would follow it was clear that at least some progress was being made and that the Soviet government was trying to improve conditions. Many Armenophiles, and particularly the relief workers operating in the Soviet Republic, began to accept the idea of Soviet Republic of Armenia as an Armenian homeland. They stressed the importance of the existence of a state called 'Armenia' for all Armenians, whatever form it took. Recognising Soviet Armenia, a region previously regarded as on the fringes of 'Greater Armenia', as a homeland meant re-imagining and redefining the region so as to render it central to Armenian identity. In addition it required practical, material efforts to reshape the region and emphasise its 'Armenianness'.

The status of Soviet Armenia as the Armenian homeland was a source of debate and conflict in the Armenian diaspora for decades to come. However during the early 1920s the British and other international relief workers espoused the idea of Soviet Armenia as a 'homeland' and worked towards making this a reality. This approach stemmed from the belief that a Soviet state was better than no Armenian state at all, as it at least guaranteed the Armenians protection from the Turks and ensured that at least some of the Armenian population could live together in part of their historic homeland.

Although the Soviet authorities had their own agenda in Armenia which centered on the socialist transformation of Armenian society, British Armenophiles continued to look to traditional symbols of Armenian identity in order to construct an image of the new state that was acceptable to them. As the national church had long been central to constructions of Armenian national identity, they placed great importance upon the fact that Etchmiadzin, seat of the Armenian patriarch, was located within the borders of the new Soviet Republic. Despite the fact that the Armenian Church faced significant restrictions under Bolshevik rule, this site was imbued with new national and spiritual significance. Northcote expressed very clearly his newfound belief that the home of the Armenian Church could also serve as a 'natural' homeland for the Armenians, suggesting that they felt an innate spiritual attachment to Etchmiadzin:

> As if prompted by some dumb racial instinct many thousands went to the little town or village of Etchmiadzin, where they camped all around the old monastery, the seat of the Catholicos, the site of the heavenly vision of St. Gregory, the very heart and soul of their race.[80]

Etchmiadzin was not the only Armenian religious or historical site to capture the attention of the Armenophiles. For Dudley Northcote the

Soviet Republic represented an 'unknown' territory filled with historical sites of undiscovered significance. During his stay in Armenia he found time to visit numerous other sites, including the churches of Hripsime and Gayane, the rock-cut monastery of Geghart, the ruins of the Hellenic temple at Garni and the island monastery at Lake Sevan. He expressed particular interest in the recently excavated remains of the early Armenian circular cathedral at Zvartnots, close to Yerevan, and was relieved to discover that, despite their animosity to the Armenian Church, the Soviet authorities, through the Commissariat of Education, were protecting these ruins.[81] Northcote evidently believed that the preservation of this heritage was essential for the preservation and development of Armenian national identity in the future and also suggested that these sites had a relevance for the world beyond Armenia. Like the Armenophile travellers and scholars of the nineteenth century he hoped to direct international attention to Armenia's glorious past: 'Civilisation of one sort or another has flourished for very many centuries in the valley of the river Arax and many indeed are the riches the past has left them. I feel sure that the district would well repay the attentions of the archaeologist and antiquary.'[82]

By drawing attention to the importance of the territory of Soviet Armenia for the development of 'civilisation' Northcote sought to counter the distance between Armenia and Europe that had been created by the imposition of Soviet rule and reaffirm Armenia's place in the 'civilised', European world. Therefore, in his reports and writings he emphasised the links and similarities between Britain and Armenia, comparing Armenian sites to sites of cultural or historical importance in Britain. The town of Etchmiadzin, he observed, was something like Oxford or Canterbury, and the monastery building itself something like Trinity College, Cambridge.

Northcote's efforts to paint Armenia as a site of special British interest were double edged. Despite his positive attitude to Armenia and the Armenians his paternalist approach was always evident and like the travel writers of the nineteenth century he objectified and exoticised Armenia. He approached Soviet Armenia in an ethnographic manner, describing the intricacies of customs, social conditions and daily life just as he had at Ba'quba Camp. For example, he described the 'primitive' methods of breadmaking and surviving traditions regarding the veiling of women.[83] In common with many other British observers he used housing conditions as one of the measures of progress and development. He reported that housing in the cities of Alexandropol (Gumryi) and Yerevan was in a terrible condition, 'even making full allowances for the much lower standard that normally prevails there as opposed to Europe'.[84] The nomadic Yezidis, one of the minorities living in the republic, he viewed as detached from the modern world, describing them as 'a picturesque people who worship the devil in the form of a peacock'.[85]

Despite such evocations of difference, the 'otherness' of the Armenians was relative. In Northcote's eyes at least, the Armenians occupied a place in-between the British and the Bolshevik Russians. He viewed the Russian communists through the lens of orientalism, reducing their political ideology and strategy to orientalist and racial characteristics. For Northcote, Soviet communism represented the opposite and other to post-war European civilisation, embodying the negative characteristics that had traditionally been identified with the 'East'. Imperial Russia, he argued, had been 'European' in orientation. Post-revolutionary Russia, however, was 'the champion of Asia against Europe'.[86] He was keen to emphasise the 'eastern' nature of the Russians, and he did so through racialising the difference between Russians and, by implication, the British and the Armenians. 'I do not think people realise how much tartar blood there is in the Russians . . . One only has to look at the prominent cheek bones and flat faces of many of the Russians to realise this.'[87] Of course this could imply that the Russians were more akin to the Turks who had persecuted the Armenians in the past than to the Armenian population that they now ruled over.

Although their doubts regarding Soviet ideology and policies remained, many of the British Armenophiles eventually came to a grudging acceptance of Soviet rule in Armenia. This acceptance was not based on a belief in the achievements of the Soviet government but a realisation that Soviet rule would not attempt to destroy, but rather offered a chance to preserve the Armenian nation and ensure its survival. For the Armenians, Northcote suggested, this was the most important thing: 'All small and persecuted races are intensely patriotic. The Armenians feel that they have at last found a national home even if it is red. It is difficult to describe how pleased they are about it.'[88]

Nonetheless, the Armenophiles did not give up hope of ever seeing the emergence of an Armenia which occupied the whole of the territories of 'historic Armenia'. This was partly because they remained dedicated to the ideal vision of an Armenian nation developed during the nineteenth century and partly because they viewed the expansion of Armenia as one way of resolving the problem of the thousands of refugees who remained in the Soviet Republic. Harold Buxton came to hope that this expansion of Armenia could be achieved through, rather than despite, the Soviet authorities. In 1922 he wrote to his BAC colleague Aneurin Williams expressing his hopes that Soviet Armenia could be expanded to include the territories of Kars, Sarikamish, Alashkert and Van. Part of the reason behind his thinking was that 'the present Armenian Soviet Government is more efficient, and more wise in its policy that the late Dashnakist Government of 1920'.[89] His perspective demonstrates the extent to which British Armenophile opinion was changing.

Relief work and the resettlement of thousands of Armenian refugees from Armenia on the territory of the Soviet Republic provided one way of preserving Armenia and transforming the Soviet state into an Armenian homeland. Resettlement of refugees, often in agricultural settlements, had the potential to create a new sense of 'roots' in the land. The refugees themselves represented a population that could rebuild and reinvigorate the damaged territory. In a sense the republic could be represented as the 'saviour' of the displaced Armenians, providing a space where the population could be protected from further harm, survive and hopefully prosper.

The influx of the refugees played a large role in the development of the new Soviet Armenian state. The city of Yerevan, which prior to the war had been little more than a small town, underwent extensive reconstruction and expansion in order to accommodate the surge in population and repair the damage and deterioration resulting from the war. The development of the city reflected the need to legitimate the Soviet state as an Armenian homeland. The landscape of Anatolia was transposed to the landscape of Soviet Armenia through the naming of the newly built regions of Yerevan which would accommodate the refugees. Taline Ter-Minassian explains that these place names not only recalled the 'national' homeland but also helped preserve regional identities, as they were funded by and named after the Compatriotic Unions based around regions or villages in Turkish Armenia.[90]

For the British relief workers in Soviet Armenia relief work provided the chance to develop Armenia in a material sense, through for example the creation of agricultural settlements, and the building of homes, schools and hospitals. Providing work for the refugees was also a central part of relief. The small British relief fund known as 'Miss Robinson's Fund' employed fifty-one women in lacemaking whilst in Yerevan, and Dudley Northcote organised refugee men to clear and plant market gardens and clear up damaged areas of the town. His work elicited the praised of Dr Armstrong Smith, from the Save the Children Fund, who was particularly impressed with the role played by the refugees themselves in these development schemes.

I was very glad to observe that the adult relief was being given in return for work and the labour of the refugees turned towards the reconstruction of the town. In other words the policy of the Lord Mayor's Fund is to help these necessitous people to regain their self respect through useful labour.[91]

Dr Armstrong Smith's comments reflect the fact that relief was regarded as offering a vital means of influencing the development of Armenian society. He hoped that the relief work of the LMF could 'materially and *morally* help towards the reconstruction of the country'.[92] His attitude reflected the approaches to refugee relief as a 'civilising mission' intended to inculcate in the refugees western values and behaviours. The LMF were themselves well aware of the role of refugee relief for the future development of Armenia. In 1923 Edward Carlile of the LMF described the purpose of their work in Armenia: 'All measures are taken to train the children both intellectually and industrially to fit them as citizens of the Armenia that is to be . . . We realise to the full how deeply the Armenian national consciousness is derived from the Armenian national Church.'[93]

Whilst the British Armenophiles continued to emphasise the role of Armenian national and religious identity the Soviet authorities sought to influence the refugees in a rather different direction. Considerable effort was put into monitoring and attempting to counter the perceived threat to their rule from returning refugees who were believed to have anti-Soviet Dashnak affiliations. A Soviet representative in Persia, V. Shumiatskii, wrote to the deputy chair of Sovnarkom Armenia, A. Mravian, expressing his concerns regarding the influence of the British on the refugee population: 'The question concerning the political filtration of refugees must be decided without delay. Filtration is needed because the British are undoubtedly recruiting dozens of agents among the refugee population', although he added that they should be easy enough to identify. Thus the Soviet authorities clearly viewed British intervention in a suspicious light and hoped to counter its possible negative effects on Soviet Armenian society.[94]

The influence of British relief agencies on the development of Soviet Armenia declined in the 1920s. The efforts of Armenophiles such as Buxton and Northcote to keep Armenia within the sphere of British interests failed and concerns for Armenia and the Armenians enjoyed little success. The dedicated few who remained involved in Armenian refugee relief for the most part turned their attention to refugee resettlement programmes in Syria.[95] The repatriation of refugees to Soviet Armenia meanwhile continued. However, these repatriations constituted a matter of intense debate amongst the Armenian diaspora. Such debates would continue throughout the Soviet period.

Aftermaths: homeland, diaspora and return

During the inter-war period British attention gradually shifted from the Armenian refugees. The presence of Soviet power in Armenia created a new kind of distance between the British public and the Armenians, rendering intervention on behalf of the Armenians less appealing to the British population and more difficult to realise. In addition the numbers of Armenians who settled in Britain after the war were relatively low and without the presence of an active diaspora it was difficult to keep an interest in the Armenian cause alive. In contrast, in France and the USA much larger diaspora communities existed.[96] Many of these communities, which had been established prior to the genocide, were extremely successful and the arrival of the refugees in the post-war period gradually enhanced their development. These diaspora communities maintained links with Soviet Armenia in a variety of ways, through family ties, the existence of Compatriotic Unions based on pre-war village communities, and also through membership of larger diasporan organisations such as the Armenian General Benevolent Union (AGBU). The development of diaspora press and political, religious and social organisations also allowed for communication and debate regarding the future of Soviet Armenia within the diaspora. This meant that although interest in the Armenians outside of the Armenian community would never again reach the levels that it had during the First World War, public and political awareness of the Armenians was maintained outside of Britain at least.

Despite the waning public interest, for Armenian diasporan organisations and international agencies, primarily the League of Nations, displaced Armenians, principally in the Middle East, still constituted a significant problem to be 'managed' and if possible 'solved'. These organisations continued to express their concern about the long-term effects of displacement on both Armenian individuals and to the fabric of the nation. As described in chapter 4, under the leadership of Nansen the League remained closely involved in the Armenian refugee problem for several years.

Although the large-scale resettlement schemes envisaged by Nansen and the League failed, the repatriation of Armenian refugees to the Soviet state did continue throughout the 1920s and early 1930s. According to Hovig Meliksetian, 42,286 Armenian refugees were repatriated to Soviet Armenia between 1921 and 1936.[97] By this time the Armenian diaspora rather than international Armenophile organisations were responsible for assisting the international agencies with this process.

Repatriation to Soviet Armenia was complicated by the fact that diaspora attitudes to Soviet Armenia were charaterised by deep divisions. Amongst the different diaspora factions, the status of the Soviet Republic as a 'homeland' remained a contested issue.[98] In general the liberal Ramkavar party and the socialist Hnchaks supported the Soviet state. The Ramkavar-backed philanthropic organisation, the AGBU, raised funds for repatriation through the 1920s, financing the building of a new town, Nubarashen, to house the incoming refugees. The Dashnak nationalists, on the other hand, were highly critical of the Soviet regime which had brought their rule in the Armenian Republic to an abrupt end. They challenged the legitimacy of the Soviet Republic as a 'homeland', opposing any form of repatriation to the region during the 1930s.

The situation changed dramatically after the Second World War when an opportunity for repatriation on a larger scale than ever before arose. In November 1945 Stalin invited the diaspora to resettle in Soviet Armenia.[99] The response to this invitation from displaced Armenians living in the Middle East, Eastern Europe and beyond was testament to the extent to which Soviet Armenia had become accepted by the Armenians as a valid homeland to which they could 'return'. In Lebanon for example, where many Armenians had been living since their displacement during the genocide, the call to repatriate was met with great enthusiasm. By February 1946 12,600 Armenians had registered to repatriate.

However the circumstances of repatriation in the post-Second World War period were very different from those of the early 1920s.[100] Although it had been portrayed as a project to reunite the Armenian nation, the Soviet authorities had their own agenda and the invitation to repatriate was intended as much to rebuild the war-weary Soviet Republic as to aid the Armenian diaspora. On the other hand, the scheme seemed to offer an option for some displaced Armenians to escape crippling poverty, for the conditions in which they lived in some parts of the Middle East were still little better then than when the refugees initially arrived after the First World War.[101]

In their appeal to Armenians to repatriate, the Soviet authorities drew upon the very discourses of homeland which had been prevalent after the First World War, discourses which stressed Armenian historical roots in the land and the link between territory and national identity. Armenian diaspora organisations that supported the repatriation also cast aside their reservations and represented Soviet Armenia as 'home'. Like the relief workers involved in repatriation to Transcaucasia in the post-war period they stressed the bonds between Armenians and the region: 'The Armenian expatriate has compellingly strong attachments for Hayastan, the land of his fathers, for Ararat, Etchmiadzin, Yerevan and the River Arax.'[102]

The AGBU idealised repatriation, describing in their journal *Houcharar* 'the return of Armenians from bondage, from a precarious existence under alien and inhospitable ties to native soil, native language, native culture'.[103] The back cover of this issue of *Houcharar* depicted a happy Armenian peasant girl standing in the shadow of that most potent symbol of the Armenian homeland, Mount Ararat. In reality Ararat lay across the border in Turkey. The image may be read as a powerful reminder of the imagined nature of 'homeland', a fluid construction with ambiguous boundaries, drawing on a range of sites and symbols.

Despite this evocation of an unbreakable bond between Armenians and the homeland, access to Soviet Armenia was in practice highly restricted. Recalling concerns expressed by their counterparts during the 1920s, Soviet repatriation authorities regarded displaced Armenians as a potential social, economic and even health threat. To minimise the risk vast amounts of information were collected about potential repatriates. Questionnaires were used to find out about individual repatriates.[104] Dashnak nationalists, thought to be potentially anti-Soviet, were screened out in the selection process.[105]

For those who did repatriate, ideals of homeland rapidly gave way to harsh social and economic realities. Conditions in Armenia proved to be as difficult for the repatriates as they were during the 1920s. A 1947 report into the conditions of those who had repatriated found that the new homes provided for repatriates lacked window panes and frames, doors or door frames. Older homes even lacked basic furniture. In the town of Leninakan, twenty-two families lived in rooms completely unfit for habitation.[106] In the 1920s the diaspora and a vigilant international community were prepared to see difficulties in refugee resettlement as an inevitable result of war and genocide. As a result they were prepared to offer as much assistance as they could manage to improve the situation. By contrast, after 1945 expectations had risen, and the treatment of the repatriates was widely regarded as a betrayal. Indeed some took the failings of repatriation as a sign that Soviet Armenia was not a valid 'homeland'.

These changing patterns of displacement and repatriation demonstrate the way that interest in the fate of Armenia and the nature of intervention in the region fluctuated with changing international circumstances. The international diaspora which flourished after the First World War by and large replaced the British Armenophiles as the main advocates of the

Armenian cause. International political change – primarily the adoption of Armenia into the Soviet orbit – brought with it a distancing of the Armenians from Britain and Europe. Armenia became part of a new kind of 'other'.

Notwithstanding these changes, the idea of Soviet Armenia as a homeland continued to exert a strong hold on Armenian imaginations. The concept of a bond between people and territory articulated in the nineteenth century remained central to constructions of Armenian identity. However, what is striking about the Armenian case is the fluidity of the concept of homeland and the flexibility of the idea of return. By the mid-twentieth century Transcaucasia, an area hitherto thought to be on the very fringes of the homeland, was now portrayed as its core.

Notes

1 See Gatrell, *A Whole Empire Walking*, chapter 7. Gatrell points out that 'to have been forcibly uprooted was itself a potent reminder that one could take pride in one's roots' (p. 143).

2 Hovannisian, *The Republic of Armenia*, Vol. 1, p. 269. Suny states that at the conference the delegations from the republic and the ANDP eventually agreed to work together despite differing agendas. Suny, *Looking Toward Ararat*, p. 128.

3 S. Pattie, 'New Homeland for an Old Diaspora', in A. Levy and A. Weingrod, *Homelands and Diasporas: Holy Lands and Other Places* (Stanford: Stanford University Press, 2005), p. 55.

4 Ibid.

5 NA FO 608/272, 74 BAC Memorandum, *Armenia and the Turkish Settlement*, 12 January 1920.

6 BAC Minute Book, *Appeal of the Armenian National Delegation to the Civilised World*, 2 May 1918.

7 ANDP, *Memorandum on the 'Armenian Question'* (1918), p. 8. During the war Nubar Pasha tried to appeal to Britain through stressing that an independent Armenia would benefit British interests in the region, providing a 'barrier' against German ambitions. British success in Mesopotamia made this less important. Somakian, *Empires in Conflict*, p. 151. The French government were also vocal in their promises to the Armenians. In July 1918 Clemenceau assured Nubar Pasha, 'Le Gouvernement de la République, comme celui du Royaume Uni n'ont jamais cesse de placer la nation Arménienne parmi les peuples dont le destins sera règle par les Allies, conformément aux lois suprêmes de l'humanité et de la justice.' (' The Government of the Republic, like that of the United Kingdom has never

ceased to place the Armenian nation amongst the peoples whose destinies will be decided by the Allies, according to the supreme laws of humanity and justice.' [My translation]) Quoted in F. Macler, *La Nation Arménienne* (Paris: Librairie, Fischbacher, 1923), p. 78.

8 ANDP, *Memorandum on the 'Armenian Question'*, p. 8. The contribution made by the Armenians in the war was also highlighted in a BAC pamphlet in 1920: C. L. Leese, *Armenia and the Allies* (London: BAC, 1920). See section, 'The War Services of the Armenians to the Allied Cause'.

9 NA FO 608/272, 76, *Armenia and the Turkish Settlement.*

10 See Hovannisian, *Republic of Armenia*, Vol. 1, pp. 259–260.

11 For the details of the Armenian claims see Hovannisian, *Republic of Armenia*, Vol. 1, p. 277–280.

12 The Armenians were never formally recognised as an ally and therefore were not given an official seat at the peace conferences. Hovannisian, *Republic of Armenia*, Vol. 2, p. 2.

13 N. Baron and P. Gatrell, 'Population Displacement, State Building and Social Identity in the Lands of the Former Russian Empire, 1917–1923', p. 51.

14 The end of war 'signalled the triumph not only of democracy but also . . . of nationalism'. M. Mazower, *Dark Continent: Europe's Twentieth Century* (New York: Vintage, 2000), p. 41.

15 A. Roshwald considers the premises and pitfalls of Wilsonianism in *Ethnic Nationalism and the fall of Empires: Central Europe, Russia and the Middle East 1914–1923* (London: Routledge, 2001), pp. 156–161. He highlights the difficulties of this approach: 'Most ethnic groups did not come in neatly wrapped territorial packages. Languages, cultures and religions were both dispersed and intermingled in a kaleidoscopic fashion . . . Cut-and-dried notions about the congruence of nation with state were far removed from the ethnographic realities the new states faced' (p. 156).

16 On the break-up of empires and nationalism see K. Barkey and M. Von Hagen, *After Empire: Multiethnic Societies and Nation Building* (Oxford: Westview Press, 1997).

17 Roshwald, *Ethnic Nationalism*, p. 161.

18 NA FO 608/78,127, Appeal from Nubar Pasha, 1919.

19 *Official Statements of War Aims and Peace Proposals, December 1916 to November 1918* (Washington DC: Carnegie Endowment, 1921), p. 231, quoted in Hovannisian, 'The Historical Dimension of the Armenian Question', p. 31.

20 Robert Cecil, letter from Foreign Office, 3 October 1918 in *Armenia's Charter. An Appreciation of the Services of the Allies Cause* (London: Spottiswode, Ballantyne and Co., 1918), p. 5. For further details see Hovannisian, 'The Allies and Armenia, 1915–18', pp. 147–150.

21 Bloxham, *Great Game of Genocide*, p. 144.

22 Nassibian, *Britain and the Armenian Question*, p. 113.

23 Their requests included: immediate occupation of strategic points by Allied troops; recognition of the Armenians as belligerents in the war; repatriation of Armenians who had fled or been thrown out by the Turks; organisation by the Allied forces of a system of relief and restoration of the women and children who had been taken away by Turks and Kurds. BAC Minute Book, 7 November 1918.

24 They also utilised the fact that the Armenians had fought on the Allied side and, in the words of one BAC pamphlet, 'rendered an inestimable service to the Allied cause': British Armenia Committee, *The Case for Armenia* (London: BAC, 1920).

25 See chapter 3 on the idea of an eastern 'taint' resulting from Ottoman rule.

26 Bryce, 'The Future of Armenia'.

27 Hacobian, *Armenia and the War*, p. 12. The emphasis on the Armenian past in justifying a future Armenian nation state is also evident in S. M. Gregory, *The Land of Ararat: 12 Discourses on Armenia, her History and her Church* (London: Chiswick Press, 1920).

28 Hovannisian, *Republic of Armenia*, Vol. 1, p. 267.

29 NA FO 608/77, 377, Toynbee's comments on Armenian delegation memorandum, 24 February 1919.

30 A. Sharp, *The Versailles Peace Settlement: Peacemaking in Paris 1919* (Basingstoke: Palgrave, 1991), p. 165.

31 Hovannissian, *The Republic of Armenia*, Vol. 1, p. 78.

32 NA FO 608/78, Minute of Conversation with Aharonian, 19 June 1919.

33 See chapter 2.

34 NA FO 608/77, Essay from Mr Louis Heck, 29 May 1919.

35 NA FO 373/5/1, Peace Conference Handbook, Armenia and Kurdistan, p. 4.

36 Ibid., p. 18.

37 Ibid., p. 14.

38 Ibid., pp. 30–31.

39 NA FO 608/77 Report on the future of Armenia, Colonel Newcombe, 1919.

40 NA FO 608/77 Comments on the report of a conversation on the future of Armenia with Colonel Newcombe, Toynbee, 1919.

41 Ibid.

42 NA FO 608/77 Notes on report of a conversation with Colonel Newcombe, Mallet, 1919.

43 FO 608/77 Report, Dr Gates, 1919.

44 FO 608/77 Report, Admiral Calthorpe, 1919.

45 On the consequences of the Greek–Turkish exchanges see R. Hirschon, *Heirs of the Greek Catastrophe* (Oxford: Berghann, 1998).

46 Suny, *Looking Toward Ararat*, p. 128.

47 Kent, 'Great Britain and the end of the Ottoman Empire 1900–1923'. On British policy in the Middle East during and after the war more generally see

D. Fromkin, *A Peace to End all Peace: The Fall of the Ottoman Empire and the Creation of the Modern Middle East* (London: Phoenix, 2000).

48 Arslanian, 'Britain and the Transcaucasian Nationalities', p. 299.
49 NA FO 608/77 Notes on report of a conversation with Colonel Newcombe, Mallet, 1919.
50 NA FO 608/78, Letter from Barton to Bryce, 27 June 1919.
51 FO 608/77, Memorandum from Tonapetean (*sic*) to British Delegation, 1919.
52 Leese, *Armenia and the Allies*, p. 14. Chapter 3 discusses British doubts about Armenian nationalism and capacities for self-rule which stretched back to the nineteenth century. Numerous British Armenophiles expressed their support for a mandate, e.g. H. Buxton, 'Armenia: Some Recent Impressions', *Contemporary Review*, Vol. 117 (Jan/June 1920), pp. 497–500. Buxton suggested that if America would not take the mandate then the British must 'step in and take up our burden'. See also Joint Council of British Societies Assisting the Armenian People, Appeal to the Assembly of the League of Nations, included in Bryce Papers, Mss Bryce, Fol. 35, August 1921.
53 On America and the mandate: L. Ambrosius, 'Wilsonian Diplomacy and Armenia: The Limits of Power and Ideology', in Winter, *America and the Armenian Genocide.* During 1919 the USA sent two commissions (the King-Crane Commission and the Military Mission led by Major General James Harbord) to investigate the situation in Armenia. They are discussed by R. Hovannisian, 'The Armenian Genocide and US Post-War Commissions', in Winter, *America and the Armenian Genocide.*
54 BAC Minute Book, 17 September 1919. The BAC corresponded with American agencies involved in the Armenophile movement, e.g. NER and The Committee for the Independence of Armenia. They were also in regular contact with Nubar Pasha, BAC Minute Book, 25 November 1919.
55 BAC Minute Book, Minute book of the Propaganda Sub-Committee of the BAC, 1 June 1920–23 November 1920. The BAC also published pamphlets on the issue of the future of Armenia, e.g. *Armenia and the Turkish Settlement: Memorandum Submitted for the Consideration of H. M. Government* (London, 1920). There was also an effort in 1920 to mobilise the Armenophile movement at an international level through the attempt to organise an international conference at Geneva in July 1920. The BAC and other organisations including the LMF were to send delegations.
56 NA FO 608/272 65, Letter from Armenian Delegation enclosing three memoranda, 12 January 1920.
57 NA FO 608/272 72, Memorandum, *Armenia and the Turkish Settlement.*
58 Arslanian, 'Britain and the Transcaucasian Nationalities', p. 299.
59 Roshwald, *Ethnic Nationalism*, p. 173.
60 Ibid.
61 Hewsen, *Armenia*, p. 244.
62 On Smyrna, the conflict between Greece and Turkey and the subsequent

population exchanges see Marrus, *The Unwanted*, pp. 97–106. On long-term implications for the Greek, Turkish and Armenian refugees, see P. Lozios, 'Ottoman Half-Lives: Long-term Perspectives on Particular Forced Migrations', *Journal of Refugee Studies*, Vol. 12, No. 3 (1999).

63 Hovannisian, 'The Historical Dimension of the Armenian Question', p. 37.
64 For an in-depth discussion of conditions in Armenia in 1919 see Hovannisian, *The Republic of Armenia*, Vol. 1, chapter 5.
65 NA FO 608/79 Report of Haskell to the peace conference, 1919.
66 NA FO 608/77 Situation in Armenia, 28 March 1919.
67 NA FO 608/78 Report of Wardrop on journey to Yerevan, 23 October 1919.
68 Ibid.
69 Northcote Papers 'Enquiry into Famine Conditions December 1921–January 1922' Copy of report from LMF to Nansen.
70 Ibid.
71 Buxton, 'Transcaucasia', p. 559.
72 Vartan Melkonian explains that whilst 7,500 Armenians were resettled in Soviet Armenia and 1,200 orphans were sent to Jerusalem, others remained in Mesopotamia where the running of the camp was transferred to Levon Shagonian. In 1929 the camp was split up and transferred to Havrez, 40 miles north of Mosul. Melkonian explained that at the time (1957) 8,000 Armenians lived in Baghdad. Melkonian, *A Historical Glimpse of the Armenians in Mesopotamia*.
73 Northcote Papers, Report from Erivan, D. S. Northcote, January 1920.
74 Northcote Papers, Letter, Northcote, February 1921.
75 ArmCheka to Sovnarkom, 10 January 1925, National Archives of Armenia (NAA) f. 113, op. 3, d. 330, l. 107; Cheka memo to Sovnarkom, 7 October 1925, f. 113, op. 3, d. 294, l. 14. I am grateful to Peter Gatrell for pointing out this material to me.
76 The work of the LMF in Transcaucasia is described in the report of Dr Armstrong Smith of the Save the Children Fund. Dr Armstrong Smith, *Famine in Transcaucasia* pp. 129–135 (extracts reprinted in Walker, *Visions of Ararat*).
77 H. Buxton, *Transcaucasia* (London: Faith Press, 1926), p. 42.
78 Northcote Papers, 'Enquiry into Famine Conditions'.
79 NAA f.430, op. 1, d. 1061, 11. 4–7, 1922.
80 Northcote Papers, *Armenia*, unpublished manuscript, 1926.
81 Northcote Papers, Report on Soviet Armenia.
82 Northcote Papers, *Armenia*.
83 Ibid.
84 Northcote Papers, Report on Soviet Armenia.
85 Ibid.
86 Northcote Papers, *Armenia*.
87 Ibid.

88 Ibid.
89 NAA f. 430, op. 1, d. 1062, 11. 1–2, letter from Buxton to Williams, 15 January 1922.
90 Taline Ter Minassian, 'Erevan, "Ville Promise": Le Rapatriement des Arméniens de la Diaspora, 1921–1948', *Diasporas*, No. 1 (2005), p. 73.
91 Armstrong Smith, *Famine in Transcaucasia*, p. 131.
92 Armstrong-Smith, *Famine in Transcaucasia*, p. 129. [My emphasis.]
93 NAA f. 430, op. 1, d. 1074, Letter from Edward Carlile to Nouradounghian, ANDP, 3 May 1923.
94 Letter dated 23 May 1924, NAA f. 113, op. 1, d. 153, ll. 49–51; Soviet representative in Tehran to Sovnarkom, 30 November 1924, NAA f. 113, op. 1, d. 127, l.63; Unsigned report to Transcaucasian Sovnarkom, 25 May 1924, NAA f. 113, op. 1, d. 310, ll. 10–12.
95 BAC papers, Correspondence regarding the settlement of Armenian refugees in Syria, 1928.
96 Tony Kushner and Katharine Knox report that only 200 genocide survivors settled in the UK whilst 63,000 settled in France. Kushner and Knox, *Refugees in an Age of Genocide* p. 71. On the Armenian community in France see M. Mandel, *In the Aftermath of Genocide: Armenians and Jews in Twentieth Century France* (Durham and London: Duke University Press, 2003).
97 Hovig Meliksetjan, *Homeland-Diaspora Relations and Repatriation* (Yerevan: Yerevan University Press 1985), p. 15.
98 For a detailed study see Panossian, *The Armenians*, chapter 6.
99 Clare Mouradian, 'L'Immigration des Arméniens de la Diaspora vers la RSS d'Arménie 1946–62', *Cahiers du Monde Russe et Soviétique*, Vol. XX, No. 1 (1997), p. 80.
100 Report of Syria and Lebanon Repatriation Committee, NAA f. 363, op. 2, d. 4. 16.
101 See Vahe Tachijian 'Le Rapatriement: Une Nouvelle Page dans la Coopération avec les Soviétiques', unpublished manuscript (Paris, 2006).
102 *Houcharar*, Vol. XXXIV, No. 15 (December 1947) p. 285.
103 *Houcharar*, Vol. XXXIII, No. 7 (August 1946) p. 253.
104 For examples see NAA f. 362, op. 2, d. 9. 39.
105 In recruiting and selecting repatriates the Soviet Armenian authorities utilised left-leaning diaspora organisations in order to form local repatriation committees. Dashnaks were excluded from this process.
106 NAA, f. 362 op. 2 d. 24 12–17. Report to the General Secretary of the Communist Party of Armenia on Housing, Work and Material Conditions of the Repatriates.

Conclusions

The Armenian past, present and
future in the British imagination

Refugeedom and being 'out of place'

The post-war period was marked by disappointments for the Armenians and their British supporters alike. Neither the establishment of Soviet rule in Transcaucasia nor the creation of a Turkish Republic were part of the Armenian future that they had envisaged. The failure of the Armenian nationalist project was accompanied by the continuation of the Armenian refugee crisis. Instead of living together as a nation in one 'homeland' the Armenian refugees were dispersed even further afield. Their plight evoked a variety of responses amongst the Armenian population at home and abroad and from the rest of the world.

The Armenian 'refugee question' anticipated many of the debates over the 'problem' of population displacement which would recur throughout the twentieth century. The issues of repatriation, resettlement and the management of large numbers of displaced persons, familiar to Northcote and his fellow relief workers, have continued to trouble relief agencies and governments since.[1]

The displacement of the Armenians and several hundred thousand others during the First World War rendered the 'refugee question' an international problem. As in the case of the 'eastern question' of the previous century, governments, humanitarians and scholars were drawn into the attempt to find solutions. Their work was augmented by that of new international bodies such as the League of Nations.[2]

Armenian refugees, as chapter 4 has shown, were not only a 'problem' in terms of the practicalities of material relief and repatriation. The condition of being a refugee has in itself been regarded as inherently damaging. As Lisa Malkki has shown, in a world where national identities are imagined as being 'rooted' in the land, displacement is imagined as a threatening or even 'pathological' condition. Her observations echo Mary Douglas's arguments regarding the 'danger' presented by things that are ambiguous or out of place and highlight their implications for understanding the way in which refugees are perceived.[3]

The fact that the refugees were a source of anxiety also relates to Zygmunt Bauman's arguments regarding 'the Jews' as a source of anxiety and hostility. The Jewish population, Bauman suggests, provoked anxiety in modern European societies because they occupied an ambivalent place in the world and did not conform to the categories or obey the boundaries so central to modernity. Bauman observed that the Jews have been 'the epitome of incongruity: a non national nation, and so cast a shadow on the fundamental principle of modern European order: that nationhood is the essence of human destiny'.[4]

In a post-war world organised according to the principles of national self-determination, where the peace conference was characterised by a 'love affair with the nation state', the displaced Armenians represented the same kind disruption of boundaries that Bauman suggests in regard to Jews.[5] Their presence threatened to disturb the fragile pattern of new nation states and national borders. This theme persisted in twentieth-century representations of the 'refugee question'.

In the case of the Armenian refugees, the idea of this population as disturbing or disrupting boundaries echoes what has been said earlier about the Armenians being characterised as 'in-between' the orientalist categories of East and West. The Armenians had long been a potential cause of anxiety for the western world, existing on the boundaries and failing to conform to established categories. As civilised Christians stranded in the 'barbaric' eastern world, they were already seen as 'out of place'. In the eyes of numerous British observers the Armenians had long been in need of attention or intervention to 'correct' what Toynbee, amongst others, viewed as a 'pathological' position.[6] The refugee crisis compounded the situation. Now that elements of the 'East', the refugees, were moving across geographical boundaries into the 'West', their physical presence was thought to be threatening to stability and order. The Armenians were now more 'out of place' than ever before.[7]

Not only did the presence of Armenian refugees blur the boundaries of states and national territories, they also blurred the boundaries of civilisation and barbarism. As refugees, even those educated or prosperous Armenians who had once been regarded as 'civilised' could no longer demonstrate the external features that had long denoted 'civilisation' to the British observer. They were now unsettled, often without work or education, without clothing or food and frequently dirty or carrying disease. Thus orientalist stereotypes and notions of civilisation and barbarism were transformed and re-used after the war and applied to new kinds of 'other', chief among which was the refugee. Orientalist discourse informed not only the image of the Armenian refugee but also the nature of humanitarian intervention and the practice of relief. This development highlights the way that demarcating between 'self' and 'other' was a dynamic, ongoing process. It extended into a variety of arenas, including the practice and conduct of humanitarian intervention.

Armenia, orientalism and the boundaries of 'self' and 'other'

Representations of the Armenian refugee as 'out of place' constituted only one point on the spectrum of British representations of Armenia. Images of the Armenian refugee provided a striking contrast, for example, to the images of Armenia as a 'cradle of civilisation' which were popularised during the late nineteenth century. Of course the difference between these two images was very much a product of altered geopolitical power relations and different hopes and fears for the future of the Armenians. However, images of Armenia did not only shift over time. At any given moment the image of Armenia and the Armenians was complex and multilayered; a number of images could co-exist or clash.

Considering the ambivalence and ambiguity in representations of the Armenians brings us back to the issues set out in chapter 1 regarding the ways in which the case of Armenia challenges the understanding of representations of the 'other' articulated in *Orientalism*. In the light of the close examination of British representations of Armenia in the previous three chapters it is now possible to consider their relationship to orientalist discourse in more depth. Said's account of orientalism is premised upon the idea of a dichotomy between East and West and the construction of an image of the East as the West's opposite and inferior.[8] Armenia fitted neither of these dichotomised categories. British observers struggled to negotiate a position for the Armenians. As 'semi-civilised' Christians living under Ottoman rule in Asia Minor they transgressed the conventional boundaries of East and West, or self and other.

The case of Armenia thus demonstrates that the binary opposition between coloniser and colonised, between metropolis and colony, civilised and barbaric assumed in *Orientalism*, does not adequately reflect the complex realities of constructing the 'other'. Representations of the other were fluid and contested rather than monolithic and static. It is important to acknowledge therefore that it is 'ambivalence rather than a simply dichotomizing and essentialising attitude which more accurately characterises the western vision of the East'.[9] What constitutes the 'other' may take a variety of forms, with different meanings. Being 'opposite' to the West is only one of them.

This is not to suggest that discourses of orientalism should be discarded completely. The categories of East and West, with all their associated images and stereotypes, played a powerful role in shaping understandings of the world. The British individuals who encountered Armenia in the late nineteenth and early twentieth centuries were directly influenced by orientalist concepts and categories. Indeed it may be because Armenia did not fit the orientalist pattern they expected, that they found both people and place so troubling.

Regions such as Armenia and the Balkans which did not conform to expected patterns were a potential source of anxiety. They created a need to redraw and reinforce the boundaries of self and other, if only to re-establish some security in British identities. In other words, underlying most British writing on Armenia was an attempt to make Armenia 'fit' into conventional worldviews, to assign it to 'East' or 'West'. This could be achieved through a number of different means. More often than not the strategy was to attempt to claim Armenia as part of the West; a strategy very much determined by prevailing political agendas and power relations. It was also shaped by the interventions of Armenians who were attempting to articulate discourses of Armenian national identity which focused on Armenia's status as a civilised nation with a glorious past.

Attempts to demonstrate bonds between Britain and Armenia and therefore 'claim' Armenia as part of the European world are highlighted in chapter 3, which considers the attempt by British Armenophiles to identify Armenia with Western Europe through the idea of shared origins. Chapter 4, on the other hand, showed a very different way of attempting to 'claim' the Armenians or return them to their rightful place, by envisaging refugee relief as a process of civilising or westernising displaced Armenians.

Although orientalism clearly played a role in British attempts to categorise or understand the Armenians, it is important to remember that the orientalist categories they utilised were neither fixed nor monolithic. The case of Armenia draws much-needed attention to the flexibility of the borders of East and West. It raises the question of where the 'self', or the West ends, and where the 'other' or East begins. This is not always as clear-cut as Said perhaps suggests. In reality there was a great deal of fluctuation in the way the divide was imagined, according to changing historical circumstances. 'Otherness,' as Michael Herzfeld has noted, 'appears as a relative quality.'[10]

The ambiguity or 'in-betweeness' which characterised British images of Armenia was in itself a form of 'otherness'. It was regarded as a predicament to be explained and solved rather than a 'natural' state of being. The image of the Armenians was therefore always measured against the 'self' in order to see how and why they had deviated from this ideal. Todorova describes the Balkans as being treated as an 'incomplete self' rather than an 'incomplete other'.[11] In a sense this is also true of British images of Armenia. There was never an acceptance that the Armenians were simply 'other', rather an exploration of how the Armenians had come to be different or distinct.

Difference was explained through an interpretation of the Armenian past which drew upon concepts of civilisation, progress and degeneration. Whilst the British, it was implied, had followed a normal course of national development, Armenian development was thought to have been 'stunted' by Ottoman rule. This interpretation was specifically linked to the politics of the 'Armenian question' and to Armenophile rhetoric aimed at freeing the Armenians from Ottoman oppression. It was part of the debate over how the Armenians could be reclaimed as part of Europe, a debate which centred on a critique of Ottoman rule and the possibilities of Armenian nationhood. Similar debates occurred about the future of the Balkans.[12] It also characterised Armenia as a region in need of European intervention. While in the case of Armenia this did not mean colonial power, it did mean a paternalist right to determine the style and pace of 'development'. Of course this effectively reinforced the British position at the pinnacle of hierarchies of development and civilisation.

The ambiguity of British images of Armenia did not mean that they were divorced from power or politics. Imagining a region as on the border, neither eastern nor western, could also be related to the maintenance of imperial power. Larry Wolff has observed that the process of inventing Eastern Europe as backward or underdeveloped was 'a style of intellectual mastery, integrating knowledge and power, perpetrating domination and subordination'.[13] The same, I suggest, is true of representations of Armenia which supported a relationship between Britain and the Armenians which may have been sympathetic but was also inherently unequal.

Images of Armenia and power were interdependent in a variety of ways. It is clear though that the ambiguity and flexibility of British images of Armenia allowed for them to be manipulated or transformed according to political necessity. This is most obvious in the aftermath of crisis, as transformed images of the region interlocked with political upheaval and the chance to create an independent Armenian nation. After the genocide of the Armenians in 1915 the British government was quick to identify with the Armenians. British propaganda drew on images of the Armenians in a highly selective manner, emphasising Christianity and civilisation and minimising negative elements. Without the body of knowledge about the Armenians gathered by scholars and travellers over the previous few decades, however, the British government would not have been able to utilise images of Armenian suffering in this way.

Although during the Great War the plight of the Armenians was superficially adopted as an official cause, in the past the sufferings of the Armenians had been used by the opposition to demonstrate the ills of British foreign policy. As a 'minority' cause they had been bound up in British politics in a different and more subtle manner. For despite the idealistic language employed by Gladstone and his followers, they did not shy away from utilising the Armenians to advance their own political agendas.[14] What is most striking however about the British espousal of the Armenian cause, in both the 1890s and after 1915, is how quickly interest could fade away and notions of responsibility for the Armenians could dissipate.

Perhaps the fact that the Armenians were not fully part of the 'self', that they were thought to exist only on the fringes of the European world, physically and culturally, made it possible for the British authorities and public to disengage politically with the Armenian cause with relative ease, without provoking widespread moral outrage. As Bloxham has observed, 'the very ambiguity of "the west" to Turkey and Armenia has shaped international responses to the destruction of the Armenians, just as it shaped perceptions of the people'.[15] This disengagement left the Armenians not as actors in the realm of international politics, but as the recipients of charity. This was a far more unequal relationship than had been imagined either by the diaspora or by the Armenophiles.

Civilisation, orientalism and the future of the Armenian nation

Over the course of the Great War and the peace settlements the image of Armenia had become closely bound up with the very real issue of Armenian self-determination. Questions of civilisation and capacities for nationhood which had preoccupied British Armenophiles for decades were at the heart of these debates. Defining the territorial boundaries of

Armenia gained a new importance. This project was complicated by the continuing dispersion of the population and with geopolitical developments. The post-war period was therefore marked by the renegotiation of Armenian identities and place in the world.

The forms of Armenian nationhood which eventually emerged met with a characteristically ambivalent response from Armenians and their British supporters alike. Western Armenians and Armenophiles doubted that the tiny Armenian Republic could replace a nation based on the ideal of 'historic Armenia' stretching across Eastern Anatolia. The imposition of Soviet rule led to further doubts about the validity of the republic, particularly amongst a western Armenian diaspora who had little time for Bolshevik ideology.[16] On the other hand, the republic at least offered some security after the events of the war, providing, in Suny's words a 'haven for Armenian refugees from around the world and for Armenian migrants from other parts of the U.S.S.R.'.[17]

The response of British Armenophiles depended on their political orientations. For those of a leftward-leaning disposition or disappointed with the emerging post-war order in Western Europe, Soviet rule may have been less problematic. For others it immediately rendered Armenia and the Armenians culturally and politically suspect. Most British Armenophiles greeted Sovietisation with resignation. Soviet rule was certainly not seen as ideal, but there was a shared sense of relief that the future of the Armenians had finally been settled.

Pragmatism characterised the reaction of Harold Buxton, long-term supporter of the Armenian cause and director of the LMF. In his book *Transcaucasia* he pointed to the fact that Soviet rule allowed for Armenian survival: 'the important and dominating fact is that an Armenia exists today, the Soviet Republic of Armenia'.[18] At the very least, Sovietisation had saved Armenia from 'extinction'.[19] Buxton's sentiments were echoed by Avalov, writing on Armenia for *The Slavonic Review* in 1925, who observed that 'its connection with the U.S.S.R. gives this diminished Armenia some guarantee against further destruction; and in the Erivan Republic the idea of a national home for the Armenians has been realised, albeit only in embryonic form'.[20]

In the aftermath of genocide and faced with the realities of the post-war geopolitical order the Armenophiles were forced to re-assess their ideals. Their ambitions for the Armenian future were refashioned to be much more modest than they had been during the war. Nonetheless, some of the concepts and categories which had played an important role in British images of Armenia remained important, albeit being deployed in different ways. In *Transcaucasia,* for example, Buxton returned to familiar Armenophile themes of Christianity and civilisation, origins and endurance, as if to remind his readers that Armenian identity had not been subsumed by Soviet identity.

Armenophiles demonstrated that although they were under Soviet rule, the Armenians were not the same as 'the Bolsheviks' in Russia. Buxton still insisted upon a lasting bond between Britain and the Armenians. The belief that the Armenians were fundamentally 'civilised' continued to characterise Armenophile writing. The relief worker Dudley Northcote, in his history of the Armenians, referred to Indo-European origins and the achievements of early Armenian kingdoms. He pointed out that the Armenian Empire of Tigranes the Great was once 'the most powerful in the East'.[21]

The Armenophiles expected British audiences to believe that Soviet power would be damaging. But they themselves had a much more ambivalent attitude. Buxton was reconciled to Soviet rule, as it had 'saved' Armenia: 'Whatever the motives of Russia may have been in resuming control over her former Caucasian provinces, it remains undeniable that in doing so she has done more for the Armenians than all the western powers together.'[22] Nonetheless there was still a sense that Soviet rule was not the 'proper' form of government for a people who, it was believed, had the potential to develop into a European-style nation state. For Northcote, Sovietisation became part of the long history of the conquest and oppression of the Armenian people. Manipulating orientalist stereotypes that had in the past been applied to the Turks, he cast the Russian Bolsheviks as another Eastern horde descending on Armenia:

> It almost seems as if the restless spirits of those wonderful old barbarians, Genghiz Khan and Tamerlane, had become re-incarnate again amongst the present Bolshevik leaders in order once more to threaten European civilisation and Christianity even as they did in days of old.[23]

Whether Soviet rule was praised or condemned it was accepted that the Armenians could not stand alone but needed the protection and support of another power. This was not just because of the threat posed by the Turks, but related also to the longstanding paternalist belief that the Armenians could not 'progress' without a guiding hand, which had been advocated by a line of British observers since Bryce's *Transcaucasia* in 1876. Thus despite their reservations it was clear to the Armenophiles that without Soviet rule Armenia, 'will be left free to decay, deteriorate and in part die out, or at best to stagnate on the threshold of civilisation.'[24] If the

European powers would not assist the Armenians, as the past few decades had demonstrated, then the best had to be made of Soviet rule.

On the other hand the continued involvement of Britain in relief work and reconstruction offered a vital means of influencing Armenian development. As Dr. Armstrong Smith of the Save the Children Fund had put it, the relief work of the LMF. could 'materially and *morally* help towards the reconstruction of the country.'[25]

It was important for British Armenophiles that the Soviet Republic, whatever its political affiliation, became a 'homeland' for the Armenians. Attempts to emphasise the role of this region as an Armenian homeland stemmed from the desire to reconcile the loss of other territories which were richer in historical or cultural associations. The perspective of Northcote on this subject, discussed in the previous chapter, was echoed by that of Harold Buxton, who stressed the 'Armenianness' of the new Republic, trying to allay fears that the Armenians had been assimilated into the Bolshevik world: 'Well over one million Armenians are already established here. It is a national home. It includes Etchmiadzin, the ancient seat of the Armenian patriarchs. Armenian is the language everywhere spoken.'[26]

The idea of Transcaucasia as homeland was articulated in a variety of ways, not least by stressing Armenian historical roots in the region. For Northcote this was about re-inscribing Armenia as a site of civilisation and a place of interest and relevance for Europe. Though his comments directly echoed those of numerous nineteenth-century travellers, by the mid-1920s Northcote had become something of a lone voice. British attention had been diverted elsewhere. Buxton could still talk of British duties towards the Armenians: 'We of Great Britain have a very direct responsibility in the matter, for our statesmen joined with our Allies in promising to the Armenian people an independent Armenian state', but by then his claims had little resonance with the rest of the population.[27]

The establishment of Soviet rule in Armenia meant that British relationships with Armenia had changed dramatically. Armenia was no longer a pressing 'problem' or 'question' in a political sense for Britain and the 'need to know' about Armenia therefore lessened. This possibly explains the relative paucity of British writing on Armenia by this time. Soviet rule had indeed brought about some kind of settlement of the 'Armenian question'. Even if it was not the desired outcome the Armenians did not seem to be under threat, as Harold Buxton put it, of 'extinction'. This obviated the need for an 'Armenophile' movement in the sense of a political pressure group.[28] The concern for 'minorities' – a concern that had emerged during the late nineteenth century – was no longer a feature of British politics. Humanitarian and imperial concerns were articulated in new ways. At the same time the emergence of international bodies such as the League of Nations provided a new forum in which such concerns could be raised.[29]

The emergence of the Turkish Republic also influenced the decline of British interest in the Armenians. In a practical sense, studying the Armenians or their history in Eastern Anatolia after the genocide became politically sensitive and extremely difficult. The British failure to protect the Armenians or prevent Turkish rule over these regions made such subjects uncomfortable and troubling. The decline of Ottoman rule also affected the possibilities for imagining Armenian identity. With the rise of the secular Turkish state, defining the 'otherness' of the Turks and the Armenians became more complex. It became more difficult and perhaps less necessary to define the Armenians as suffering Christians, an outpost of civilisation in the East. Attention gradually shifted from the Turks to the Soviets as the 'opposite' or 'other' of a civilised world that was defined by democracy, nationalism and freedom.

Once again the Armenians were caught 'in-between'. As Northcote and Buxton had made clear, they were distinct from the Soviet world but postwar politics had made clear that they were not part of the European or western world of nation states either. As Robert Hayden and Milica Bakic Hayden have pointed out the Soviet world could itself become a replacement 'other': 'In this century, an ideological "other", communism, has replaced the geographical/cultural "other" of the Orient. The symbolic geography of eastern inferiority, however, remains.'[30] However, the Armenians, who were dispersed far beyond the Soviet nation in France, America and beyond, did not fit easily into this new category either.

As the twentieth century progressed, the imaginative distance between the Armenians and the British grew. That the image of the Armenians was so ambivalent in the first place allowed Armenia to slip from British consciousness.[31] It was not until the late 1980s that the Soviet Union and the outbreak of war between Armenia and Azerbaijan over the territory of Nagorno-Karabagh briefly drew attention to Armenia. Once again the region was characterised, like the Balkans, as a site of violence and also a site of mass population displacement, a place which was inherently unstable.

When Armenia gradually began to impinge upon British consciousnesses once again it was not only through 'news' of the Karabagh conflict but also through a variety of other means, including travel writing. That this was the case was indicative of the gulf which had grown between Britain and Armenia since the British 'forgetting' of the fate of the Armenians during the First World War.

Armenia and the Armenians have once again become exotic and mysterious, a backdrop for stories of exploration and adventure such as Philp Marsden's account of his travels through the Armenian communities of Europe and the Middle East, which ends with his experiences of the Karabagh conflict.[32] The title of Marsden's work, *The Crossing Place*, illustrates the extent to which perceptions of Armenia have remained the same. *The Crossing Place* is suggestive of Armenia's place 'in-between' East and West, Christianity and Islam and civilisation and barbarism. Colin Thubron's description of his encounter with Armenia in *Among the Russians* is also permeated by this sense of Armenia as a borderland and as in-between East and West. In his description of the temple at Garni (a site which had been carefully described by Northcote around 60 years previously) Thubron emphasises the contrast between the Hellenic style structure and the 'oriental' decoration which covered its columns: 'An oriental exuberance pervaded the temple's friezes, where whirls of stone foliage ran riot among the lion masks and undermined Ionic capitals.'[33] Thus Armenia is still often portrayed by western observers as occupying an unusual and 'special' position.

Representations of Armenia are open to continual processes of manipulation and reconstruction. For example, in their hope to eventually join the European Union, many representatives of Armenian authorities are keen to portray Armenia as a modern nation state, with much in common with the states of Western Europe. The Armenian diaspora meanwhile has its own images of the Armenian Republic, images which tend to focus on the ancient sites of Armenian heritage and Christianity and gloss over the Soviet past. Meanwhile British perceptions of Armenia now range from complete unfamiliarity to images of 'ethnic conflict' to images of ancient Christianity. Despite the coming of independence in 1991 the ambiguous image of Armenia is still embedded in complex power relations as Armenia continues to negotiate a place in the post-Soviet world.

Notes

1 For a survey of the problem in the twentieth century see, for example, Kushner and Knox, *Refugees in an Age of Genocide*.

2 Sir John Hope Simpson, *The Refugee Problem: Report of a Survey* (London: Oxford University Press, 1939).

3 Malkki, 'National Geographic', p. 34, and see M. Douglas, *Purity and Danger* (London: Routledge, 2002).

4 Bauman, 'Allosemitism' p. 153.

5 Mazower, *Dark Continent*, p. 51.

6 Bryce and Toynbee, *The Treatment of the Armenians*, p. 595.

7 For a recent case study see Maud Mandel, *Armenians and Jews in Twentieth-Century France* (Durham, NC: Duke University Press, 2003).

8 'For Orientalism was ultimately a political version of reality whose structure promoted the difference between the familiar (Europe, the West, "us") and the strange (the Orient, the East, "them").' Said, *Orientalism*, p. 43.

9 Moore-Gilbert, *Postcolonial Theory*, p. 70.

10 Herzfeld, *Anthropology through the Looking Glass*, p. 13. Herzfeld refers to the modern anthropology of Greece but his point seems relevant – he goes on to suggest that this realisation does not so much solve problems but initiates a critique of exoticism.

11 Todorova, *Imagining the Balkans*, p. 18.

12 This is addressed in Todorova, *Imagining the Balkans*, chapter 1. See also Mazower, *The Balkans*, chapter 3 and Hupchick, *Constantinople to Communism*, Part Three.

13 Wolff, *Inventing Eastern Europe*, p. 9.

14 See chapter 3.

15 Bloxham, *Great Game of Genocide*, p. 9.

16 The Dashnak government of the Armenian Republic had had a 'decidedly western European orientation' and its supporters were hostile towards the Soviet regime. Suny, *Looking toward Ararat*, p. 127.

17 Suny, 'Soviet Armenia, 1921–1991', in Herzig and Kurkchiyan, *The Armenians*, p. 115.

18 Buxton, *Transcaucasia*, p. 56.

19 Ibid.

20 Z. Avalov, 'The Caucasus Since 1918', *The Slavonic Review*, Vol. III (1924–25), p. 331.

21 D. S. Northcote, unpublished manuscript, *Armenia*, 1926. Northcote Papers, British Library.

22 Buxton, *Transcaucasia*, p. 129.

23 Northcote, *Armenia*.

24 Avalov, 'The Caucasus', p. 335.

25 Armstrong-Smith, 'Famine in Transcaucasia', p. 129. [My emphasis.]

26 Buxton, *Transcaucasia*, p. 53.

27 Ibid., p. 63.

28 Supporters of the Armenians now branched out in other directions. The Buxtons, for example, were by this point equally involved in other humanitarian ventures such as the Save the Children Fund.

29 There had been some crossover between supporters of the League and the

Armenophiles. Bryce was involved in both causes. Bryce died in 1924, depriving the Armenophile movement of one of its leaders.

30 M. Bakic-Hayden and R. Hayden, 'Orientalist Variations on the Theme "Balkans": Symbolic Geography in Recent Yugoslav Cultural Politics', *Slavic Review*, Vol. 51, No. 1 (Spring 1992), p. 4.

31 This was of course different for the Armenian diaspora in Britain. Relations between diaspora and homeland over the twentieth century have been complex and are beyond the scope of this work. See Razmik Panossian 'Homeland–Diaspora Relations and Identity Differences', in Herzig and Kurkchiyan, *The Armenians* and on the diaspora in Britain, V. Amit, 'Armenians and Other Diasporas: Trying to Reconcile the Irreconcilable', in N. Rapport, ed., *British Subjects: An Anthropology of Britain* (Oxford: Berg, 2002).

32 P. Marsden, *The Crossing Place, A Journey Among the Armenians* (London: Flamingo, 1994).

33 C. Thubron, *Among the Russians* (London: Penguin, 1983), p. 176.

Bibliography

Primary sources

Unpublished materials

Armenian National Archive, Yerevan

British Armenia Committee Papers, British and Foreign Anti-Slavery Archives, G506, Rhodes House Library, Oxford

National Archive, Kew, London: FO 286; FO 373; FO 608; FO 96; FO 881; FO 424; INF 4

Northcote Papers, British Library, London

Viscount Bryce Papers, Bodleian Library, Oxford

Published materials (i): newspapers and journals

Ararat: A Searchlight on Armenia

Contemporary Review

Folklore

Hansard

Houcharar

Journal of the Royal Geographical Society

New Near East

Slave Market News

*The Daily News**

The Friend of Armenia

The Geographical Journal

*The Graphic**

The Manchester Guardian

The Nineteenth Century

The Sphinx

The Times

* Viewed as part of the Press Cuttings Collection of the Nubarian Library, Paris.

Bibliography

Published materials (ii): books, articles and pamphlets

Abbot, K. E., 'Notes of a Tour in Armenia in 1837', *JRGS*, Vol. 12 (1842)

A Practical Scheme for the Solution of the Armenian Question (Manchester: Guardian Printing Works, 1890)

Ainsworth, W. F., *Travels and Researches in Asia Minor, Mesopotamia, Chaldea and Armenia* (London: John W. Parker, 1842)

Armenia's Charter: An Appreciation of the Services of Armenians to the Allied Cause (London: Spottiswode, Ballantyne & Co., 1918)

Armenian National Delegation, *Memorandum on the Armenian Question* (Paris, 1918)

Armenian Red Cross and Refugee Fund, *Annual Reports: 1915–20* (London: Armenian Red Cross and Refugee Fund)

Armstrong Smith, Dr, *Famine in Transcaucasia* (1922), extracts reprinted in C. J. Walker, *Visions of Ararat* (London: I. B. Tauris, 1997)

Aslan, G., *Armenia and the Armenians from the Earliest Times until the Great War* (London: Macmillan & Co., 1920)

Austin, H. H., *The Baqubah Refugee Camp: An Account of Work on Behalf of the Persecuted Assyrian Christians* (London: Faith Press, 1920)

Avalov, Z., 'The Caucasus Since 1918', *The Slavonic Review*, Vol. III (1924–25)

Barkley, H., *A Ride through Asia Minor and Armenia: Giving a Sketch of the Characters, Manners and Customs of both the Mussulman and Christian Inhabitants* (London: John Murray, 1891)

Barton, J., *The Story of Near East Relief, 1915–30: An Interpretation* (New York: Macmillan, 1930)

Benson, E. F., *Crescent and Iron Cross* (London: Hodder & Stoughton, London, 1918)

Bent, J. T., 'Travels Among the Armenians', *Contemporary Review*, Vol. 70 (December 1896)

Bishop, I., *Journeys in Persia and Kurdistan*, 2 vols (London: John Murray, 1891)

Bliss, E. M., *Turkey and the Armenian Atrocities* (London: T. Fisher Unwin, 1896)

Blunt, F. J., *The People of Turkey: Twenty Years Residence among Bulgarians, Greeks, Turks and Armenians. By a Consul's Wife and Daughter* (London: John Murray, 1878)

Brant, J. 'Journey Through a Part of Armenia and Asia Minor in the Year 1835', *JRGS*, Vol. 6 (1836)

British Armenia Committee, *Armenia and the Turkish Settlement: Memorandum Submitted for the Consideration of H.M. Government* (London: British Armenia Committee, 1920)

British Armenia Committee, *The Case For Armenia* (London: British Armenia Committee, 1920)

Bryce, J., *Russia and Turkey* (London, 1876)

Bryce, J., *Transcaucasia and Ararat* (London: Macmillan & Co., 1877)

Bryce, J., *The Attitude of Great Britain in the Present War* (London: Macmillan & Co., 1916)

Bibliography

Bryce, J., 'The Future of Armenia', *Contemporary Review*, Vol. 114 (December 1918)

Bryce, J., and A. J. Toynbee, *The Treatment of the Armenians in the Ottoman Empire* (London: Hodder & Stoughton, 1916)

Burnaby, F., *On Horseback through Asia Minor* (London: Sampson, Low & Co., 1877)

Buxton, H., *The Armenian Church* (London: Spottiswode, Ballantyne & Co., 1919)

Buxton, H., 'Armenia: Some Recent Impressions', *Contemporary Review*, Vol. 117 (January/June 1920)

Buxton, H., 'Transcaucasia', *Contemporary Review*, Vol. 121 (January/June 1922)

Buxton, H., *Transcaucasia* (London: Faith Press, 1926)

Buxton, N., MP and Rev. H. Buxton, *Travels and Politics in Armenia* (London: Smith, Elder and Co., 1914)

Chamichian, M., *History of Armenia from BC 2247 to the year of Christ 1780 or 1229 of the Armenian Era*, 3 vols, trans. Johannes Advall (Calcutta: Bishop's College Press, 1829)

Childs, W. J., *Across Asia Minor on Foot* (London: Blackwoods, 1917)

Clayden P. W., *Armenia: The Case against Salisbury. A Journalist's Glance Back over Twenty Years* (London: H. Marshall & Son, 1897)

Commission of Inquiry into the German Atrocities, *Evidence and Documents laid before the Committee on Alleged German Outrages* (Appendix to the report which has been published separately) (London, 1915)

Commission of Inquiry into the German Atrocities, *Report of the Committee on Alleged German Outrages appointed by his Britannic Majesty's Government and Presided over by the Right Honourable Viscount Bryce* (London, 1915)

Coneybeare, F. C., 'Notes on Some Early Ecclesiastical Practices in Armenia', *Folklore*, Vol. 18, No. 4 (December 1907)

Creagh, J., *Armenians, Koords and Turks*, 2 vols (London: Samuel Tinsley & Co., 1880)

Curzon, R., *Armenia: A Year at Erzeroom and on the Frontiers of Russia, Turkey and Persia*, 2 vols (London: John Murray, 1854)

De Brosset, M. F., *Les Ruines d'Ani: Histoire et Description* (St Petersburg: Imprimerie de l'Académie Impériale des Sciences, 1860)

Dillon, E. J., 'The Condition of Armenia', *Contemporary Review*, Vol. 68 (August 1895)

Douglas, J. A., *Death's Ride in Anatolia and Armenia* (London: Faith Press, 1920)

Duke of Argyll, *Our Responsibilities for Turkey* (London: John Murray, 1896)

Eastern Question Association, *Papers on the Eastern Question* (London: Cassell, Peter & Galphin, 1877)

Freeman, E. A., *The Eastern Question in its Historical Bearings* (Manchester: National Reform Union, 1876)

Freeman, E. A., *The Ottoman Power in Europe: Its Nature, its Growth and its Decline* (London: Macmillan, 1877)

Freshfield, D. W., *Travels in the Central Caucasus and Bashan including Visits to Ararat and Tabreez and Ascents of Kazbeh and Elbruz* (London: Longmans, Green & Co., 1869)

Further Memoranda on the Armenian and Assyrian Refugees in Mesopotamia (in continuation of publication no. 36170) (Baghdad: Government Press, 1921)

Garnett, L., *The Women of Turkey and their Folklore*, 2 vols (London: David Nutt, 1890)

Garnett, L., 'Women under Islam', *The Nineteenth Century*, Vol. 37 (January 1895)

Germany, Turkey and Armenia: A Selection of Documentary Evidence Relating to the German Atrocities from German and Other Sources (London: J. J. Keilher and Co., 1917)

Gladstone, W. E., *Bulgarian Horrors and the Question of the East* (London: John Murray, 1896), reprint of 1876 edition

Gladstone, W. E., *Mr Gladstone on the Armenian Question* (reprint of his speech at Chester Town Hall, 6 August 1896)

Glennie, J. S. S., 'Introduction' in L. Garnett, *The Women of Turkey and their Folklore*, 2 vols (London: David Nutt, 1890)

Greene, F. D., *The Armenian Crisis and the Rule of the Turk* (New York: G. P. Putnam's Sons, 1896)

Gregory, S. M., *The Land of Ararat: 12 Discourses on Armenia, her History and her Church*, (London: Chiswick Press, 1920)

Hacobian, A. P., *Armenia and the War* (London: Hodder & Stoughton, 1917)

Hagopian, G., 'Appeal to the British Nation', in Stevenson, F. S., *The Case For The Armenians* (London: Harrison & Sons, 1893)

Hamilton, W., 'Extracts from Notes Made on a Journey in Asia Minor 1836', *JRGS*, Vol. 7(1837)

Hamilton, W., 'Observations on the Position of Tavium', *JRGS*, Vol. 7 (1837)

Hamilton, W., *Researches in Asia Minor, Pontus and Armenia. With Some Account of Their Antiquities and Geology* (London: John Murray, 1842)

Harris, J. H., *Salving the Outcasts of War* (reprinted from the *Contemporary Review*, 1929)

Harris, J. R. and H. B. Harris, *Letters from the Scenes of the Recent Massacres in Armenia* (London: James Nisbet and Co., 1897)

Harrison, F., *Cross and Crescent* (London, 1876)

Hepworth, G., *Through Armenia on Horseback* (London: Ibister & Co., 1898)

Hodgetts, E. A. B., *Round about Armenia: The Record of a Journey across the Balkans, Through Turkey, the Caucasus and Persia in 1895* (London: Sampson, Low, Marston and Co., 1896)

Hogarth, D. G., *The Wandering Scholar in the Levant* (London: John Murray, 1896)

Hubbard, G. E., *From the Gulf to Ararat: An Expedition through Armenia and Kurdistan* (London: Blackwell, 1916)

International Association of the Friends of Armenia, *Armenia: England's Responsibility* (London: International Association of the Friends of Armenia,

Information Bureau, No. 12)

Jerazian, B., *The Armenian Merchants and the Armenian Community in Manchester* (Manchester: Local Studies Collection, Central Library)

Johnson, C. F., *The Armenians* (Blackburn: G. Toulmin & Sons, 1916)

Kerr-Porter, R., *Travels in Georgia, Persia, Armenia & Ancient Babylonia*, 2 vols (London: Longman, Hurst, Reese, Orme and Brown, 1821)

Kinneir, J. M., *Journey through Asia Minor, Armenia and Koordistan in the Years 1813 and 1814* (London: John Murray, 1818)

Layard, A. H., *Discoveries in the Ruins of Nineveh and Babylon. With Travels in Armenia* (London: John Murray, 1853)

Layard, A. H., *The Condition of Turkey and Her Dependencies: A Speech Delivered in the House of Commons, Friday 29 May, 1863* (London: John Murray, 1863)

Leese, C. L., *Armenia and the Allies* (London: British Armenia Committee, 1920)

Lepsius, J., *Le Rapport Secret sur les Massacres d'Arménie* (Paris: Payot, 1917)

Lord Mayor's Fund, *Armenians: Saving the Remnant* (London: Lord Mayor's Fund, 1917)

Lynch, H. F. B., 'The "Armenian question": Part II, in Russia', *Contemporary Review*, Vol. 66 (July 1894)

Lynch, H. F. B., *Armenia Travels and Studies*, 2 vols (London: Longmans, Green & Co., 1901)

MacColl, M., *England's Responsibility towards Armenia* (London: Longmans, Green & Co., 1895)

MacDonald, A., *The Land of Ararat or up the Roof of the World* (London: Eden, Remmington & Co., 1893)

Memoranda on the Armenian and Assyrian Refugees at Present in Camp at Ba'quba Mesopotamia (Baghdad: Government Press, 1919)

Morgan, J. H., *German Atrocities: An Official Investigation* (London: T. Fisher Unwin, 1916)

Morgenthau, H., *Ambassador Morgenthau's Story* (Detroit: Wayne State University Press, 2003)

Morier, J., *A Second Journey through Persia, Armenia and Asia Minor, to Constantinople* (London: Longman, 1812)

Mugerditchian, E., *From Turkish Toils: The Narrative of an Armenian Family's Escape* (London: C. Arthur Pearson Ltd., 1918)

Nansen, F., *Armenia and the Near East* (New York: Da Capo Press, 1976), reprint of 1928 publication

Nazarbek, Avetis, 'Zeitun', *Contemporary Review*, Vol. 69 (1896)

Niepage, Dr M., *The Horrors of Aleppo . . . Seen by a German Eye-Witness* (London: T. Fisher Unwin Ltd., 1917)

Pasha, N., *A Practical Scheme for the Solution of the Armenian Question* (Manchester: Guardian Printing Works, 1890)

Pears, E., *40 Years in Constantinople: The Recollections of Sir Edwin Pears 1873–1915* (London: Herbert Jenkins, 1916)

Bibliography

Percy, H. A. G., *Notes From a Diary in Asiatic Turkey* (London: E. Arnold, 1898)

Probyn, J. W., 'Armenia and the Lebanon', in Eastern Question Association, *Papers on the Eastern Question* (London: Cassell, Peter & Galphin, 1877)

Raffi, A., ed., *Armenia and the Settlement* (Report of Public Meeting to express sympathy with the Armenian Cause, held at Central Hall Westminster, 19 June 1919) (London, 1919)

Ramsay, Mrs W. M., *Everyday Life in Turkey* (London: Hodder & Stoughton, 1897)

Ramsay, W. M., *Impressions of Turkey during Twelve Years Wanderings* (London: Hodder & Stoughton, 1897)

Rawlinson, Sir H., *England and Russia in the East* (London: John Murray, 1875)

Robinson, E. J., *The Truth about Armenia* (1913)

Robinson E. J., *Armenia and the Armenians* (1917)

Rolin-Jaequemyns, G., *Armenia, the Armenians and the Treaties* (London: John Heywood, 1891)

Russell, G. W. E., *The Offence of the Cross* (1896)

Russell, G. W. E., 'Armenia and the Forward Movement', *Contemporary Review*, Vol. 71 (January 1897)

Saint-Martin, J. A. de, *Mémoires Historiques et Géographiques Sur L'Arménie*, 2 vols (Paris, 1819)

Shiel, J. 'Notes on a Journey from Tabriz, Through Kurdistan, Via Van, Bitlis Se'eert and Erbul to Suleimanyeh in July and August 1836', *JRGS*, Vol. 8 (1838)

Shiell, A. G., *The Armenian Agony, An Open letter to the Prime Minister* (Brighton: A. G. Shiell, 1896)

Shoemaker, M. M., *The Heart of the Orient: Saunterings Through Georgia, Armenia, Persia and Turkey* (London: G. P. Putnam's Sons, 1904)

Simpson, Sir J. H., *The Refugee Problem: Report of a Survey* (London: Oxford University Press, 1939)

Southgate, H., *Narrative of a Tour through Persia, Mesopotamia and Armenia* (New York: Appleton & Co., 1840)

Stead, W. T., ed., *The Haunting Horrors in Armenia* (London: 'Review of Reviews', 1896)

Stevenson, F. S., *The Case for the Armenians* (London: Harrison & Sons, 1893)

The Conference and the Armenians (London: R. Clay, Sons & Taylor, 1878)

The Cry of Armenia (1895)

The Martyrdom of a Nation (London: Lord Mayor's Fund, 1916)

The New Armenia. Claims at the Peace Conference. By the Special Correspondent of *The Times*, reprinted from *The Times*, 31 December 1918 (London: Spottiswode, Ballantyne & Co., 1919)

Toynbee, A. J., *Armenian Atrocities: The Murder of a Nation* (London: Hodder & Stoughton, 1915)

Toynbee, A. J., *The Belgian Deportations* (London: T. Fisher Unwin, 1916)

Toynbee, A. J., *The Murderous Tyranny of the Turks* (London: Hodder & Stoughton, 1917)

Toynbee, A. J., *Turkey: A Past and a Future* (London: Hodder & Stoughton, 1917)

Tozer, H. F., *Turkish Armenia and Asia Minor* (London: Longmans Green & Co., 1881)

Ussher, J., *A Journey from London to Persepolis including Wanderings in Dagestan, Georgia, Armenia etc.* (London: Hurst & Blackett, 1865)

Ward, M. H., *The Deportations in Asia Minor, 1921–22* (London: Anglo-Hellenic League; British Armenia Committee, 1922)

Watson, W., *The Purple East: A Series of Sonnets on England's Desertion of Armenia* (London: John Lane, 1896)

Wilbraham, R., *Travels to the Transcaucasian Provinces of Russia and along the Southern Shores of Lakes Van and Urmiah* (London, 1839)

Williams, W. L., *Armenia: Past and Present: A Study and Forecast, With an Introduction by T. P. O'Connor MP* (London: P.S. King & Son, Ltd., 1916)

Wintle, W. J., *Armenia and Its Sorrows* (London: Andrew Melrose, 1896)

Secondary sources

Abrahamian, L., *Armenian Identity in a Changing World* (Costa Mesa, CA: Mazda, 2006)

Abrahamian, L. and N. Sweezy, eds, *Armenian Folk Arts, Culture and Identity* (Bloomington: Indiana University Press, 2001)

Allen, T. and H. Morsink, eds, *When Refugees go Home* (London: UNRISD in association with James Currey, 1994)

Ambrosius, L., 'Wilsonian Diplomacy and Armenia: The Limits of Power and Ideology', in J. Winter, ed., *America and the Armenian Genocide of 1915* (Cambridge: Cambridge University Press, 2003)

Amit, V., 'Armenians and Other Diasporas: Trying to Reconcile the Irreconcilable', in N. Rapport, ed., *British Subjects: An Anthropology of Britain* (Oxford: Berg, 2002)

Anderson, B., *Imagined Communities* (London: Verso, 1991), revised edition

Anderson, M., *Noel Buxton: A Life* (London: George Allen and Unwin, 1952)

Anderson, M. S., *The Eastern Question 1774–1923: A Study in International Relations* (London: Macmillan, 1966)

Arslanian, A. H., 'Britain and the Transcaucasian Nationalities during the Russian Civil War', in R. G. Suny, ed., *Transcaucasia: Nationalism and Social Change* (Ann Arbor: University of Michigan, 1983)

Astourian, S., 'In Search of their Forefathers: National Identity and the Historiography and Politics of Armenian and Azerbaijani Ethnogeneses', in D. Schwartz and R. Panossian, eds, *Nationalism and History: The Politics of Nation Building in Post-Soviet Armenia, Azerbaijan and Georgia* (Toronto: University of Toronto, Centre for Russian and East European Studies, 1994)

Atkinson, J., I. Banks and J. O'Sullivan, eds, *Nationalism and Archaeology* (Glasgow: Cruthie Press, 1996)

Bibliography

Audoin-Rouzeau, S. and A. Becker, *1914–1918: Understanding the Great War* (London: Profile, 2002)

Bakic-Hayden, M. and R. Hayden, 'Orientalist Variations on the Theme "Balkans": Symbolic Geography in Recent Yugoslav Cultural Politics', *Slavic Review*, Vol. 51, No. 1 (Spring 1992)

Balakian, P., *The Burning Tigris: The Armenian Genocide* (London: William Heinemann, 2004)

Balakrishnan, G., *Mapping the Nation* (London: Verso, 1996)

Bardakjian, K., *The Mekhitarist Contribution to Armenian Culture and Scholarship* (Cambridge, MA: Harvard College Library, 1976)

Bardakjian, K., 'Armenia and the Armenians through the Eyes of English Travellers of the Nineteenth Century', in R. Hovannisian, ed., *The Armenian Image in History and Literature* (California: Undena Publications, 1981)

Barkan, E., *The Retreat of Scientific Racism* (Cambridge: Cambridge University Press, 1992)

Barkey, K. and M. Von Hagen, *After Empire: Multiethnic Societies and Nation Building* (Oxford: Westview Press, 1997)

Baron, N. and P. Gatrell, 'Population Displacement, State Building and Social Identity in the Lands of the Former Russian Empire, 1917–1923', *Kritika: Explorations in Russian and Eurasian History*, Vol. 4, No. 1 (Winter 2003)

Baron, N. and P. Gatrell, eds, *Homelands: War, Population and Statehood in Eastern Europe and Russia, 1918–1924* (London: Anthem Press, 2004)

Barthes, R., *Mythologies* (London: Vintage, 2000), first published 1957

Baud, M. and W. Van Schendel, 'Toward a Comparative History of Borderlands', *Journal of World History*, Vol. 8, No. 2 (1997)

Bauman, Z., 'Allosemitism: Premodern, Modern, Postmodern', in B. Cheyette and L. Marcus, eds, *Modernity, Culture and the Jew* (Cambridge: Polity Press, 1998)

Bentley, M., *The Liberal Mind 1919–1929* (Cambridge: Cambridge University Press, 1977)

Best, G., *War and Law since 1945* (Oxford: Clarendon Press, 1994)

Bloxham, D., 'Determinants of the Armenian Genocide', in R. Hovannisian, ed., *Looking Backward, Moving Forward: Confronting the Armenian Genocide* (New Brunswick, NJ: Transaction, 2003)

Bloxham, D., 'The Armenian Genocide of 1915–1916: Cumulative Radicalization and the Development of a Destruction Policy', *Past and Present*, No. 181 (November 2003)

Bloxham, D., *The Great Game of Genocide: Imperialism, Nationalism and the Destruction of the Ottoman Armenians* (Oxford: Oxford University Press, 2005)

Boswell, D. and J. Evans, *Representing the Nation: A Reader* (London: Routledge, 1999)

Bouatchidze, G., *La Vie de Marie Brosset* (Paris: Editions du Petit Véhicule, 1996)

Bourke, J., *Dismembering the Male: Men's Bodies, Britain and the Great War* (London: Reaktion Books, 1996)

Bibliography

Bourke, J., *An Intimate History Of Killing: Face to Face Killing in Twentieth Century Warfare* (London: Granta, 1999)

Bournoutian, G. A., *A Concise History of the Armenian People* (Costa Mesa, CA: Mazda, 2003)

Burney, C. and D. M. Lang, *The People of the Hills: Ancient Ararat and Caucasus* (London: Weidenfeld and Nicholson, 1991)

Calahan, P., *Belgian Refugee Relief in England during the First World War* (New York: Garland, 1982)

Chamberlain, J. E. and S. L. Gilman, eds, *Degeneration: The Dark Side of Progress* (New York: Columbia University Press, 1985)

Cheyette, B. and L. Marcus, eds, *Modernity, Culture and the Jew* (Cambridge: Polity Press, 1998)

Cheyette, B. and N. Valman, 'Introduction', in *The Image of the Jew in European Liberal Culture 1789–1914* (London: Vallentine Mitchell, 2004)

Cheyette, B. and N. Valman, eds, *The Image of the Jew in European Liberal Culture 1789–1914* (London: Vallentine Mitchell, 2004)

Cheyette, B., *Constructions of the Jew in English Literature and Society: Racial Representations 1875–1945* (Cambridge: Cambridge University Press, 1996)

Cheyette, B., 'Introduction' in B. Cheyette, ed., *Between 'Race' and Culture: Representations of 'the Jew' in English and American Literature* (Stanford: Stanford University Press, 1996)

Cheyette, B., ed., *Between 'Race' and Culture: Representations of 'the Jew' in English and American Literature* (Stanford: Stanford University Press, 1996)

Chorbajian, L., ed., *The Making of Nagorno Karabagh: From Secession to Republic* (Basingstoke: Palgrave, 2001)

Cirakman, A., *From the 'Terror of the World' to the 'Sick Man of Europe': European Images of Ottoman Empire and Society from the Sixteenth Century to the Nineteenth* (Oxford: Peter Lang, 2002)

Clarke, J. I. and H. Bowen-Jones, *Change and Development in the Middle East: Essays in Honour of W.B. Fisher* (London: Methuen, 1981)

Clarke, P., *Hope and Glory: Britain 1900–1990* (London: Penguin, 1996)

Clifford, J., 'On Orientalism', in J. Clifford, *The Predicament of Culture: Twentieth-Century Ethnography, Literature, and Art*, (Cambridge, MA: Harvard University Press, 1988)

Clifford, J. *The Predicament of Culture: Twentieth-Century Ethnography, Literature, and Art* (Cambridge, MA: Harvard University Press, 1988)

Cohn, B., *Colonialism and its Forms of Knowledge: The British in India* (Princeton: Princeton University Press, 1996)

Conwell-Evans, T. P., *Foreign Policy from a Back Bench: A Study Based on the Papers of Noel Buxton* (London: Oxford University Press, 1932)

Cornell, S., *Small Nations and Great Powers: A Study of Ethnopolitical Conflict in the Caucasus* (Richmond: Curzon, 2000)

Bibliography

Dadrian, V. N., *The History of the Armenian Genocide: Ethnic Conflict from the Balkans to Anatolia to the Caucasus* (Oxford: Berghan, 1995)

Dadrian, V. N., *German Responsibility in the Armenian Genocide: A Review of the Historical Evidence of German Complicity* (Watertown, MA: Blue Crane Books, 1996)

Davey, A., *The British Pro-Boers 1877–1902* (Cape Town: Tafelberg, 1978)

Davis, L. A., *The Slaughterhouse Province: An American Diplomat's Report on the Armenian Genocide, 1915–17*, edited by S. K. Blair (New York: A. D. Caratzas, Orpheus Publications, 1989)

Davison, R. H., 'The Armenian Crisis (1912–1914)', *American Historical Review*, 53 (April 1948)

De Groot, J., 'Sex and Race: The Construction of Language and Image in the Nineteenth Century', in, C. Hall, ed., *Cultures of Empire: A Reader* (Manchester: Manchester University Press, 2000)

Dolukhanov, P., 'Archaeology and Nationalism in Totalitarian and Post-Totalitarian Russia', in J. Atkinson, I. Banks and J. O'Sullivan, eds, *Nationalism and Archaeology* (Glasgow: Cruthie Press, 1996)

Douglas, M., *Purity and Danger* (London: Routledge, 2002)

Douglas, R., 'Britain and the Armenian Question, 1894–97', *Historical Journal*, Vol. 19, No. 1 (March 1976)

Driver, F., *Geography Militant, Cultures of Exploration and Empire* (Oxford: Blackwell, 2001)

Dudnik, S., K. Hagemann and J. Tosh, eds, *Masculinities in Politics and War: Gendering Modern History* (Manchester: Manchester University Press, 2004)

Dyer, G., 'Turkish Falsifiers and Armenian Deceivers: Historiography and the Armenian Massacres', *Middle Eastern Studies*, Vol. 12, no. 1 (1976)

Eley, G. and R. G. Suny, 'Introduction: From the Moment of Social History to the Work of Social Representation', in G. Eley and R. G. Suny, eds, *Becoming National: A Reader* (Oxford: Oxford University Press, 1996)

Eley, G. and R. G. Suny, eds, *Becoming National: A Reader* (Oxford: Oxford University Press, 1996)

Elliott, M. E., *Beginning Again at Ararat* (London and Edinburgh: Fleming H. Revell Company, 1924)

Etmekjian, J., *The French Influence on the Western Armenian Renaissance* (New York: Twayne Publishers Inc., 1964)

Fabian, J., *Time and the Other: How Anthropology Makes Its Object* (New York: Columbia University Press, 2002)

Fein, H., *Denying Genocide: From Armenia to Bosnia* (London: LSE, Occasional Papers in Comparative and International Politics, 2001)

Fleming, K. E., 'Orientalism, The Balkans and Balkan Historiography', *American Historical Review*, Vol. 105, No. 4 (2005)

Fromkin, D., *A Peace to End all Peace: The End of the Ottoman Empire and the Creation of the Modern Middle East* (London: Phoenix, 2000)

Bibliography

Gatrell, P., *A Whole Empire Walking: Refugees in Russia during World War I* (Bloomington: Indiana University Press, 1999)

Gatrell, P. and J. Laycock, 'Armenia: The "Nationalisation", Internationalisation and Representation of the Refugee Crisis', in N. Baron and P. Gatrell, eds, *Homelands: War, Population and Statehood in Eastern Europe and Russia 1918– 24* (London: Anthem Press, 2004)

George, J., *Merchants in Exile: The Armenians in Manchester, England, 1835–1935* (London: Gomidas Institute, 2002)

Gilroy, A., ed., *Romantic Geographies: Discourses of Travel, 1775–1844* (Manchester: Manchester University Press, 2000)

Grabill, J., *Protestant Diplomacy in the Near East* (Minneapolis: University of Minnesota Press, 1971)

Graham-Brown, S., *Images of Women: The Portrayal of Women in Photography of the Middle East, 1860–1950* (London: Quartet, 1958)

Grant, K., *A Civilised Savagery: Britain and the New Slaveries in Africa 1884–1926* (London: Routledge, 2005)

Grayzel, S., *Women's Identities at War: Gender, Motherhood and Politics in Britain and France during WW1* (London and Chapel Hill: North Carolina University Press, 1999)

Greenshields, T. H., 'The Settlement of Armenian Refugees in Syria and Lebanon, 1915–1939', in J. I. Clarke and H. Bowen-Jones, *Change and Development in the Middle East: Essays in Honour of W. B. Fisher* (London: Methuen, 1981)

Gullace, N., 'Sexual Violence and Family Honor: British Propaganda and International Law during the First World War', *American Historical Review*, Vol. 102, No. 3 (June 1997)

Gullace, N., *The Blood of Our Sons: Men, Women and the Renegotiation of Citizenship during the Great War* (Basingstoke: Palgrave, 2002)

Gupta A., and J. Ferguson, eds, *Culture, Power, Place: Explorations in Critical Anthropology* (London: Duke University Press, 1997)

Hall, C., 'Thinking the Postcolonial, Thinking the Empire', in C. Hall, ed., *Cultures of Empire: A Reader* (Manchester: Manchester University Press, 2000)

Hall, C., ed., *Cultures of Empire: A Reader* (Manchester: Manchester University Press, 2000)

Harris, R., 'The "Child of the Barbarian": Rape, Race and Nationalism in France during the First World War', *Past and Present*, No. 141 (November 1993)

Haste, C., *Keep the Home Fires Burning* (London: Allen Lane, 1977)

Herzfeld, M., *Anthropology through the Looking Glass: Critical Ethnography in the Margins of Europe* (Cambridge: Cambridge University Press, 1987)

Herzig, E., *The New Caucasus: Armenia, Azerbaijan and Georgia* (London: Royal Institute of International Affairs, 1999)

Herzig, E. and M. Kurkchiyan, eds, *The Armenians: Past and Present in the Making of National Identity* (London: RoutledgeCurzon, 2005)

Bibliography

Hewsen, R., *Armenia: A Historical Atlas* (Chicago and London: University of Chicago Press, 2001)

Higonnet, M., J. Jenson, S. Michel and M. Collins-Weitz, eds, *Behind the Lines: Gender and the Two World Wars* (London: Yale University Press, 1987)

Hirschon, R., *Heirs of the Greek Catastrophe* (Oxford: Berghann, 1998)

Hobsbawm, E., 'Mass Producing Traditions: Europe 1870–1914', in E. Hobsbawm and T. Ranger, eds, *The Invention of Tradition* (Cambridge: Cambridge University Press, 1983)

Hobsbawm, E., *The Age of Empire, 1875–1914* (London: Abacus, 1987)

Hobsbawm, E., *Nations and Nationalism since 1780: Programme, Myth, Reality* (Cambridge: Cambridge University Press, 1990)

Hobsbawm, E. and T. Ranger, eds, *The Invention of Tradition* (Cambridge: Cambridge University Press, 1983)

Hofmann, T. and G. Koutcharian, 'Images that Horrify and Indict: Pictorial Documents on the Persecution and Extermination of Armenians from 1877 to 1922', *Armenian Review*, Vol. 45, No. 1–2 (1992)

Holquist, P., 'New Terrains and New Chronologies: The Interwar Period Through the Lens of Population Politics', *Kritika: Explorations in Russian and Eurasian History*, Vol. 4, No. 1 (Winter 2003)

Horne, J., 'Masculinity and Politics in the Age of Nation-States and World Wars', in S. Dudnik, K. Hagemann and J. Tosh, eds, *Masculinities in Politics and War: Gendering Modern History* (Manchester: Manchester University Press, 2004)

Horne, J. and A. Kramer, *German Atrocities: A History of Denial* (London and New Haven: Yale University Press, 2001)

Housepian-Dobkin, M., 'What Genocide, What Holocaust? News from Turkey, 1915–1923: A Case Study', in R. Hovannisian, ed., *The Armenian Genocide in Perspective* (New Brunswick, NJ: Transaction, 1986)

Hovannisian, R., *Armenia on the Road to Independence* (Berkeley and Los Angeles: University of California Press, 1967)

Hovannisian, R., 'The Allies and Armenia, 1915–18', *Journal of Contemporary History*, Vol. 3, No. 1 (January 1968)

Hovannisian, R., *The Republic of Armenia*, 4 vols (Berkeley: University of California Press, 1971–1996)

Hovannisian, R., 'The Historical Dimension of the Armenian Question', in R. Hovanisian, ed., *The Armenian Genocide in Perspective* (New Brunswick, NJ: Transaction, 1986)

Hovannisian, R., 'Confronting the Armenian Genocide', in R. Hovannisian, ed., *Looking Backward, Moving Forward: Confronting the Armenian Genocide* (New Brunswick, NJ: Transaction, 2003)

Hovannisian, R., 'The Armenian Genocide and US Post-War Commissions', in J., Winter, ed., *America and the Armenian Genocide of 1915* (Cambridge: Cambridge University Press, 2003)

Bibliography

Hovannisian, R., ed., *The Armenian Image in History and Literature* (California: Undena Publications, 1981)

Hovannisian, R., ed., *The Armenian Genocide in Perspective* (New Brunswick, NJ: Transaction, 1986)

Hovannisian, R., ed., *The Armenian Genocide, History, Politics, Ethics* (London: Macmillan, 1992)

Hovannisian, R., 'The Republic of Armenia', in R. Hovannisian, ed., *The Armenian People from Ancient to Modern Times, Vol. 2* (St. Martin's Press, New York, 1997)

Hovannisian, R., ed., *The Armenian People From Ancient to Modern Times, Vol. 2*. (New York: St. Martins, 1997)

Hovannisian, R., ed., *Looking Backward, Moving Forward: Confronting the Armenian Genocide* (New Brunswick, NJ: Transaction, 2003)

Hovannisian, R., ed., *The Armenian People from Ancient to Modern Times, Vol. 1, The Dynastic Periods* (Basingstoke: Palgrave Macmillan, 2004)

Hupchick, P., *The Balkans: From Constantinople to Communism* (London: Palgrave, 2002)

Hyndman, J., *Managing Displacement: Refugees and the Politics of Humanitarianism* (Minnesota: University of Minnesota Press, 2000)

Jones, S., *The Archaeology of Ethnicity* (London: Routledge, 1997)

Kabbani, R., *Imperial Fictions: Europe's Myths of Orient* (London: Pandora 1994)

Kaplan, S., 'Documenting History, Historicising Documents: French Military Officials' Ethnological Reports on Cilicia', *Comparative Studies in Society and History*, Vol. 44, No. 2 (2002)

Kaplan, S., 'Territorializing Armenians: Geo-Texts and Political Imaginaries in French Occupied Cilicia, 1919–1922', *History and Anthropology*, Vol. 15, No. 4 (December 2004)

Kaprelian-Churchill, I., 'Armenian Refugee Women: The Picture Brides, 1920–1930', *Journal of American Ethnic History*, Vol. 13, No. 3 (1993)

Kasparian, A. O., *Armenian Needlelace and Embroidery* (Virginia: EPM Publications, 1983)

Keddie, N. R. and B. Baron, eds, *Women in Middle Eastern History: Shifting Boundaries of Sex and Gender* (London: Yale University Press, 1991)

Kent, M., 'Great Britain and the End of the Ottoman Empire 1900–1923', in M. Kent, ed., *The Great Powers and the End of the Ottoman Empire* (London: Frank Cass, 1996) second edition

Kent, M., ed., *The Great Powers and the End of the Ottoman Empire* (London: Frank Cass, 1996), second edition

Kerr, S. E., *The Lions of Marash* (Albany: State University of New York Press, 1973)

Kevonian, D., *Réfugies et la Diplomatie Humanitaire: Les Acteurs Européens et la Scène Proche Orientale Pendant l'Entre Deux Guerres* (Paris: Publications de la Sorbonne, 2004)

Kévonian-Dyrek, D., 'Les Tribulations de la Diplomatie Humanitaire, La Société des Nations et les Réfugies Arméniens', in Hans-Lukas Kieser, ed., *Die*

Bibliography

Armenische Frage und die Schweiz : 1896–1923 (Zurich: Chronos Verlag, 1999)

Kevorkian, R., *Revue d'Histoire Arménien Contemporain (Numéro Spécial): L'Extermination des Déportés Arméniens Ottomans dans les Camps de Concentration de Syrie-Mesopotamie (1915–1916): La Deuxième Phase du Génocide* (Paris: Bibliothèque Nubar, 1998)

Kevorkian, R., ed., *Ani, Capitale de l'Arménie en l'An Mil* (Paris: Paris Musées, 2001)

Kieser, Hans-Lukas, ed., *Die Armenische Frage und die Schweiz: 1896–1923* (Zurich: Chronos Verlag, 1999)

Kingsley-Kent, S., *Making Peace: The Reconstruction of Gender in Inter-War Britain* (Princeton: Princeton University Press, 1993)

Kirakosian, A. J., *Velikobritania i Armenianski Vopros: 90–e Gody XIX Veka* (Erevan: Aiastan, 1990)

Kirakosian, A. J., ed., *The Armenian Massacres, 1894–1896: U. S. Media Testimony* (Detroit: Wayne State University Press, 2004)

Kohl, P. and C. Fawcett, eds, *Nationalism, Politics and the Practice of Archaeology* (Cambridge: Cambridge University Press, 1995)

Kohl, P. and Gocha R. Tsetskhladze, 'Nationalism, Politics and the Practice of Archaeology in the Caucasus', in P. Kohl and C. Fawcett, eds, *Nationalism, Politics and the Practice of Archaeology* (Cambridge: Cambridge University Press, 1995)

Korte, B., *British Travel Writing: From Pilgrimage to the Postcolonial* (London: Macmillan, 2000)

Kouymjian, D., 'Destruction des Monuments Historiques Arméniens, Poursuite de la Politique Turque de Génocide', in Tribunal Permanant des Peuples, *Le Crime de Silence: Le Génocide Des Arméniens* (Paris: Flammarion, 1984)

Kouymjian, D., 'Confiscation and Destruction: A Manifestation of the Genocidal Process', *Armenian Forum*, Vol. 1, No. 3 (Autumn 1998)

Kuper, L., *Genocide: Its Political Use in the Twentieth Century* (London: Penguin, 1982)

Kuper, L. 'The Turkish Genocide of the Armenians 1915–17', in R. Hovannisian, ed., *The Armenian Genocide in Perspective* (New Brunswick, NJ: Transaction, 1986)

Kurkchiyan, M., 'The Karabagh Conflict: From Soviet Past to Post-Soviet Uncertainty', in E. Herzig and M. Kurkchiyan, eds, *The Armenians: Past and Present in the Making of National Identity* (London: RoutledgeCurzon, 2005)

Kushner, T. and K. Knox, *Refugees in the Age of Genocide: Global, National and Local Perspectives during the Twentieth Century* (London: Frank Cass, 1999)

Kyadjian, Edmond, *Archag Tchnobian et la Mouvement Armenophile en France* (Marseille: Centre National de Documentation Pédagogique, 1986)

Laity, P., *The British Peace Movement, 1870–1914* (Oxford: Clarendon Press, 2001)

Lang, D. M., *Armenia: Cradle of Civilisation* (London: George Allen and Unwin, 1980), third edition

Bibliography

Lang, D. M., *The Armenians: A People in Exile* (London: Hyman, 1988)

Lang, D. M. and Walker C. J., *The Armenians* (London: Minorities Rights Group, 1976)

Lentin, R., ed., *Gender and Catastrophe* (London: Zed Books, 1997)

Leonard, T. C., 'When News Media is Not Enough: American Media and Armenian Deaths', in J. Winter, ed., *America and the Armenian Genocide of 1915* (Cambridge: Cambridge University Press, 2003)

Levene, M., 'Creating a Modern Zone of Genocide. The Impact of Nation and State Formation on Eastern Anatolia 1878–1923', *Holocaust and Genocide Studies*, Vol. 12, No. 3 (1998)

Levene, M. and P. Roberts, eds, *The Massacre In History* (Oxford: Berghan, 1999)

Levy, A. and A. Weingrod, *Homelands and Diasporas: Holy Lands and Other Places* (Stanford: Stanford University Press, 2005)

Lewis, B., *The Emergence of Modern Turkey* (Oxford: Oxford University Press, 1961)

Lewis, R., *Gendering Orientalism: Race, Femininity and Representation* (London: Routledge, 1996)

Lewis, R., *Re-Thinking Orientalism: Women, Travel and the Oriental Harem* (London: I. B. Tauris, 2004)

Lewis, R. and S. Mills, 'Introduction', in R. Lewis and S. Mills, eds, *Feminist Postcolonial Theory: A Reader* (Edinburgh: Edinburgh University Press, 2003)

Lewis, R. and S. Mills, eds, *Feminist Postcolonial Theory: A Reader* (Edinburgh: Edinburgh University Press, 2003)

Libaridian, G., 'Objectivity and the History of the Armenian Genocide', *Armenian Review*, 31 (Spring 1978)

Libaridian, G., *The Challenge of Statehood: Armenian Political Thinking Since Independence* (Watertown, MA: Blue Crane Books, 1999)

Libaridian, G., *Modern Armenia: People, Nation, State* (London: Transaction, 2004)

Loescher, G., *The UNHCR and World Politics: A Perilous Path* (Oxford: Oxford University Press, 2001)

Loew, L., *Critical Terrains: French and British Orientalisms* (Ithaca and London: Cornell University Press, 1991)

Lozios, P., 'Ottoman Half-Lives: Long-term Perspectives on Particular Forced Migrations', *Journal of Refugee Studies*, Vol. 12, No. 3 (1999)

Loizos, P., 'Misconceiving Refugees', in Renos K. Papadopoulos, ed., *Therapeutic Care for Refugees: No Place Like Home* (Karnac: London and New York, 2001)

Macfie, L., *The Eastern Question, 1774–1923* (London: Longman, 1996)

Mackenzie, J. M., *Propaganda and Empire* (Manchester: Manchester University Press, 1984)

Mackenzie, J. M., *Imperialism and Popular Culture* (Manchester: Manchester University Press, 1986)

Bibliography

Mackenzie, J. M., *Orientalism: History, Theory and the Arts* (Manchester: Manchester University Press, 1995)

Macler, F., *La Nation Arménienne* (Paris: Librairie Fischbacher, 1923)

Macmillan, M., *The Peacemakers* (London: John Murray, 2001)

Maisels, C. K., *Archaeology in the Cradle of Civilisation* (London: Routledge, 1993)

Malkki, L., 'National Geographic: The Rooting of Peoples and the Territorialization of National Identity Among Scholars and Refugees', *Cultural Anthropology*, Vol. 7, No. 1 (1992)

Malkki, L., 'Speechless Emmisairies: Refugees, Humanitarianism and De-historicization', *Cultural Anthropology*, Vol. 11, No. 3 (1996)

Mamoulia, G., 'Les Premières Fissures de L'URSS d'Apres Guerre: Le Cas de la Georgie et du Caucase du Sud: 1946–7', *Cahiers du Monde Russe*, Vol. 46, No. 3 (2005)

Mamoulia, G., 'Les Crises Turque et Iranienne 1945–7: L'Apport des Archives Caucasiennes', *Cahiers du Monde Russe*, Vol. 45, No. 1–2 (2004)

Mandel, M., *In the Aftermath of Genocide: Armenians and Jews in Twentieth-Century France* (Durham, NC: Duke University Press, 2003)

Maranci, M., *Medieval Armenian Architecture: Constructions of Race and Nation* (Leuven: Peeters, 2001)

Marrus, M., *The Unwanted: European Refugees from the First World War through the Cold War* (Philadelphia: Temple University Press, 2002)

Marsden, P., *The Crossing Place: A Journey Among the Armenians* (London: Flamingo, 1994)

Marsh, P., 'Lord Salisbury and the Ottoman Massacres', *Journal of British Studies*, Vol. 11, No. 2 (May 1972)

Masterman, C. F. G., ed., *The Heart of the Empire: Discussions of Problems of Modern City Life In England* (London: T. Fisher Unwin, 1901)

Matthew, H. C. G., *A Short Oxford History of the British Isles: The Nineteenth Century* (Oxford: Oxford University Press, 2000)

Matthew, H. C. G., ed., *The Gladstone Diaries, Vol. IX, January 1875–December 1880* (Oxford: Clarendon Press, 1986)

Mazower, M., *Dark Continent: Europe's Twentieth Century* (New York: Vintage, 2000)

Mazower, M., *The Balkans* (London: Phoenix, 2000)

Mazower, M., 'Travellers and the Oriental City', *Transactions of the Royal Historical Society*, 12 (2002)

Meliksetjan, H., *Homeland–Diaspora Relations and Repatriation* (Yerevan: Yerevan University Press, 1985)

Melkonian, V., *A Historical Glimpse of the Armenians in Mesopotamia from the Earliest Times to the Present Day* (Basra: Times Press, 1957)

Melman, B., *Women's Orients: English Women and the Middle East, 1718–1918* (London: Macmillan, 1995), second edition

Bibliography

Melman, B., 'Introduction', in B. Melman, ed., *Borderlines, Genders and Identities in War and Peace* (London: Routledge, 1998)

Melman, B., ed., *Borderlines: Genders and Identities in War and Peace* (London: Routledge, 1998)

Melson, R., 'Provocation or Nationalism: A Critical Enquiry into the Armenian Genocide of 1915', in R. Hovannisian, ed., *The Armenian Genocide in Perspective* (New Brunswick, NJ: Transaction, 1986)

Melson, R., *Revolution and Genocide: On the Origins of the Armenian Genocide and the Holocaust* (London and Chicago: University of Chicago Press, 1992)

Messinger, G. S., *British Propaganda and the State in the First World War* (Manchester: Manchester University Press, 1992)

Miller, D. E. and L. Touryan Miller, eds, *Survivors: An Oral History of the Armenian Genocide* (Berkeley: University of California Press, 1999)

Mills, S. *Discourses of Difference: An Analysis of Women's Travel Writing and Colonialism* (London: Routledge, 1991)

Milton-Cooper Junior, J., 'A Friend in Power? Woodrow Wilson and Armenia', in J. Winter, ed., *America and the Armenian Genocide of 1915* (Cambridge: Cambridge University Press, 2003)

Moore-Gilbert, B., *Postcolonial Theory: Contexts, Practices, Politics* (London: Verso, 1997)

Moore-Gilbert, B., G. Stanton and W. Maley, eds, *Postcolonial Criticism* (London: Longman, 1997)

Moranian, S. E., 'The Armenian Genocide and American Missionary Relief Efforts', in J. Winter, ed., *America and the Armenian Genocide of 1915* (Cambridge: Cambridge University Press, 2003)

Moscrop, J. J., *Measuring Jerusalem. The Palestine Exploration Fund and British Interests in the Holy Land* (London: Leicester University Press, 2000)

Mouradian, C., 'L'Immigration des Arméniens de la Diaspora vers la RSS d'Arménie 1946–62', *Cahiers du Monde Russe et Soviétique*, Vol. XX, No. 1 (1997)

Naimark, N., *Fires of Hatred: Ethnic Cleansing in Twentieth Century Europe* (London: Harvard University Press, 2001)

Nalbandian, L., *The Armenian Revolutionary Movement: The Development of Armenian Political Parties through the Nineteenth Century* (Berkeley: University of California Press, 1963)

Nassibian, A., *Britain and the Armenian Question* (London: Croom Helm, 1984)

Panossian, R., 'The Past as Nation: Three Dimensions of Armenian Identity', *Geopolitics*, Vol. 7, No. 2 (2002)

Panossian, R., 'Homeland–Diaspora Relations and Identity Differences', in E. Herzig and M. Kurkchiyan, eds, *The Armenians: Past and Present in the Making of National Identity* (London: RoutledgeCurzon, 2005)

Panossian, R., *The Armenians: From Kings and Priests to Merchants and Commissars* (London: Hurst, 2006)

Bibliography

Papadopoulos, Renos K., ed., *Therapeutic Care for Refugees: No Place Like Home* (Karnac: London and New York, 2001)

Pattie, S., 'Armenians in Diaspora', in E. Herzig and M. Kurkchiyan, eds, *The Armenians: Past and Present in the Making of National Identity* (London: RoutledgeCurzon, 2005)

Pattie, S., 'New Homeland for an Old Diaspora', in A. Levy and A. Weingrod, *Homelands and Diasporas: Holy Lands and Other Places* (Stanford: Stanford University Press, 2005)

Pick, D., *Faces of Degeneration: A European Disorder, c. 1848–1918* (Cambridge: Cambridge University Press, 1989)

Pipes, R., *The Formation of the Soviet Union* (Cambridge, MA: Harvard University Press, 1964), revised edition

Poliakov, L., *The Aryan Myth: A History of Racist and Nationalist Ideas in Europe* (London: Sussex University Press, 1971)

Ponsonby, A., *Falsehood in Wartime: Containing an Assortment of Lies Circulated throughout the Nations during the Great War* (Sudbury: Bloomfield, 1991), reprinted from 1928 edition

Porter, B., *Critics of Empire: British Radical Attitudes to Colonialism in Africa 1895–1914* (London: Macmillan, 1968)

Porter, D., 'Orientalism and its Problems', in P. Williams and L. Chrisman, eds, *Colonial Discourse and Post-Colonial Theory: A Reader* (London: Harvester Wheatsheaf, 1993)

Power, S., *A Problem from Hell: America and the Age of Genocide* (New York: Basic Books, 2002)

Pratt, M. L., *Imperial Eyes: Travel Writing and Transculturation* (London: Routledge, 1992)

Rabinow, P., ed., *The Foucault Reader* (London: Penguin, 1984)

Ranger, T., 'Studying Repatriation as Part of African Social History', in T. Allen and H. Morsink, eds, *When Refugees go Home* (London: UNRISD in association with James Currey, 1994)

Rapport, N., ed., *British Subjects: An Anthropology of Britain* (Oxford: Berg, 2002)

Reade, J., 'Hormuzd Rassam and his Discoveries', *Iraq*, 55 (1993)

Redgate, A. E., *The Armenians* (Oxford: Blackwell, 1998)

Robbins, K., ed., *Political Diplomacy and War in Modern British History* (London: Hambledon Press, 1994)

Roessel, D., *In Byron's Shadow: Modern Greece in the English and American Imagination* (Oxford: Oxford University Press, 2002)

Roper, M., 'Between Manliness and Masculinity: The War Generation and the Psychology of Fear in Britain 1914–1915', *Journal of British Studies*, Vol. 44, No. 2 (April 2005)

Roshwald, A., *Ethnic Nationalism and the fall of Empires: Central Europe, Russia and the Middle East 1914–1923* (London: Routledge, 2001)

Bibliography

Ryan, J., *Picturing Empire: Photography and the Visualisation of the British Empire* (London: Reaktion Books, 1997)

Saab, A. P., *Reluctant Icon: Gladstone, Bulgaria and the Working Classes, 1856–1878* (Cambridge, MA: Harvard University Press, 1991)

Said, E., *Culture and Imperialism* (London: Vintage, 1994)

Said, E., *Orientalism* (London: Penguin, 1995), originally published 1978

Sanasarian, E., 'Gender Distinction in the Genocidal Process, A Preliminary Study of the Armenian Case', *Holocaust and Genocide Studies*, Vol. 4, No. 4 (1989)

Sarkiss, H. J., 'The Armenian Renaissance 1500–1863', *Armenian Review*, Vol. 23, Part 3, reprinted from the *Journal of Modern History* (December 1937)

Sarkissian, A. O. 'Concert Diplomacy and the Armenians 1890–1897', in A. O. Sarkissian, ed., *Studies in Diplomatic History* (London: Longman, 1961)

Sarkissian, A. O., ed., *Studies in Diplomatic History* (London: Longman, 1961)

Schwartz, D. and R. Panossian, eds, *Nationalism and History: The Politics of Nation Building in Post-Soviet Armenia, Azerbaijan and Georgia* (Toronto: University of Toronto, Centre for Russian and East European Studies, 1994)

Schwarz, H. and S. Ray, eds, *A Companion to Postcolonial Studies* (Oxford: Blackwell 2000)

Searle, G. R., *The Liberal Party, Triumph and Disintegration, 1886–1929* (Basingstoke: Macmillan, 1992)

Seton-Watson, R., *Disraeli, Gladstone and the Eastern Question* (London: Macmillan & Co., 1935)

Shannon, R., *Gladstone and the Bulgarian Agitation, 1876* (London: Thomas Nelson, 1963)

Shannon, R., *Gladstone: Heroic Minister, 1865–1898* (London: Allen Lane, 1999)

Sharp, A., *The Versailles Peace Settlement: Peacemaking in Paris 1919* (Basingstoke: Palgrave, 1991)

Shemmassian, V. L., 'The League of Nations and the Reclamation of Armenian Genocide Survivors', in R. Hovannisian, ed., *Looking Backward, Moving Forward: Confronting the Armenian Genocide* (New Brunswick, NJ: Transaction, 2003)

Simcowantz, A., 'The Etchmiadzin Manuscripts during the First World War', *Armenian Review*, Vol. 36, No. 4 (1983)

Skran, C., *Refugees in Inter-War Europe: The Emergence of a Regime* (Oxford: Clarendon Press, 1995)

Slide, A., *Ravished Armenia and the Story of Aurora Mardiganian* (London: The Scarecrow Press, 1997)

Smith, R. W., 'The Armenian Genocide: Memory, Politics and The Future', in R. Hovannisian, ed., *The Armenian Genocide: History, Politics, Ethics* (London: Macmillan, 1992)

Soffer, R., 'Nation, Duty, Character and Confidence: History at Oxford 1850–1914', *Historical Journal*, 30 (1987)

Bibliography

Somakian, M., *Empires in Conflict: Armenia and the Great Powers 1895–1920* (London: I. B. Tauris, 1995)

Spaull, H., 'Mothering Children for the League of Nations: Froken Jeppe', in H. Spaull, *Women Peacemakers* (London: Harrap, 1924)

Spaull, H., *Women Peacemakers* (London: Harrap, 1924)

Stepan, N., *The Idea of Race in Science* (London: Macmillan, 1982)

Stocking, G. W., *Race, Culture and Evolution, Essays in the History of Anthropology* (Chicago: University of Chicago Press, 1968)

Stocking, G. W., *Victorian Anthropology* (London: Collier Macmillan, 1987)

Suny, R. G., ed., *Transcaucasia: Nationalism and Social Change* (Ann Arbor: University of Michigan, 1983)

Suny, R. G., *Looking Toward Ararat: Armenia in Modern History* (Bloomington and Indianapolis: Indiana University Press, 1993)

Suny, R. G., 'Constructing Primordialism: Old Histories for New Nations', *Journal of Modern History*, Vol. 73, No. 4 (December 2001)

Suny, R. G., 'Soviet Armenia, 1921–1991', in E. Herzig and M. Kurkchiyan, eds, *The Armenians: Past and Present in the Making of National Identity* (London: RoutledgeCurzon, 2005)

Sykes, A., *The Rise and Fall of British Liberalism, 1776–1988* (London: Longman, 1997)

Tachijian, Vahe, 'Le Rapatriement: Une Nouvelle Page dans la Coopération avec les Soviétiques', unpublished manuscript (Paris: 2006)

Ter Minassian, A., *Nationalism and Socialism in the Armenian Revolutionary Movement* (Cambridge, MA: Zoryan Institute, 1983)

Ter Minassian, A., 'Elites Arméniennes en Suisse. Le Rôle de Genève dans la Formation des Elites Arméniennes au début du XXieme Siècle', in Hans-Lukas Kieser, ed., *Die Armenische Frage und die Schweiz : 1896–1923* (Zurich: Chronos Verlag, 1999)

Ter Minassian, T., 'Erevan, "Ville Promise": Le Rapatriement des Arméniens de la Diaspora, 1921–1948', *Diasporas*, No. 1 (2005)

Ternon, Yves, *Les Arméniens: Histoire d'un Génocide* (Paris: Seuil, 1977)

Texier, C. *Description de l'Armenie* (Paris, 1942)

Thane, P., 'The British Imperial State and the Construction of National Identities', in B. Melman, ed., *Borderlines: Genders and Identities in War and Peace* (London: Routledge, 1998)

Thubron, C., *Among the Russians* (London: Penguin, 1983)

Todorova, M., *Imagining the Balkans* (Oxford: Oxford University Press, 1997)

Toynbee, A. J., *Acquaintances* (London: Oxford University Press, 1967)

Tribunal Permanant des Peuples, *Le Crime de Silence: Le Génocide Des Arméniens* (Paris: Flammarion, 1984)

Trigger, B., *A History of Archaeological Thought* (Cambridge: Cambridge University Press, 1989)

Bibliography

Walker, C. J., *Armenia: The Survival of a Nation* (London: Croom Helm, 1980)

Walker, C. J., *Visions of Ararat: Writings on Armenia* (London: I. B. Tauris, 1997)

Walkowitz, J., *City of Dreadful Delight: Narratives of Sexual Danger in Late-Victorian London* (London: Virago, 1992)

Ward, M., *European Atrocity, African Catastrophe: Leopold II, the Congo Free State and its Aftermath* (London: RoutledgeCurzon, 2004)

Wheatcroft, A., *Infidels: A History of the Conflict between Christianity and Islam* (London: Penguin, 2004)

Williams, P. and L. Chrisman, 'Colonial Discourse and Post-Colonial Theory: An Introduction', in P. Williams and L. Chrisman, *Colonial Discourse and Post-Colonial Theory: A Reader* (London: Harvester Wheatsheaf, 1993)

Williams, P. and L. Chrisman, eds, *Colonial Discourse and Post-Colonial Theory: A Reader* (London: Harvester Wheatsheaf, 1993)

Wilson, T., 'Lord Bryce's Investigation into the German Atrocities in Belgium 1914–15', *Journal of Contemporary History*, Vol. 14, No. 3 (July 1979)

Wilson, T., *Myriad Faces of War: Britain and the Great War* (Cambridge: Polity, 1986)

Winter, J., 'Catastrophe and Culture: Recent Trends in the Historiography of the First World War', *Journal of Modern History*, Vol. 64, No. 3 (1992)

Winter, J., 'Under Cover of War: The Armenian Genocide in the Context of Total War', in J. Winter, ed., *America and the Armenian Genocide of 1915* (Cambridge: Cambridge University Press, 2003)

Winter, J., ed., *America and the Armenian Genocide of 1915* (Cambridge: Cambridge University Press, 2003)

Wolff, L., *Inventing Eastern Europe: The Map of Civilization on the Mind of the Enlightenment* (Stanford, CA: Stanford University Press, 1994)

Zimansky, P., *Ancient Ararat: A Handbook of Urartian Studies* (Delmar, NY: Caravan Books, 1998)

Unpublished theses

Greenshields, T. H., *The Settlement of Armenian Refugees in Syria and Lebanon, 1915–1939*, unpublished PhD thesis, University of Durham, 1978

Kevonian, D., *Réfugies et Diplomatie Humanitaire: Les Acteurs Européens et la Scène Proche Orientale Pendant l'Entre Deux Guerres*, unpublished thesis, Pantheon-Sorbonne, 1998

Index

Note: 'n.' after a page reference indicates the number of a note on that page.

Aharonian, A. (representative of Armenian Republic to the Peace Conference) 187, 200
ARA (American Relief Administration) 157
AAA (Anglo-Armenian Association) 9, 33–34, 52, 60, 74, 86n.9
ANDP (Armenian National Delegation, Paris) 102
  and mandate 196
  petition 198
  post-war aims and activities 184–187
  and repatriation 168
Ani 62–63
  cathedral 63–64
Ararat 48, 55–58, 211
Armenian Church
  attacks on 124
  under Bolshevik rule 204
  critiques of 65
  divisions 53
  and nationality 52–53, 123
  rituals 66
Armenian diaspora
  and Armenian 'homeland' 184–185
  and 'Armenian question' 45–46
  and genocide 6
  and history 5–6
  during inter-war period 209

and peace conference delegations 187
  and Soviet Armenia 210–211
Armenian Nationalism 51–52
  British opinions of 121
  nationalist parties 51
'Armenian question' 9–10, 44–46, 73, 85
  and 'eastern question' 3, 7–8
  and Soviet rule 226–227
  transformation into a 'national' cause 103
Armenian Red Cross and Refugee Fund 102
Armenian renaissance 28, 47
Armenian Republic 144, 185
  conditions 200–201
  formation of 146
  Sovietisation 199
atrocity stories 107
  and First World War 109–112
  and 'new journalism' 82–83
Azerbaijan 4, 14n.13

BAC (British Armenia Committee) 85, 102
  and Armenian mandate 197–198
  pamphlet 133
  and strategic importance of Armenia 187

Baghdad 154
Baku 167
Balkan Committee 98n.185, 104–105
'Balkanism' 31, 32–34
Balkans 2–3, 32–33
    nationalism 8
Ba'quba refugee camp 153, 158
    discipline 161
    disease 154, 160, 168
    closure 169–172
Barton, J.
    and mandate 197
Bauman, Z. 30, 219
Bishop, I. 48–49
    on Armenians and British 54
    on female dress 68
Boghos Nubar Pasha 102, 184, 186
Bryce, J. Viscount
    on Armenian nationalism 52
    on German atrocities 111, 138n.47,
        48
    on Ottoman massacres 102, 108
    and pro-Boer movement, 39n.30
    Russia and Turkey 40n.38
    Transcaucasia and Ararat, 48
    *Treatment of Armenians in the
        Ottoman Empire* 105
    see also Ararat; EQA; Armenian
        Church; rituals; veiling
'Bulgarian horrors' 3, 8–9, 82
Buxton, N. 27, 40n.31
Buxton, H. 152, 154 177n.50
    on conditions in Transcaucasia
        201–202
    on problems of relief in Soviet
        Armenia 203
    on Soviet rule 225, 226, 227

children
    as archetypal image of Armenian
        massacres 125–126
    in atrocity narratives 111, 129
    at Ba'quba camp 162

in British press 83
and extermination 132
and missionary work 76–77
rescue of 148–151
Cilicia
    and Armenian state 184
    evacuation 199
Clayden, P. W. 79
cleanliness 64
Clifford, J.
    on *Orientalism* 27
Contemporary Review 82, 201–202
conversion 61–62, 65, 92n. 83
    of Armenian women 130
'cradle of civilisation' 34, 55–56, 60, 220
Crusades 46, 62
Curzon, Sir R. 60

Dashnaks
    and Armenian Republic 146, 184
    attitude to Soviet Armenia 210
degeneration 73–74
deportations 118
    gendered 126
    pattern of 9–10
Dillon, E. J. 82
Disraeli, B. (Prime Minister)
    and imperialism 25
    Liberal critiques 24

'eastern question' 2–3, 13–14n.13
    history of 7–9
    historiography 3, 40n.38
    and Ottoman violence 99
    and race 54–55
EQA (Eastern Question Association)
    45
Etchmiadzin 66–67, 204–205

Friends of Armenia 9, 80, 84
    Friend of Armenia
        cover image 126
        settlement of refugees 169–170

Garni 205, 228
genocide
    Armenian history 4–6, 7
    and Armenian identity 5
    denial 6–7
    memorial 6
    UN definition 116
    Georgia, 146
German atrocities 110–111, 114, 125
    see also atrocity stories
Germany
    influence on 1915 massacres 114
Gladstone, W. E.
    and Armenian cause 78–79
    see also 'Bulgarian horrors'
'Greater Armenia' 185, 190
    and Soviet Armenia 203–204
Greece
    British attitudes to 36, 75–76
    British heritage 35
    independence 7–8

harem 69–70, 83
    and Armenian women 149–50
Haskell, W. (Colonel) (Allied High
    Commissioner for Armenia)
    157–158, 166, 200
Herzfeld, M. 35, 42n.65, 75–76, 223
    see also Greece
Hnchaks 51, 184
Hobsbawm, E. 39n.28
    Invention of Tradition 42n.61, 51
    Nations and Nationalism 88n.36
homeland
    Armenian 184, 199
        and peasantry 75
        and post-war world 169, 185–186
        and repatriation 164, 165
    in former Ottoman Empire 191
    and nationalist discourses 51
Hovannisian, R. G.
    and genocide 5–6
    and Soviet Republic 210

illuminated manuscripts 62
Indo-European 58, 91n.69
    and Van cuneiforms 59–60

Jeppe, K. 149
Jews 29–30, 219
*Journal of the Royal Geographical
    Society* 47

Karabagh 4, 227–228
Kars 146, 199, 207

Layard, Sir A. H. 58–59, 60
League of Nations
    and Armenian refugees 209–210
    Commission of Inquiry for the
        Protection of Women and
        Children in the Near East
        149
    and displaced persons 163–164
Liberals (Liberal Party)
    and Armenian cause 78–79
    and First World War 119
    'forward movement' 79
    and minorities 8, 24–25
    and 1894–1896 massacres 9
Lloyd George, D. (Prime Minister)
    anti-Turkish sentiments 190
    support for the Armenians
        188
LMF (Lord Mayor's Fund) 103,
    155–156
    appeal posters 126
    in Soviet Armenia 208
Lynch, H. F. B.
    Ani 64
        cathedral 63
    Armenian population distribution
        50
    on race 58

MacColl, M. (Canon) 76, 78, 80,
    97n.171

Macedonia 24, 108
  see also Balkan Committee
Manchester Guardian 103, 114, 116,
    120, 124
mandate 196–198
Mardiganian, A. 130–131, 151
Marsden, P.
  The Crossing Place 228
martyrdom 62, 123, 149
massacres
  Adana 9, 85, 129
  1894–1896 9, 44, 77
    and religion 81
    British response to 78–83
    Rendel and Helen Harris on 29
  1915 10
    Allied joint declaration on 101
    Armenian men 132–133
    Armenian women 129–132
    as attack upon 'civilisation'
        122
    as 'extermination' 116–117
    as war atrocity 109–110
    religion 113, 123–125
Masterman, C. F. G. 104–105
Mekhitarists 28, 62
missionaries 53, 76–77
  refugee relief 156–57
Mudros armistice 144, 146

Nansen, F.
  passports 164
  and resettlement schemes 170
Near East Relief 156–57
  New Near East 153, 157, 161, 163
Northcote, D. S. 160
  Armenian refugees
    national customs 160–161
    and closure of camp 171
  Ba'quba camp 167–168
  Russian Bolsheviks 206, 225
  resignation 171
  Soviet Armenia 202, 226

historical sites 204–205
  relief work 207

Ottoman Empire 8–9
  Armenians in 75, 77
  and barbarism 27, 81, 108, 112
  and British foreign policy 8, 23,
      104
  and Christian minorities 24, 107,
      108
  critique of 36, 69, 73–74, 83,
      112–113
  Gladstone on 78
  and Germany 114
  post-war 190–196
  races of 54–55
  See also Treaty of Sevres; Treaty of
      Lausanne; Treaty of Berlin;
      Harem; 'eastern question'

pan-Turkism 117, 140n.78
philhellenism 7–8
photographs
  of Armenian monasteries 124
  of refugees 163
  of genocide 140n.81
  and 'native dress' 68
progress 71–74
  Armenian capacity for 24, 65
  and Christianity 123
  and Empire 36
  and housing conditions 205–206
  and Soviet rule 203–204, 225
  and treatment of women 70–71
Propaganda Bureau 104–105

Ramkavar party
  and Soviet Republic 210
rape 81–82, 129–131
refugees
  female 148–150
  male 150
  in Middle East 145

refugees (*cont.*)
oral testimony 155
'otherness' 151–152
as 'problem' 152, 154, 159, 166,
218–220
self-help 161–162
in Transcaucasia 145–146,
156–157
repatriation 145–146, 164–165
from Ba'quba 167–170, 202
problems 166
after Second World War
210–211
1920s and 1930s 209
Robinson, E. 102, 121–122
Rosebery, Earl of (Prime Minister)
78
rules of war 110
Russell, G. W. E. 79
Russia
British fears 23
condition of Armenians in 74–75
Russian Revolution 146
Russo-Turkish war 44, 62

Said, E.
and Foucault 20, 22, 26
on minorities 26
Orientalism 21, 22, 27, 36
critiques
Lewis, R. 22, 23
Mackenzie 38n.17
Porter, 22, 38n.16
Salisbury, Marquis of (Prime
Minister) 79, 96n.163, n.164
San Stefano 9, 44
Save the Children 203, 207
self-determination 119, 188
Armenian 183 193
see also mandate; Wilson, W.
Slave Market News 149
Smyrna
attack on 199

Greek landing 167
and Treaty of Sevres 198
Soviet Republic (of Armenia)
as Armenian homeland 204, 207
210–211, 224, 226
refugee crisis 202–203
Stead, W. T. 78, 82, 97n.174
Stevenson, F. S. 33, 74
Suny, R. G.
and Armenian historiography
5, 7

Tanzimat reforms 8
Tbilisi 52, 146
Thubron, C.
Among the Russians 228
time 72
Times 103, 114, 115, 116, 130
Toynbee, A. J. 18
*Armenian Atrocities: The Murder of
a Nation* 105, 117
and massacres 115, 117
and population of Eastern Anatolia
195
*Treatment of the Armenians in the
Ottoman Empire* 19,
104–107
on Turkish rule 112–113
Transcaucasian Federation 146
Treaty of Berlin 9
Article 61 44–45, 80
Treaty of Lausanne 199
Treaty of Moscow 199
Treaty of Sevres 198
Turkish nationalism 197, 198
Turkish Republic 199, 202

Urartu 58–59

Van 58–59
Versailles Peace Conference 187–188,
192
'victim nations' 119–120

Wilson, Sir H. 167
Wilson, W. (President of USA) 188
   and Armenian Mandate 197
   and Armenian Boundaries 198
Wolff L. 31, 32, 222
women
   as martyrs 83, 129, 131
   orientalist representations of 67–68
   traditional dress 68–69
   rescue of 149–151
   veiling 70

Xenephon 61

Yerevan
   capital of First Armenian Republic
     146
   Wardrop, O. on 200–201
   development of 207
Young Turk regime 85, 113
Young Turk Revolution 9, 117

Zvartnots 205